Celebrities in American Elections

Celebrities in American Elections

Case Studies in Celebrity Politics

Richard T. Longoria

LEXINGTON BOOKS
Lanham • Boulder • New York • London

Published by Lexington Books
An imprint of The Rowman & Littlefield Publishing Group, Inc.
4501 Forbes Boulevard, Suite 200, Lanham, Maryland 20706
www.rowman.com

86-90 Paul Street, London EC2A 4NE
British Library Cataloguing in Publication Information Available

Library of Congress Cataloging-in-Publication Data

Names: Longoria, Richard T., 1977- author.
  Title: Celebrities in American elections : case studies in celebrity
    politics / Richard T. Longoria.
  Description: Lanham : Lexington Books, [2022] | Includes bibliographical
    references and index. | Summary: "The author explains why entertainment
    celebrities win and lose elections in the United States. Celebrities
    have the talent, fame, and resources to succeed in politics, but they
    often lose when the political environment is not favorable to their
    candidacy"-- Provided by publisher.
  Identifiers: LCCN 2022031899 (print) | LCCN 2022031900 (ebook) | ISBN
    9781666923155 (cloth) | ISBN 9781666923179 (paperback) | ISBN
9781666923162 (ebook)
  Subjects: LCSH: Political candidates--United States--Public opinion--Case
    studies. | Celebrities--Political activity--United States--History--Case
    studies. | Entertainers--Political activity--United States--Case
    studies. | Politics and culture--United States--Case studies.
  Classification: LCC JK1967 .L66 2022 (print) | LCC JK1967 (ebook) | DDC
    324.973--dc23/eng/20220812
  LC record available at https://lccn.loc.gov/2022031899
  LC ebook record available at https://lccn.loc.gov/2022031900

Contents

List of Textboxes and Tables

Acknowledgments

The author would like to express his gratitude to the many people who made this work possible. His colleagues at The University of Texas Rio Grande Valley read early drafts of the manuscript and provided valuable advice during the publication phase of this project. Colleagues at other institutions served as discussants for draft chapters presented at academic conferences and provided suggestions that improved the project. The anonymous reviewers identified critical issues that the author missed and provided insightful critiques of the manuscript. The Roper Center for Public Opinion Research houses the iPoll database that provided some of the polling data presented here. Selected portions of "George Murphy: A Celebrity Politician," by Richard T. Longoria, which appeared in the *Southern California Quarterly* 104, no. 2 (Summer 2022), have been reprinted here with the permission of *Southern California Quarterly*.

Introduction

In March 2022, Volodymyr Zelensky, the president of Ukraine and a former TV comedian, was being praised for his handling of the Russian invasion of his country. Arnold Schwarzenegger, the action movie hero who was elected governor of California, released a video message to the Russian people asking them to oppose the war in Ukraine. Dr. Oz, the TV doctor, was running for the US Senate in Pennsylvania and Herschel Walker, the former NFL player, was running for the US Senate in Georgia. Stacy Abrams, a candidate for Georgia governor, made a guest appearance on *Star Trek: Discovery*. Barack Obama, now a documentary film producer, was releasing a new series on Netflix. How did we get here? Why is there such a profound intermingling of politics and the entertainment industry?

Since the early days of Hollywood, the entertainment industry has played an active role in American politics. Celebrities play an important role in our society and they have valuable talents that lend themselves well to politics. Indeed, some have argued that entertainment and politics are not distinct realms. They share many of the same attributes. Entertainers, therefore, have ready entrance into the political arena. They have the talent, fame, and resources to help them succeed in electoral politics. They also benefit from "celebrity slack," they get away with transgressions that would doom non-celebrities. Ultimately, the political environment seems to be the most important factor in determining whether a celebrity can win elected office.

Chapter 1 reviews the academic literature on celebrity. The broad overview draws from the disciplines of sociology, anthropology, media studies, marketing, and social psychology. Celebrities can use multiple techniques to draw attention to themselves. Some draw attention because of their exceptional good looks, some draw attention because they wear outlandish costumes, some draw attention because they stoke dramatic conflict with others. These techniques are managed by agents and publicists who are skilled at creating fame for their clients. Celebrities can use their "attention capital" to sell movies, music, and consumer products. The celebrities discussed in this book use these techniques to sell policy ideas to voters.

1

Chapter 2 reviews the literature in celebrity politics and outlines the framework used throughout the remainder of this book. Celebrities have the talent, fame, and resources to win elections. Their ease in front of cameras and audiences allows them to build a personal brand that is marketable. Their very high name recognition means that voters already understand who the celebrity is, they benefit from earned media. Their elite status provides them access to a social network that is beneficial for fundraising. These are tremendous advantages that non-celebrity candidates don't have, but they are not enough by themselves to win an election. The political environment is the decisive factor. The unique circumstances of the time and place is the reason that some celebrities win while others lose. Most of the celebrities were able to survive scandals that non-celebrity candidates likely would not have survived. The case study chapters are organized in chronological order by date of election.

Chapter 3 explores the rise of Ronald Reagan. He was a teen heartthrob in the 1930s and a television star during the advent of television in the 1950s. When Americans first started watching television, they were watching Ronald Reagan. On screen he portrayed an affable nice guy and a heroic federal agent. Over the years he carefully crafted a persona that resonated with audiences and electorates. He was the president of the Screen Actors Guild and learned about politics from the perspective of the labor organizer that he was. As a politician he believed his role was to read the scripts his advisors had given him, using his acting skills to deliver political monologues.

Chapter 4 focuses on Clint Eastwood. Eastwood is a legendary actor whose tough guy persona was revered by audiences. He received global media attention when he decided to run for mayor in his small California town. With his immense wealth, and fame, he trounced the incumbent mayor. His well-publicized marital infidelities proved to be no barrier to his electoral success.

Chapter 5 explores Fred Grandy. Grandy was best known for his role as "Gopher" in television's *The Love Boat*. The Harvard educated actor re-branded himself to distance himself from the inept and bumbling character he played on TV. Grandy was the focus of the media's, and his opponents' attention throughout the campaign. The election was about Fred Grandy. His skill in front of cameras was an asset and voters attended his events to see a celebrity.

Chapter 6 discusses Sonny Bono. Bono came to fame as part of the Sonny and Cher duo. He appeared on television and in movies. He was skilled at manipulating public perceptions of himself and gaining attention. He would be elected mayor of Palm Springs, California and win a seat in the US House of Representatives. His unusual lifestyle would be overlooked by the voting public.

Chapter 7 examines the unexpected election of Jesse Ventura to the governorship of Minnesota. Jesse "The Body" Ventura was a professional wrestler known for his vanity and over the top attire. He co-starred with Arnold Schwarzenegger in *Predator* and became an actor in his own right. His hostility toward reporters and ridicule of opponents would serve as a model that Donald Trump would later replicate. His bombastic tone and hyper-masculine boasting endeared him to many of his supporters. The peculiarity of Minnesota election laws helped Ventura succeed.

Chapter 8 considers the dramatic story of Arnold Schwarzenegger. Schwarzenegger is a seven-time Mr. Olympia champion and Hollywood movie star known the world over. He typically portrays a muscle man hero who saves the world from disaster. He was a skilled self-promoter who understood how to capture the public's attention. He was elected governor of California by promising to save the state from its own disaster. Accusations of sexual harassment did not prevent him from being elected.

Chapter 9 explores the election of comedian Al Franken to the US Senate. Franken began in stand-up comedy to become a writer for *Saturday Night Live*. He would eventually serve as a cast member on the show and later host his own radio program. His skill in front of live audiences helped him succeed in politics just as it helped him succeed in comedy. He acknowledges that his stardom helped him succeed in politics and argued that getting financial support from "Big Comedy" was better than support from "Big Oil" and "Big Pharma." Minnesota voters were willing to overlook Franken's offensive and obscene conduct that were intended as jokes by the award-winning comedian.

Chapter 10 looks at the second celebrity to become president, Donald Trump. Trump rose to prominence as a real estate developer who actively sought out media coverage of his business endeavors. He became known for his lavish lifestyle and earned additional earnings by licensing his name for various products. He participated in WrestleMania and was the star of *The Apprentice* before seeking public office. He billed himself as a savvy businessman but did have financial problems. His use of racially divisive appeals helped him with Republican voters. With outlandish bravado, he made vulgar, demeaning, and degrading statements against others. He remained enormously popular with his core constituency.

Chapter 11 discusses the politicians who became entertainers—Fred Thompson, Sarah Palin, and Jerry Springer. Their talent in front of audiences and television cameras allowed them to use their skills in multiple industries. It also considers celebrities who have lost elections—Shirley Temple, Ben Jones, Gary Coleman, Linda McMahon, Roseanne Barr, Cynthia Nixon, Stacey Dash, and others. Celebrities lose if they are running in an unfavorable district or state for their party, if they have a public persona not suited to the political environment of the moment, or if their bid is viewed as a publicity stunt. Despite the many advantages that celebrities have, these cases suggest that the political environment is the difference between winning and losing for celebrity candidates.

Chapter 12 provides an overview of the important lessons to be learned from the case studies in this book. It also presents the arguments for and against celebrity politics. Some believe that the celebrification of our politics poses a danger to democracy, while others believe it could enhance democracy. Both sides make valid claims as the celebrification of our politics is not good or bad in and of itself. There are costs and benefits to the new media and political environment we find ourselves in.

Chapter 1

Celebrity Society

Corner and Pels define celebrification as system where "celebrity power is progressively being translated from the popular entertainment industries towards more 'serious' fields such as business, politics, art and science" (Corner and Pels 2003, 8). The lines between these industries become blurred and causes "an intermeshing of formerly distinct values and codes" (Corner and Pels 2003, 8). The process of celebrification only occurred because humans invented the mass media. By the time Ronald Reagan was elected president in 1980, the process of celebrification was well underway. His election marked a new era in American society. American politics became celebrified.

To say that something is a process does not diminish its historical precedents. For example, bureaucratic organizational structures are a key component of Max Weber's modernization theory (Weber 1947). Bureaucracies were formed in the nineteenth century as part of modernization, but new bureaucracies continue to be formed in the twenty-first century. The Department of Homeland Security and the US Space Force are recent developments in an ongoing process. Celebrity influence on US politics began in the 1920s and continues a hundred years later.

The same decade that saw the election of Ronald Reagan witnessed the rise of Madonna as a global pop star. Madonna figured out that a person could sell records by exposing every detail of their private lives to the mass media; that behaving outrageously could garner attention and that it could sell out stadiums for her performances. Madonna did on purpose what Elizabeth Taylor had done accidently in an earlier era (Cashmore 2014). The celebrity society was now coming of age. More recently, Lady Gaga, a self-proclaimed master of the "sociology of fame," expertly used the tools that were available to her to propel herself to global stardom. She used a blueprint that was developed by her predecessors. It is not an accident that some people become famous, while most do not.

It is in this new celebrity society that Ronald Reagan, Clint Eastwood, Fred Grandy, Sonny Bono, Jesse Ventura, Arnold Schwarzenegger, Al Franken, and Donald Trump won elected office. They became the leaders and representatives of the American people. They were celebrities transformed into politicians—*polebrities*. They were able to win, first, because our society had changed and allowed them to win. Second, they were able to win because polebrities have *the power trifecta*, three characteristics that make them ideal candidates for public office. They have the talent, fame, and resources to make them successful campaigners. The political environment, items like a state's election laws or idiosyncratic elements of particular electoral contests, also plays a critical role in electoral success. It is not an accident that some people win elections and others lose.

To understand how it is that celebrities become elected officials, we need to first understand the nature of celebrity. The historical development of celebrity society is discussed in this chapter. The celebrification of our politics follows from the celebrification of our society. Donald Trump is merely the most recent example of celebrities actively seeking and winning a political election. The celebrities lead and Americans follow them because the domains of entertainment and politics are no longer distinct.

WHAT IS CELEBRITY?

Daniel Boorstin's definition of celebrity is tautological. For him, a celebrity is someone who is famous for being famous. Boorstin argues that in the past fame was associated with greatness, people became well known because they were born great, monarchs, or because they achieved greatness, war heroes. But today, the link between fame and greatness has been broken. He says, "the machinery of information has brought into being a new substitute for the hero, who is the celebrity, and whose main characteristic is his well-knownness. In the democracy of pseudo-events, anyone can become a celebrity, if only he can get into the news and stay there" (Boorstin 1992, 72). He goes on, "The hero was distinguished by his achievement; the celebrity by his image or trademark. The hero created himself; the celebrity is created by the media. The hero was a big man; the celebrity is a big name" (Boorstin 1992, 74). What is worse is the self-reinforcing nature of celebrity, "With the mushroom-fertility of all pseudo-events, celebrities tend to breed more celebrities. They help make and celebrate and publicize one another. Being known primarily for their well-knownness, celebrities intensify their celebrity images simply by becoming widely known for relations among themselves" (Boorstin 1992, 78).

This definition of celebrity as someone well known, but devoid of any merit, i.e., talent, was adopted by Ellis Cashmore. "A peculiarity of celebrity culture is the shift of emphasis from achievement-based fame to media-driven renown" (Cashmore 2014, 12). Americans have been persuaded that, "people with no talent, no obvious gifts, nor any characteristic worthy of distinction were deserving of our serious attention just because they were in the media" (Cashmore 2014, 13). In our celebrity obsessed culture, "literally worthless individuals . . . commanded interest for nothing in particular" (Cashmore 2014, 13). Perhaps more alarmingly, they were being venerated and practically deified by the mass public (Rojek 2004).

Not everyone is so pessimistic about celebrities. Robert van Krieken makes a distinction between fame and celebrity. Fame is about having, "relatively high public visibility and recognition," while celebrity is, "fame—being visible, recognized and well known—plugged into networks of mass communication, themselves circuits of desire and commerce" (van Krieken 2012, 18). Celebrity is fame with commercial value. In particular, "Celebrity is a quality or status characterized by a capacity to attract attention, generating some 'surplus value' or benefit derived from the fact of being well known (highly visible) in itself in at least one public arena. It can be either positive or negative, including notoriety" (van Krieken 2012, 24). Celebrities have at least one talent, they can attract attention. This ability to attract attention has instrumental value to those who are trying to get the public to buy a product or vote for a political candidate. Simply put, a celebrity is someone who has the talent to attract the public's attention.

As will be explored in further detail later, this can be done in a few different ways. Physically attractive people grab our attention, so top fashion models like Chrissy Teigen become celebrities. Being physically attractive is also helpful in movie acting; since movies aim to capture the audience's attention and create an entertaining fantasy world. Arnold Schwarzenegger and Clint Eastwood succeeded as actors because of their physical appearance. If one is not physically attractive, one could wear strange costumes to attract attention. Performers such as Lady Gaga, and before her Sonny Bono, used unusual outfits to get themselves noticed. If that is not appealing, engaging in outrageous behavior, or making controversial statements, is another method to get people's attention. Howard Stern and Donald Trump used that method. At their core, these controversial statements are made to stoke conflict and conflict is inherently dramatic. Some people are athletically talented and garner public attention for their skilled play. Michael Jordan and Serena Williams are famous for their dominance in their respective sports. Some athletes do express their political views publicly and use their celebrity to call attention to important issues.

Fred Inglis makes a distinction between renown and celebrity. For Inglis, celebrity only comes into being with the rise of the mass media, urban democracy, and radical individualism. At the heart of his idea of celebrity is a "powerful contradiction." Celebrity "combines knowability with distance" (Inglis 2010, 11). Celebrities are well known. They enter our homes through the television, radio, and internet. We know the intimate details of their personal lives and professional achievements. As such, celebrities wield what Marshall calls "affective power" (Marshall 1997, 185). Fans become emotionally attached to their favorite celebrities. Yet, most people will never actually meet a celebrity in person. Stars "appear both hugely familiar and quite untouchable" (Inglis 2010, 231).

Celebrities play an important role in our society. Inglis argues that "The star has been appointed to perform our significant actions for us" (Inglis 2010, 231). Marshall believes, "celebrities are human agents in the public sphere who act as proxies" (Marshall 1997, 249). "The celebrity figure is constructed . . . to represent the public" (Marshall 1997, 242). They are spokespersons, both literally and figuratively, for interest groups, companies, ideas, causes, and, increasingly, political parties. They are trend setters and leaders that other people follow. Celebrities have become the representatives of our group identities.

Following Durkheim's (1996) theory of structural functionalism, Turner argues that celebrity has several important social functions. First, celebrities are like real people in that they replace the void left by our atomized and more isolated social existence created by modernity. People have "para-social" relationships with celebrities that they never actually meet in person. They even mourn the death of celebrities and weep as though a loved one has died; this is because the celebrity was a real part of their life and operated as a person known to them personally. Second, celebrities help set the standard for what is considered normal behavior. Celebrity antics can be praised or ridiculed in a way that informs the public about the line between acceptable and unacceptable actions. Third, celebrity functions to perpetuate a culture of individualism and consumerism. Fourth, celebrities can create ideal-type images, such as the bad boy, good girl, nerd, jock, preppy, hipster, etc., which embody social types that others can emulate to form their own social identities. The celebrity helps structure our society, they help define individuals' role in that society, and they facilitate interaction between members of that society (Turner 2014).

The media outlets that focus on celebrity gossip are an integral part of this system. Millions of people purchase magazines, watch television programs, and visit websites that focus on celebrity gossip (West and Orman 2003). Turner notes, "Gossip is a way of sharing social judgements and of processing social behavior, and this is true whether it involves people we know directly or people we know solely through their media presence. Gossip is also one of the fundamental processes employed as a means of social and cultural identity formation" (Turner 2014, 119). The commentators who discuss celebrities' actions can praise or deride the behavior. Readers and watchers can then emulate or ridicule the celebrity. While their primary function may be to entertain the public, their latent functions may be just as important. Celebrities play a role in our society that should not be dismissed as trivial. They are important and deserve serious attention from sociologists and political scientists.

CELEBRITY SOCIETY

Robert van Krieken argues that the celebrity society that we live in today has its roots in court society. He states, "In court society, individual existence and identity is profoundly representational—they consist of how one exhibits one's position and status, and this process of exhibition and performance is highly competitive and constantly fluctuating" (van Krieken 2012, 34). The court society is, "characterized by theatricality, performativity and the competitive organization of power and social mobility around the strategic projection of symbolically constituted identity" (van Krieken 2012, 30). The courtesans performed their roles and vied for social status that was conferred by the monarch. Favored courtesans rise in rank while disfavored courtesans risk exile from court.

In the eighteenth century, "Court society and its psychological disposition had gained still more ground, with celebrities such as Cibber and Garrick embodying the principle that one was never offstage" (van Krieken 2012, 50). Those with fame realized that they were perpetually being judged and that they must always stay in character. Even the development of modern governments was to some extent dependent on these elite constructed narratives, "The formation of nation-states in the nineteenth century was dependent on the construction of narratives organized around charismatic individuals which obeyed the central rules of the celebrity story" (van Krieken 2012, 120).

Democratization meant that fame and rank would now be conferred by the mass public instead of the monarch. It meant that one's performance now needed to be directed at everyone. Only with modern mass communication, including "the printing press . . . photography, radio, film, television and the Internet" could celebrity be created (van Krieken 2012, 32). Max Weber's (1947) rationalization and bureaucratization of social life meant that "the celebrity production process" saw the "appearance of 'experts' in public relations, publicity and image-management" (van Krieken 2012, 26). The stagecraft that started in court society was becoming professionalized.

This led to the creation of what Boorstin called "pseudo-events." He believes that we now live in a world where "pseudo-events" take the place of reality. These events are manufactured happenings that are planned and choreographed to create a spectacle that will be distributed by the mass media. Press conferences, national party conventions, and campaign rallies are stagecraft for the political performer. The problem is that Americans conflate the real and the unreal, they often do not understand the difference or even care to distinguish between the two.

> Until recently we have been justified in believing Abraham Lincoln's familiar maxim: "You may fool all the people some of the time; you can even fool some of the people all the time; but you can't fool all of the people all the time." This has been the foundation-belief of American democracy. Lincoln's appealing slogan rests on two elementary assumptions. First, that there is a clear and visible distinction between sham and reality, between the lies a demagogue would have us believe and the truths which are there all the time. Second, that the people tend to prefer reality to sham, that if offered a choice between a simple truth and a contrived image, they will prefer the truth. Neither of these any longer fits the facts. Not because people are less intelligent or more dishonest. Rather because great unforeseen changes—the great forward strides of American civilization—have blurred the edges of reality. The pseudo-events which flood our consciousness are neither true nor false in the old familiar senses. The very same advances which have made them possible have also made the images—however planned, contrived, or distorted—more vivid, more attractive, more impressive, and more persuasive than reality itself. (Boorstin 1992, 49)

Too many Americans live "in a world where fantasy is more real than reality" (Boorstin 1992, 49). This presents an amazing opportunity for the master performer, someone who can manufacture preferred subjective realities to replace the disliked objective realities that Americans experience. In this new America, the ability to craft a convincing pseudo-event is a skill that successful politicians must have.

Boorstin discusses how the subjects of the news and the reporters of the news work in tandem to create the news. They collaborate to produce "synthetic facts," "contrived reality," and "counterfeit happenings." Emphasizing the performative nature of this endeavor he states, "More and more news events become dramatic performances in which 'men in the news' simply act out more or less well their prepared script. The story prepared 'for future release' acquires an authenticity that competes with that of the actual occurrences on the scheduled date" (Boorstin 1992, 33). Today's reporters are given the text of the speech before a politician delivers it so that they can prepare their report of the speech prior to it being given. Politicians inform the media about what is going to happen, then they perform the happening, then the reporters report what happened.

All this preplanned stagecraft substitutes the real for what the powerful want the masses to believe is real. Boorstin blames citizens themselves for having unrealistic expectations. To meet these expectations the powers that be must give grander and grander performances. They must plan, manage, and entertain.

> We refuse to believe that advertising men are at most our collaborators, helping us make illusions for ourselves. In our moral indignation, our eagerness to find the villains who have created and frustrated our exaggerated expectations, we have underestimated the effect of the rise of advertising. We think it has meant an increase of untruthfulness. In fact, it has meant a reshaping of our very concept of truth. (Boorstin 1992, 217)

With a complicit public, a public that prefers the unreal, the best political candidates will be those that are the most skilled at putting on a show that is liked better than the alternative show. Elections become reality TV programs where the public gets to vote to decide the winner.

Some argued that this susceptibility to illusion is part of the American character. Kurt Anderson believes that "America was created by people resistant to reality checks and convinced they had special access to the truth, a place founded to enact grand fantasies" (Anderson 2017, 78). The earliest European settlers were drawn to America because they were promised that mountains of gold were waiting for the taking. Unfortunately for them, "People kept coming and believing, hopefulness becoming delusion. It was a gold rush with no gold" and many of them died (Anderson 2017, 28). America was founded by people who were exceptionally susceptible to advertising.

The fame celebrities have does not occur accidentally, nor is it merely the case of taking notice of the talented among us. Fame occurs through a concerted media campaign to produce a particular type of fame. Celebrity is created by the media, coordinated by an industry (publicists and public relations professionals), and consumed by audiences. There are at least three ways a person can draw attention to themselves to get people and the mass media to notice them. These are good looks, crazy costumes, and fake fighting.

GOOD LOOKS

Physical attractiveness is not a talent per se. However, it does confer on those who have it social advantages. When a physically attractive person walks into a room, people notice. In the social psychology literature, the question is not whether physically attractive people have advantages, but rather how large the "halo effect" is (Thorndike 1920; Nisbett and Wilson 1977; Kaplan 1978; Lucker, Beane, and Helmreich 1981; Ogden 2013; Shinada 2014; Talamas, Mavor, and Perrett 2016). Physically attractive politicians are perceived to be more competent, qualified, and trustworthy than less attractive politicians and there is evidence to suggest that more attractive politicians garner more votes than less attractive politicians (Efrain and Patterson 1974; Budesheim and DePaola 1994; Surawski and Ossoff 2006). For those individuals whose job it is to recruit political candidates, finding a physically attractive person to run will increase the odds of winning.

The Hollywood studios are in the fantasy creation business and as such they employ physically attractive stars to complete their task. Hollywood has created the standard for envisioning the ideal female body and the ideal male body (Holmes and Redmond 2006). Recruiting political candidates from Hollywood's A-list is not a foolhardy endeavor. Humans are hard wired to take notice of "pretty people." If the task at hand is to get people's attention, then we need to recognize that some people are better positioned to do this than others. We can argue about the ethics of this and even whether it is rational to use physical beauty as a proxy for competence. But when the task is garnering attention, being good looking is a trait that helps.

The esteemed John Adams, one of America's early political luminaries, understood the importance of physical beauty. He wrote,

> Every personal quality, and every blessing of fortune, is cherished in proportion to its capacity of gratifying this universal affection for the esteem, the sympathy, admiration and congratulations of the public. Beauty in the face, elegance of figure, grace of attitude and motion, riches, honors, every thing is weighed in the scale, and desired, not so much for the pleasure they afford, as the attention they command. . . . Why are the personal accomplishments of beauty, elegance and grace, held in such high estimation by mankind? Is it merely for the plea-sure which is received from the sight of these attributes? By no means . . . those attractions command the notice and attention of the public—they draw the eyes of spectators: this is the charm that makes them irresistible. . . . Beauty and address are courted and admired, very often, more than discretion, wit, sense, and many other accomplishments and virtues of infinitely more importance to the happiness of private life. (Adams 1805, 29)

Physical beauty is important because it draws the attention of the public. As a politician, he knew he had to get people to pay attention and he under-stood the advantages of physical beauty in this regard. He also understood that there may be many characteristics that were more valuable than beauty, but that beauty might carry the day none-the-less. Celebrities like Arnold Schwarzenegger and Clint Eastwood were successful in Hollywood because of their good looks. After they secured the public's attention, they decided to start talking about politics.

Some magazines have been known to "airbrush" or "photoshop" images to make models look better than they actually look. It is the image that sells, not the person behind the image. Today, there is an entire industry associated with image creation and management (McDonald 2006). "Publicists, agents, managers, and the gamut of other personnel exploiting, working for, or attending to the needs of the entertainers became self-taught guardians of images" (Cashmore 2014, 31). Cosmetic surgeons are also in the business of image management. Many celebrities are naturally good looking, but many also have cosmetic enhancements to create the right image. This obsession with the manufacture of a personal image has resulted in fourteen million Americans undergoing cosmetic procedures every year. It is the culmination of a consumer culture where everything, even good looks, can be bought and sold (Cashmore 2014). These are real people, but they are a little bit fake too. Americans understand that creating the right image is important for individual success. It can help a person find a mate and, also, a job.

CRAZY COSTUMES

Lady Gaga, an international pop superstar, understands celebrity as an academic exercise. She studied "the sociology of fame" and said, "I art direct every moment of my life" (*60 Minutes*). Her outrageous, and attention grabbing, costumes are intentional pieces of performance art. In this regard she is modelling the nineteenth century dancer and actress Lola Montez who "was an important early pioneer of the eccentric female celebrity identity" (van Krieken 2012, 61). Lady Gaga's eccentricity is displayed by wearing a dress made of meat or a hat shaped like an old-fashioned telephone. The costume is intentionally strange, its intent is to garner attention. "One of my greatest artworks is the art of fame. I'm a master of the art of fame," she told Anderson Cooper in a *60 Minutes* interview. "Part of my mastering of the art of fame, part of it is getting people to pay attention to what you want them to pay attention to. And not pay attention to the things you don't want them to pay attention to" (*60 Minutes*). When Lady Gaga walks into a room everyone looks at her. She understands that fame is the currency she possesses and uses her music, costumes, and media appearances to direct the audience's attention. Later chapters will show how Jesse Ventura and Sonny Bono used costumes to garner attention for themselves.

If one cannot rely on their natural good looks to gain attention, costumes do the trick. Indeed, everyday wardrobing decisions are a kind of costuming done for the purpose of image management. For ordinary people,

Clothes and cosmetics are the easiest place to begin. Chosen with a little care, they express dignity or informality, intensity or casualness, rebellion or propriety, liberality or conservatism, fashionableness or insouciance. Dark suits with pinstripes are said to make the man more authoritative, light brown suits make him approachable, impeccably shined shoes make him punctilious. (Sternberg 1998, 13)

Ordinary Americans take their cues from celebrities and learn how to adopt a persona that will project the right image.

To be sure, the labor performer can rarely afford the personality technicians that celebrities count on, such as agents, publicists, PR firms, personal managers, personal promoters, press secretaries, spin doctors, spokespersons, advance men, speech writers, image consultants, therapists and personal groomers, including assorted costumers, cosmeticians, cosmetic surgeons, voice coaches and hairstylists. (Sternberg 1998, 11)

Still, there are steps they can take to creatively display the correct self-image. In addition to their sartorial decisions, they can also practice their voice, movements, gestures, body positions and eye contact techniques. "To truly advance his value on the market, the ambitious performer must be willing to calculatedly adapt persona to the desires of the audience" (Sternberg 1998, 18). This is true of actors, politicians, and ordinary folks who want to make the right impression on others.

FAKE FIGHTING

Garnering attention is a skill that can be learned and utilized to orchestrate desired responses from the audience. Costumes draw attention, but so do outrageous comments or public feuding. Celebrities will often engage in a war of words with another celebrity to create a hostile rivalry that creates public drama. The goal is for each of the rivals to make the news for their hostility toward the other, making people pay attention to them. P.T. Barnum reportedly said, "If you want to attract a crowd, start a fight." In today's media environment, however, the audience is everyone on earth. For celebrities and politicians, the grand audience is the public writ large, the more people pay attention to them the more influential they are. Once they have the audience's attention, they can sell them a product or sell them a cause.

It is worth some time here to explore the history of professional wrestling and its role in American society because this form of entertainment was instrumental to the success of both Jesse Ventura and Donald Trump. The stagecraft they learned from professional wrestling provides insights into their public behaviors as political candidates. While it is certainly odd to include a discussion of professional wrestling in an academic endeavor it is necessary to understand the broader context that led to the rise of two of the most controversial celebrity politicians.

Wrestling as a sport can be traced to the first Olympiad in ancient Greece. The Romans adopted this sport but used it as a spectacle to amuse the masses. These early wrestling matches eventually became the gladiatorial contests that ancient Rome is famous for. The sport and spectacle then diffused throughout Europe as the Roman Empire expanded. It made its way to America when Irish immigrants brought "scuffling" with them as a form of entertainment. Enterprising tavern owners would hire traveling "scufflers" who would fight in front audiences. The fight would draw a crowd who would purchase liquor and make wagers on the fight. If professional wrestling has the aura of a bar room brawl, that is because that's where professional wrestling in America began (Beekman 2006).

In the early 1900s carnival owners also used this technique to draw a crowd. "The shift toward wrestlers working in collusion . . . emerged from the carnival subculture. The effects of carnivals on the development of modern professional wrestling are immense. Most carnivals and many circuses of the period included an athletic show (or, more commonly, 'at show') attraction that included boxers, wrestlers, and strongmen" (Beekman 2006, 39). The owners would often hire people with deformities or other unusual characteristics as part of a traveling "freak show." One of the "freaks" would be an unusually large man who would challenge audience members to a fight. A carnival employee would play the role of "audience member" in a staged fight that appeared unrehearsed. Wrestling promoter Jack Pfefer decided that this approach could be used on its own. He traveled from town to town with wrestlers who would fight in front of paying audiences. "As a self-proclaimed showman, Pfefer not only relied on gimmick wresters to sell tickets but also took great pleasure in publicly acknowledging how he used them to dupe the gullible public" (Beekman 2006, 74). He did not pretend the fights were real and he referred to his wrestlers as his "freaks" because he was selling a type of performance art for audience consumption (Beekman 2006).

In the 1940s and 1950s, when television was getting started, professional wrestling was regularly broadcast to mass audiences. Because of technological limitations sports like baseball did not present well on TV. The ball was too small, and cameras were not able to zoom in on the action or move fast enough to follow the play. Sports that took place in an arena could be captured relatively well from a camera in a fixed location so boxing and wrestling were the sports that broadcasters utilized. Wrestling promoters realized that fights were better and more interesting when they had a back-story, so they manufactured "heat" or hostility between various wrestlers who, of course, would settle their differences in the ring (Beekman 2006).

Various wrestling promoters copied the idea and professional wrestlers became adept at creating personas and wearing costumes that would distinguish them from other wrestlers. Wrestlers who were skilled at creating a good performance gained popularity and could command higher wages for each appearance. "Gorgeous George," according to Beekman, "can be viewed as the first modern professional wrestler in that he abandoned antiquated notions of striving to become world champion to achieve celebrity . . . wrestlers such as George truly became entertainers, as opposed to athletes" (Beekman 2006, 88).

Professional wrestling on TV then became a "masculine melodrama" where good guys and bad guys would fight it out. The wrestlers would adopt good guy and bad guy personas with correspondingly exaggerated good and bad characteristics. The good guy would not always win, sometimes the bad guy would win, usually by cheating or by using some kind of deception. The jilted good guy would challenge their opponent to a rematch where, of course, the wrong would be righted. The rematch ensured that more tickets would be sold to live events and TV viewers would tune in again. Storylines would be developed for each wrestler that would leave the audience curious about outcomes and resolutions to various conflicts between the wrestlers. Professional wrestling for men was like soap operas for women, the audience would have to tune in again to learn what happens to their favorite characters (Barthes 2005; de Garis 2005; Jenkins III 2005a).

At the beginning of the 1980s the World Wrestling Federation (WWF), National Wrestling Alliance (NWA), and American Wrestling Association (AWA) were the three largest wrestling promotions in America. Vince McMahon (his wife, Linda McMahon, would serve in the Trump administration) consolidated the regional system of wrestling promotions into a single national enterprise called the WWF. The regional system was increasingly difficult to maintain because wrestling matches were now being nationally broadcast on cable television. McMahon's first move was to acquire the NWA with its flagship promotion *Georgia Championship Wrestling* which was broadcast nationally on the TBS network. He then set his sights on the AWA. When Hulk Hogan left the AWA for the WWF after appearing in *Rocky III* the AWA's fate was sealed. Having lost their top talent, the AWA could not compete with McMahon's WWF (Beekman 2006).

To understand how promoters and publicists create "pseudo-events" to increase their client's attention capital one needs to look no farther than a 1984 collaboration between the WWF and MTV.

A chance encounter between singer Cyndi Lauper and WWF heel manager "Captain" Lou Albano led to the WWF performer appearing in her "Girls Just Want to Have Fun" music video. In the spring of 1984, the video went into heavy rotation on Music Television (MTV), the explosive new arbiter of teenage culture. McMahon and Lauper's management then built a feud between Lauper and Albano over his alleged sexist attitudes. Both cut promos that ran on WWF programs and MTV. The cross-promotion helped both sides. Lauper's album sold 6 million copies, and the WWF broke out of the wrestling ghetto and into mainstream popular culture. McMahon proclaimed his product "Rock 'n' Wrestling" and built the Lauper-Albano feud into a major wrestling event. The feminist angle eventually led well-known figures such as Gloria Steinem and Geraldine Ferraro to make public statements in support of Lauper. On July 23, 1985, the match between Lauper's proxy, Wendi Richter, and the ageless Fabulous Moolah, drew the largest audience in MTV history. (Beekman 2006, 125)

This cultural moment in America was entirely fabricated. The good guys and bad guys were defined, the conflict was stoked, people of import expressed opinions on the matter, and the nation watched the spectacle. Both sides orchestrated the event for calculated monetary gain.

The media consultants that work for modern political campaigns are well versed in these techniques because the entertainment and political industries both require mass marketing. They understand the aphorism, "If you want to draw a crowd, start a fight." The practitioners in each industry rely on the same skill set to succeed. Fights between opponents are exciting because the audience wants to know who will win. There is an inherent drama to the spectacle of wrestling matches and political contests.

The WWF was marketed to a mass audience of both adults and children. *Hulk Hogan's Rock 'n' Wrestling* was a Saturday morning cartoon that provided simple narratives of right and wrong, consistent with professional wrestling's long-standing tradition of pitting good guys against bad guys. The selling of action figures and other toys provided additional revenues in excess of $200 million annually (Beekman 2006). In 1998, the WWF earned approximately $500 million from retail sales of licensed products (Hauser 2002). Jesse Ventura, having learned from the McMahon business model, sold Jesse Ventura action figures to raise money for his political campaign (Jenkins III 2005b).

WrestleMania 1 "not only included wrestling matches but also a spate of celebrities as accoutrements. Muhammad Ali, Billy Martin, Mr. T. and Liberace, among others, appeared on the show" (Beekman 2006, 126). The event, in which Jesse Ventura appeared, grossed $4 million in 1985. Two years later WrestleMania 3 earned more than $10 million in pay per view buys alone (Beekman 2006). WrestleMania 29 featuring a match between

John Cena and Dwayne "the Rock" Johnson, now a Hollywood actor, had more than 1 million viewers and earned $72 million (Dawson 2017). In 1998, the WWF had 4.3 million pay-per-view sales from which it earned $130 million (Hauser 2002). Its primetime TV offerings drew 5 million viewers (Sammond 2005b). By 2001, McMahon's company had yearly revenues of $456 million. The WWF changed its name to WWE in 2002 to settle a lawsuit from the World Wildlife Fund (Beekman 2006). These figures are presented to show that professional wrestling has a significant fan base. Later chapters will show that these fans can be transformed into voters who can impact election outcomes.

In 1989, to avoid sports licensing fees, McMahon announced that WWF matches were not a sport, but rather entertainment and therefore not subject to sports industry regulations. Like Pfefer before him, McMahon admits that the fights are not real and lets the audience in on the production of the spectacle (Beekman 2006). Mazer found that wrestling fans "evaluate the performance as performance" (Mazer 2005, 71). "With a knowledge and ferocity that would impress any theater producer or teacher, they argue about the believability of characters and evaluate storylines . . . [t]hey note the shifts in dramaturgical practice" (Mazer 2005, 78). High-brow Americans might have their Broadway plays, but low-brow Americans have their WrestleManias. Both are live action entertainment. "There is no more a problem of truth in wrestling than in theater. In both, what is expected is the intelligible representation of moral situations which are usually private" (Barthes 2005, 26). Viewed in this way Donald Trump's dishonesty can be viewed as a ploy to excite his followers to root for him as he battles his political rivals (Trump performed in WrestleMania 23). Today's WWE hires professional writers to develop scripts and choreographers to plan the fights. Wrestlers, like actors in a live action play, rehearse their lines and actions to prepare for their in-ring performances (Sammond 2005a).

The performances take a heavy toll on the wrestlers. According to Beekman, "A frighteningly high percentage of wrestlers die before the age of 40 because of hardcore matches and outrageous stunts and gimmicks. . . . For the past half-decade, an average of approximately ten wrestlers under 40 die every year. Most wrestling deaths are either suicides or drug related" (Beekman 2006, 142–43). One particularly tragic event was during the *Over the Edge* event in 1999. Owen Hart was supposed to descend from the rafters, but when his harness broke, he fell to his death in front of a stadium full of spectators and countless others watching on live television. The show went on and spectators and viewers were not told about Hart's death until after its conclusion (Beekman 2006; Mazer 2005). The wrestlers take serious risks with their bodies to wow their audiences with spectacular feats of strength and agility, but for many the costs are severe. For others, the benefits are enormous. The top wrestlers become celebrities that allow them to use their skills in other industries. Wrestler Jesse "The Body" Ventura pursued an acting career and was successfully elected the governor of Minnesota. Wrestler Dwayne "The Rock" Johnson has become a successful actor himself and has recently fielded questions about running for president (Reilly 2021).

BRANDING

In a society where creating and maintaining illusions is paramount, image management is key to one's success. Erving Goffman's social theory seems especially relevant in a celebrified society. Goffman's symbolic interaction is based on the projection of an image of the self. Humans develop a self-presentation to interact with each other. These self-images are the representations of the self that individuals wish to project to others in the social world. Every person creates a type of front or mask that superficially displays what the individual wants displayed in the social realm. Individuals behave as performers in front of an audience to garner the desired reaction from others (Goffman 1959, 2005). This skill at projecting the right image leads to social success.

Reputation building is now known as "branding." A brand is a mark that distinguishes one product from another. A brand with a reputation for quality will have an advantage over a brand with a reputation for being unreliable. As if consumerism had not already gone too far (Marcuse 2013), humans are now marketed in the same way brands once were.

> Self-branding involves the self-conscious construction of a meta-narrative and meta-image of self through the use of cultural meanings and images drawn from the narrative and visual codes of the mainstream culture industries. The function of the branded self is purely rhetorical; its goal is to produce cultural value and, potentially, material profit. . . . The practice of self-branding is clearly expressed and delineated in current management literature as a necessary strategy for success in an increasingly complex corporate world. (Hearn 2008, 198)

Celebrities are highly skilled at creating a personal brand that is easily recognized and admired by audiences. Politicians too must develop a reputation, a brand, that people want to support. This coincidence is one more feature of social celebrification.

CONCLUSIONS

This is the cultural milieu that allows polebrities to develop. The image that people seek to create of themselves is fake and contrived. But this is true of every social actor. Every personal interaction is an interaction with someone else's mask. Everyone is involved in some type of fakery, but this pretense is the reality we live in. The fake and the real is not a binary choice, it is a continuum where things are more, or less, real, and fake. Van Krieken argued that "The court's patronage of secular, professional theatre proved quickly to be a double-edged sword, because the skilled actor demonstrated how all of life can be 'acted' with greater or lesser talent, including the role of the monarch" (van Krieken 2012, 48). Real actors can pretend to be real political leaders. Denzel Washington is Malcolm X, Daniel Day-Lewis is Abraham Lincoln, Gary Oldman is Winston Churchill. Actors can create the illusion of being a good political leader, simply transfer that into the real world and things will be great. Democracy has given the masses the power to make the fake real. People have realized that actors could be real political leaders.

Chapter 2

Celebrity Politics

C. Wright Mills argues that celebrities are part of the power elite. For him, "celebrities are The Names that need no further introduction" (Mills 2000, 72). Celebrities are "synthetic," and their talent is "their appearance value and their skill combined into what is known as A Personality" (Mills 2000, 75). Celebrities come primarily from the entertainment industry. Actors, musicians, models, and professional athletes now occupy the upper strata of the social hierarchy. So much so that the highest status males would now rather date and marry a model than a blue blood debutante. "The hierarchy of publicity has replaced the hierarchy of descent and even of great wealth," according to Mills (73). This status system of American prestige serves two social functions. First, "they serve to keep a propertied class intact" (Mills 2000, 88). Second, and most importantly, "Prestige buttresses power, turning it into authority, and protecting it from social challenge" (Mills 2000, 89). Celebrity is an integral part of the power system in American society.

Mills acknowledges that celebrities are created by the mass media and understands the celebrification of American politics.

> More serious public figures too, must now compete for attention and acclaim with the professionals of the mass media. On provincial levels, politicians play in hillbilly bands; on national levels, they are carefully groomed and coached for the TV camera, and, like other performers, the more important of them are subject to review by entertainment critics. (Mills 2000, 75)

The modern American politician must use the means of celebrity to successfully navigate our new political environment.

This chapter will review the literature on politics as a kind of performance art. It will also discuss how politics has been celebrified, how entertainment and politics are no longer distinct realms. Indeed, the entertainment industry has a long history of political involvement. Professionals in each industry readily switch between the two and join forces to achieve political and social aims. Lastly, it will create a framework, used in subsequent chapters, to understand why it is that celebrities win elections in American politics.

Many authors have argued that entertainment and politics have now merged. Building on that work this book argues that celebrities have an advantage in electoral politics because they have the necessary skills. These skills include gaining attention, comfort with live audiences, ease in front of cameras, and the ability to build a personal brand. As we will see in chapter 11, these skills can work in the other direction. Politicians with these skills can become celebrities. Celebrities also have the fame and resources to help them win elections. Critically, the political environment separates the successful celebrity candidates from the unsuccessful ones. This suggests that celebrity is insufficient on its own to win electoral contests.

Van Zoonen has developed a concept called "Fan Democracy." She argues that in many respects voters behave like fans (van Zoonen 2005). As one would expect fans have a very favorable view of the celebrities they admire, and high favorability ratings are very useful in the political arena. Building on these insights this book argues that celebrities have a fan base that they can transfer into the political arena. The fans can be activated as voters to impact electoral outcomes. The celebrity politicians profiled in this book begin their electoral contests with many advantages that ordinary candidates do not have.

POLITICS AS PERFORMANCE

Marshall notes the convergence between entertainment and politics, "In politics, a leader must somehow embody the sentiments of the party, the people, and the state. In the realm of entertainment, a celebrity must somehow embody the sentiments of an audience" (Marshall 1997, 203). Both entertainer and politician are in some sense "working the crowd." Schweiger and Adami argue that "To orientate himself or herself on the complicated market of different candidates and parties, the voter uses much the same patterns as when comparing brands. . . . The candidate has to be accepted as a branded product of a company called a political party" (Schweiger and Adami 1999, 350). In this way the Democratic donkey and Republican elephant serve as company logos that convey meanings to the voters as consumers of political products.

The "celebrification" of society has meant that, "institutions such as parties and ideologies primarily serve as brands, while the only future for political personality is that of celebrity" (Corner and Pels 2003, 8). Mirroring Mills, Corner and Pels argue that "A performative politics foregrounds the politician as an actor, whose performance on the public stage is continuously judged" (Corner and Pels 2003, 10). Alexander used this framework to analyze the

2008 presidential campaign, arguing that "the struggle for power becomes theatrical. Candidates work to present compelling performances of civil competence to citizen audiences" (Alexander 2010, 9). Similarly, Street contends,

> The art of politics becomes the art of performance, the art of being a celebrity. It is important, therefore, to develop the concepts and tools that enable us to understand better how political ideas are enacted, and how audiences—"the people"—are created in the act of performance. And how, in turn, the passions of the citizen-fan are elicited and orchestrated. (Street 2019, 17)

In the same vein as Goffman and van Krieken, Alexander believes that candidates seek to become symbolic representations of political ideals (Alexander 2010). The literature strongly suggests that a celebrified society necessitates a celebrified politics.

Celebrities and politicians are especially skilled at projecting exactly the image they wish to project. Drake and Higgins argue that "Through political campaigning and image management, the politician—like the celebrity—aims to appeal to a mass audience" (Drake and Higgins 2006, 88). Today, "Any analysis of political persona must recognize that performance, involving varying degrees of self-consciousness and calculated deceit, is a constituent factor of social life" (Corner 2000, 387). In 1886, Theodore Roosevelt staged a photograph of himself apprehending criminals. Historians have discovered that the "criminals" in the photograph were Roosevelt's own staff (Corner 2000). Television has only enhanced the need for image management. The skills needed to win a nominating convention before the television era are far different from the skills needed to win a direct primary by appealing to television viewers (Wray 1999). Politicians must work at creating a public persona that will resonate with the electorate, one that will convey the right message and win them votes.

Street argues that we need to rethink the field of political marketing. Political marketing is not like a commercial business, selling oil, it is like show-business, selling performances. "Politicians may be commodities, just like pop and film stars are commodities, but the way they are sold does not fit into the pattern set by consumer goods. Instead, they belong to the field of cultural goods, which are significantly different in kind and character from other consumer products" (Street 2003, 92). This means that "The business of political communication is about turning politicians into celebrities in order to organise the sentiments they want to represent. Spin doctors are the equivalent of PR people in film and record companies, managing the image of, and access to, their stars" (Street 2003, 92).

Street has developed a useful typology that can be used to understand celebrity politics. The first type is the celebritized politician (CP1), a "traditional politician . . . who engages with the world of popular culture in order to enhance or advance their pre-established political functions and goals" (Street 2004, 437). The second type is the politicized celebrity (CP2), "the entertainer who pronounces on politics and claims the right to represent peoples and causes, but who does so without seeking or acquiring elected office" (Street 2004, 438). CP1s can be divided into two groups: traditional politicians who take on the trappings of celebrity—think of Bill Clinton playing the saxophone or Tony Blair posing with his guitar—and celebrities turned politicians, like Ronald Reagan or Arnold Schwarzenegger. CP2s are entertainers from the film, music, or sports industries who advocate for social or political causes, like Jane Fonda or Bono. Political parties and candidates seek out celebrity spokespersons or endorsers to communicate their message to targeted demographics. For Street, celebrity politics is a legitimate means of democratic representation. CP1s use the modern means of media communication at their disposal to broadcast their message to the public and CP2s represent citizens who seek government action on certain issues (Street 2004, 2012). Celebrity politics is not fundamentally different from the politics of the past just because the method of communication has changed. It still amounts to various interests attempting to wield government authority in their favor.

CELEBRIFIED POLITICS

According to West and Orman we have entered an era where entertainment has become politics and politics has become entertainment. In this new era of celebrity politics,

> Prominent individuals use fame either to run for elected office or influence those who do. They are able to draw on their platform to raise money for themselves and other politicians. In a media-centered political system, celebrities are adept at attracting attention. They make great copy, and reporters love to build stories around glamorous celebrities. (West and Orman 2003, 6)

They use the term "famed nonpoliticos" to describe celebrities who, "piggyback fame in one sector onto political life." These celebrities, "are seen as political 'white knights.' Since their prominence comes from outside the political world, these individuals have a high degree of public trustworthiness and star power to boot" (West and Orman 2003, 4). They harness their celebrity status to effect political change by acting as lobbyists for various causes, or by seeking elected office themselves.

The earliest examples of Hollywood actors winning elected office are Helen Douglas and George Murphy. Douglas won a seat in the US House of

Representatives in 1944 and Murphy became a US senator in 1964 (Longoria 2022). They paved the way for Ronald Reagan to be elected governor of California in 1966. After Reagan many more celebrities would seek elected office. As this book goes to press Dr. Oz is running for the US Senate in Pennsylvania and Herschel Walker is running for the US Senate in Georgia (Yang 2022).

Louis B. Mayer laid the foundation for a long-lasting relationship between Hollywood and Washington. Mayer co-founded Metro-Goldwyn-Mayer (MGM) studios in 1924. He was active in Republican politics and was, what we would call today, a "bundler" for the Herbert Hoover campaign in 1928. He solicited and collected large contributions from Hollywood luminaries such as Cecil B. DeMille and Joseph Schenck. Mayer used his position to spearhead Hoover's radio campaign, he used this new media to get the GOP message to voters. Because of his fundraising prowess he secured a position in Hoover's closest circle of advisors. As a studio executive he would invite governors, senators, and congressmen to tour MGM. While there, he would make sure that the GOP politicians were photographed with the movie stars, creating press for both the politician and the star. While Mayer was certainly ideological, he did find practical uses for his political connections. When MGM needed to borrow battleships or fighter planes to make a war movie, Mayer called his friend the President (Brownstein 1990; Ross 2011).

Mayer used his skills from the movie making business to change the very nature of American politics.

> Mayer's greatest contribution to the 1932 election was to inject showmanship and celebrity into the GOP convention and the presidential campaign. It was not evident to party leaders that elections could be a form of entertainment. But it was to Mayer, and he worked hard to make them so. Understanding that voters, like moviegoers, wanted a good show, he taught Republicans how to produce and sell a more effective drama for a mass audience. He staged the convention, now being broadcast on national radio, just as thoughtfully as he would one of his film productions . . . Mayer introduced a festive element by providing live music during delegate demonstrations, screening a talking film of Hoover, and arranging for balloons to flutter down onto the convention floor following the Chief's nomination. (Ross 2011, 69)

He also ordered the film stars under his employ to attend Hoover campaign rallies. He knew many people would take time out of their day to see a movie star they admired, and it gave partisans an opportunity to persuade the voter to support the Republican ticket.

Because of his efforts Mayer became chairman of the California GOP in 1932. He was very active in the race for California governor between Upton Sinclair and Frank Merriam (Brownstein 1990). Moviegoers who saw an

MGM feature film would first have to sit through a newsreel. MGM news-reels during the election featured a "reporter" interviewing "citizens," and asking them questions about the governor's race.

> MGM hired a series of minor actors to play the part of ordinary voters. Thalberg and Mayer understood that casting, costuming, accents, and makeup could all be used to shape the ideological impact of the sham newsreels. Interviewees supporting Merriam were well-dressed, attractive, American-looking citizens who had jobs and property and spoke in a clear and cogent manner. Sinclair's supporters were disgruntled, dirty, riffraff who occasionally stammered or spoke with foreign accents and lauded communism and socialism. (Ross 2011, 75)

Mayer invented fake news. During his tenure as the simultaneous head of the California Republican Party and MGM Studios, MGM became the GOP's propaganda division. Mayer's innovations were soon copied by the Democrats and today's political parties continue to rely on Hollywood-style production techniques.

What Mayer did for Republicans, Jack Warner of Warner Brothers did for Democrats. "Warner Bros. was known in the thirties as the studio of 'social consciousness,' and—more especially—as the studio of the New Deal, one that flashed big posters of FDR and the Blue Eagle during Cagney's dance act in *Gold Diggers of 1933*" (Wills 2017, 111). Warner Brothers Studios produced a series of movies celebrating the federal government, especially praising the new crime fighting FBI. Ronald Reagan played heroic federal agent Brass Bancroft in a series of action-adventure movies in 1939 (Vaughn 1994; Wills 2017). Today's political parties and interest groups are in the propaganda business in what O'Shaughnessy calls a "marketing-propaganda hybrid" (O'Shaughnessy 1999, 736). It has been this way for a century.

When not running for office themselves, or holding partisan leadership positions, celebrities lobby for various causes or fundraise for favored politicians. Charles Dickens, Ralph Waldo Emerson, and Henry David Thoreau used their fame to support the abolition of slavery. Stars such as Humphrey Bogart and Judy Garland made appearances at FDR campaign rallies. Marlon Brando worked with UNICEF to provide famine relief in India, advocated for Native American causes, and marched with Dr. Martin Luther King, Jr. to promote civil rights. Jane Fonda was a prominent anti-Vietnam War activist. Paul Newman and Burt Lancaster were civil rights activists. Muhammed Ali opposed the Vietnam War and advocated for African American civil rights. Audrey Hepburn was concerned with alleviating African poverty. John Wayne became the president of the right-wing Motion Picture Alliance. Charlton Heston became president of the National Rifle Association (NRA), and Tom Selleck was an NRA board member. Robert Redford supported energy conservation. George Clooney used his fame to bring attention to the atrocities in Darfur. Angelina Jolie has brought attention to the plight of refugees from West Africa and has adopted children from developing countries. Martin Sheen opposes nuclear weapons and supports the homeless. Richard Gere is the chairman of The International Campaign for Tibet which seeks Tibetan self-determination and reports on human rights abuses. Sigourney Weaver has sought to protect gorillas in wildlife conservation efforts. Michael J. Fox has become an advocate to bring awareness to Parkinson's disease. The singer Bono from the band U2 has focused his efforts on developing nation aid and debt relief and is the co-founder of the One Campaign and Debt, Aids, Trade, Africa (DATA). Unlike other celebrities, Bono has also used direct lobbying of government officials to achieve his political aims. The list could go on, but the point should be clear. Celebrities have a long tradition of social and political activism in the United States and internationally (Street 2002; West and Orman 2003; Huddart 2005; Rabidoux 2009; Tsaliki et al. 2011; van Krieken 2012; Wheeler 2013; Totman 2017).

Today, celebrity agents and publicists look for causes that their client can become involved with. The selection of the cause is important because it is used to add another dimension to their public persona. Not only is so and so a great actor, but they want to save the environment too! Getting behind a cause increases the star's fame, it provides new opportunities for publicity, and, when done correctly, improves the star's reputation (Littler 2008; Stanley 2014).

> Celebrities have a type of power that is influential in the political arena, celebrity activists have popularized campaigns as they have provided credibility for political agendas among target audiences. It has demonstrated how CP2s have orchestrated fund-raising for causes, have brought attention to policy debates and have attracted public support for social movements. In addition, the audience's capacity to consume celebrity activities has increased due to the collapse of trust in the political classes. This politicization of celebrities has reflected how celebrity culture has expanded in western democracies. (Wheeler 2013, 97)

As society itself becomes celebritized, it should be no surprise that our politics begins to get celebritized. Celebrities enter politics because it is the logical next step of our cultural development.

In addition to overt methods of political involvement there are more subtle ways Hollywood can affect the American political landscape. Hollywood can act as a trendsetter. In the early days this was done to curry favor with Washington elites. The movie industry was worried about anti-trust legislation because of their monopolistic control over the production process. They were also concerned with censorship. In the 1930s, Warner Brothers inserted pro-New Deal propaganda into their movies to sell the public on FDR's policies and get on the government's good side. In the 1940s, the industry moved to root out communist influences by making actors sign a loyalty pledge and by blacklisting actors with leftist views. The 1960s and 1970s experienced many prominent actors getting involved in anti-war and civil rights causes. In the 1980s, there were many action movies that had Soviet villains. Today, the communists have been replaced by jihadis, but the theme remains the same— a muscle man hero saves the world (Ross 2011; Scott 2011).

In some cases, entertainment is explicitly political. Musicians such as Bob Dylan, Tracy Chapman, Bob Marley, Public Enemy, NWA, Rage Against the Machine, and Prophets of Rage have songs that express political values and speak to social ills. Satire and comedy are often used to ridicule political authority. Professional sports shape ideals of masculinity and perpetuate gender bias. They can also unite the citizens of a country when their national team plays against a political rival, think of USA vs. Russia or England vs. India. The entertainment people consume is not apolitical. Political culture and political ideals are transmitted through forms of entertainment (Street 2001). Van Zoonen argues that "television culture . . . through its entertainment genres in particular . . . provides narratives and perspectives that express and make sense of politics" (van Zoonen 2003, 101). Television remains the number one source of political information for most Americans (Wray 1999).

The indirect influence is most evident on the issue of gay rights. The situation comedy *Ellen* was the first instance of an openly gay lead character on national television. After that, *Queer Eye for the Strait Guy* and *Will & Grace* featured openly gay characters. These shows, "treated homosexuality as something normal, or even aspirational—they made it cool to be gay or to have gay friends" (Stanley 2014, 235). When Joe Biden came out in favor of same sex marriage, he credited *Will & Grace* for educating the American public on the issue. When President Obama followed suit to support same sex marriage, donations from Hollywood to the Obama campaign followed the announcement. Hollywood can promote policy changes directly through political action or indirectly by trying to influence public opinion, often both methods are used simultaneously (Stanley 2014).

Scott correctly argues that "Film—Hollywood, cinema more generally— has also become an integrated source of discourse for the political culture" (Scott 2011, 31). Similarly, Dahlgren argues that television blurs the line between informational civic affairs programming and entertainment programming. Situation comedies, soap operas, drama series, and other entertainment programing often feature value conflicts over "premarital sex, sexual preference, abortion, gene manipulation, interethnic relations, and so on" that inform or tap into political controversies (Dahlgren 2009, 135). There simply is not a distinct line that separates our entertainment from our politics.

Political values are expressed on both the small and large screens; political controversies provide ready-made drama for use by screenwriters.

Eli Attie worked in the Clinton White House and became Al Gore's chief speechwriter. Later, Attie become a writer for the TV show *The West Wing*. When he was tasked with creating a Latino presidential candidate for the show, he modeled the character on a little-known politician from Illinois—Barack Obama. The Matthew Santos character was a "principled, charismatic ethnic minority presidential candidate who, against the odds, captured the White House. When Obama won his party's nomination three years later in spookily similar circumstances, Axelrod wrote Attie, "We're living your scripts!" (Stanley 2014, 135). Hollywood can prime the American electorate to accept particular causes or candidates. Things that once seemed unimaginable, like same sex marriage or a black president, are imagined by Hollywood, promoted in TV and movies, and made imaginable, even unspectacular, events when they actually happen. Hollywood can break down social barriers and change the way people think.

Stuart Stevens is a graduate of UCLA film school and was a script writer for the television shows *Northern Exposure*, *Commander in Chief*, and *K Street*. He was also a top-level Republican consultant and strategist who worked on presidential, US senate, state, and local elections. He wrote campaign speeches for Republican candidates and now regrets intentionally stoking the flames of white racial resentment as part of the Republicans' southern strategy (Stevens 2020). Attie and Stevens demonstrate that campaign speech writers and television script writers move back and forth between the entertainment and political industries rather easily and in both directions.

Both liberals and conservatives take their cues from Hollywood created archetypes. The liberal hero archetype is embodied by Malcolm X, Harvey Milk, and Erin Brockovich in their biopic films. "The liberal hero is someone who is rational and informed and who elevates politics with their presence—wonks willing to confront the ignorance of the mob head-on" (Stanley 2014, 136). Conservatives rely on the cowboy archetype, "the cowboy represents everything they think they represent: honor, masculinity, faith in God, resistance to authority, guns, self-reliance, the common man made heroic" (Stanley 2014, 161). Together these two archetypes create the script for our political screenplay. Our politicians play the roles to greater or lesser effect, but American ideals are shaped by Hollywood fantasy.

These heroic fantasies then get imposed on the political system. For the vast majority of voters, the candidates they vote for are only known through their on-screen representations. They are as real, or as fictional, as the other characters they see on the screen.

> The more power a person has on the screen, or the more influence behind it, the more they can shortcut the process of persuading an electorate that they have earned their passage into politics. The instant answers that movieland and TV-land offer—from the bromides of agony-counseling talk shows to the quick-fix baddy-bashing of blockbusters—can seem, to an impressionable, needy or overoptimistic populace, the template for political problem-solving. (Andrews 2003, 250)

In other words, voters do not draw a distinction between real and fictional characters. Some actors have complained because they are recognized for the characters they play, rather than themselves. Many fans who know the character would be hard pressed to remember the name of the actor. They believe that real life problems can be solved in the same way as the fictional problems they encounter in their entertainment. If only they could find their idealized hero in the real word, they could solve real life problems.

Many authors have discussed the convergence between entertainment and politics (Marshall 1997; Street 2001; Corner and Pels 2003; West and Orman 2003; Drake and Higgins 2006; Street 2012; Wheeler 2013; Stanley 2014; Turner 2014; Majic, O'Neill, and Bernhard 2020). For some this is because celebrities and politicians are psychologically similar, "Moviemakers and politicians are very similar types of people: Vain, ambitious, egotistical performers who love crowds, they're drawn to one another's charisma. Their alliances have often tipped over into interdependence; they are hooked on each other's power and money" (Stanley 2014, 18). This natural similarity makes it easier for them to form friendships because both parties understand how their coordinated efforts are mutually beneficial.

Hollywood was very active in the 2012 election. Celebrities donated to Obama, campaigned for him, and, also, stirred up the culture war to promote liberal views. That same year, former US Senator Chris Dodd chaired the Motion Picture Association of America (MPAA) and lobbied for anti-piracy legislation to protect the entertainment industry's profits (Stanley 2014). The convergence between Washington and Hollywood is profound. Elites of the political and entertainment industries regularly switch places in this new era of celebritized politics.

Wheeler argues that the political parties themselves have changed in order to succeed politically in our celebritized society,

> The centralized "cartel" parties who were employed by states to realize policies have been superseded by "expert–celebrity" parties who enact a discursive set of exchange relations aimed at achieving good governance. Although good governmental performance remains a requisite for re-election, so is the presentation of the party, the government and the policy. In an expert–celebrity party, members are not sources of policy ideas but are valued instead by their ability

to communicate the "message" of reform to convince the electorate to cast their vote. Thus, to speak to the electorate, parties have employed the media tools of celebrity, such as the appearances of leaders on popular television programmes, personalized web sites and political blogs. This reflexivity has meant that politicians have "celebritized" themselves to engage in a more personalized and less ideological set of political communications. (Wheeler 2013, 22)

The political class has adapted to the media environment. Just like celebrities, politicians reveal the intimate aspects of their personal lives to develop rapport with their audience (Stanyer 2007). Meanwhile, the political leader is merely a spokesperson for a political party that advocates for a group of allied interests.

For Wheeler, the "celebritization of politics has brought about alternative forms of political engagement which indicate cultural changes in the concepts of citizenship and participation" (Wheeler 2013, 114). He believes we need to look at politics in a new way, but he remains optimistic,

the mass escalation of celebrity politics may indicate a realistic means through which to promote political engagement. The dialogue between celebrity politicians and the public has allowed for new opportunities for political participation. This has reflected a growing willingness within the audience to accept celebrities as authentic political figures because of a decline in trust in the political classes and the public's greater identification with stars, brought about by the celebritization of popular culture. (Wheeler 2013, 114)

Celebrities offer an alternative that ordinary politicians do not. They can increase civic engagement and reach out to audiences that are typically ignored. They have more appeal and provide an alternative to a mass public that is frustrated by the status quo in American politics.

POLEBRITIES

Building on the theory developed by Goffman, Turner believes that "the systems used to produce celebrity in the entertainment and sports industries are very similar to those now used to produce the public persona of the politician. The need for the successful politician to build a public face means that the conventions of celebrity must collude with those of party politics" (Turner 2014, 149). This convergence is what allows for the development of *polebrities*, celebrities that become politicians. For those that are seriously interested in policy for the common good or who wish to express their ideological commitments, the trick is to find a good spokesperson. This spokesperson needs to entertain, convince, and garner the approval of the mass public. They do not need to strictly adhere to reality, they simply must capture the public's attention and make agreeable statements to gain the public's support.

Celebrities can be good politicians because they have the talent, fame, and resources to make them successful political campaigners—this is *the power trifecta* that polebrities possess. Their most important talent is their skill in stagecraft or image management, they can come to personify desired characteristics. They are good at reading scripts and portraying characters; they give convincing performances. Celebrities are also skilled at dealing with the media, their livelihood depends on it. Celebrities are well known; in politics we say they have high levels of name recognition. This means they get large amounts of earned media that other candidates do not receive. They can use this fame as a platform to espouse political ideas and have the public pay attention to them. Celebrities are millionaires who have the financial resources and personal contacts to finance a viable political campaign. Celebrities can win elections because they are in a better position to do so than run of the mill candidates.

Wright argues that celebrities have seven advantages that ordinary politicians don't have. They are "Name recognition, favorability, outsider status, fundraising ability, media attention, a large and passionate following, and relatability" (Wright 2019, 17). This book boils it down to three—talent, fame, and resources. Wright uses an experimental survey design while this book uses the case study approach. The case studies of winning candidates confirm that Wright's analysis was correct. Where we differ is with the importance of the political environment in determining outcomes. Wright is correct when she argues that a celebrity's "character is often judged by the standards to which entertainers adhere, or the lack thereof, rather than a stricter code of conduct we generally expect our government representatives to follow" (Wright 2019, 24). This is referred to as "celebrity slack" in this book and the case studies demonstrate its veracity.

However, as chapter 11 demonstrates, in the real world more celebrities lose elections than win them suggesting that their numerous advantages are not enough by themselves to win. Counting elected celebrity politicians who failed in seeking other offices yields more losers than winners. In those cases, traditional political experience and celebrity fame combined were still not enough to win. In addition, many of the winners won with pluralities not majorities, which does not suggest overwhelming enthusiasm for celebrity candidates but rather the good fortune of a plurality wins system in races with three or more candidates. This was the case for Bono, Ventura, Schwarzenegger, Franken, and Trump. Even the majority winners got lucky. Reagan benefitted from Governor Brown's blunders during the campaign. Fred Grandy was able to win because the incumbent was forced to drop out of the race after being bitten by a tick and contracting Lyme disease. Ben Jones, who lost most of his elections, got lucky when the incumbent was indicted propelling him to a fortuitous victory. The threat of an "emerging celebocracy" may be overblown (Wright 2019, 29).

TALENT

There are four talents that celebrities have that make them superior political candidates. First, they are good at attracting attention from the media and the public. Second, they are good in front of live audiences. Third, they are good in front of cameras. Fourth, and perhaps most importantly, they are good at developing a personal brand that resonates with audiences. The first talent was discussed at length in chapter 1, the next two are discussed in the case study chapters, so this section will primarily emphasize brand building.

Reagan, Eastwood, and Schwarzenegger were able to capture audience attention in their movies because of their good looks. Sonny Bono and Jesse Ventura used crazy costumes to gain the attention of their audiences. Donald Trump used outrageous comments, fake fighting, to draw attention to himself. Al Franken, as a stand-up comedian, was highly skilled at reading an audience's emotions and tailored his presentations to capture his audience. Reagan, as well, learned how to perform in front of live audiences when he traveled the country as the spokesman for GE. All the celebrities profiled in this book appeared on television or in movies. They felt comfortable in front of cameras and were effective communicators through that type of media. All of them, also, developed a persona that audiences understood implicitly. They developed images that conveyed a particular meaning to audiences.

Because of the performative nature of the celebrity society, actors have a tremendous advantage in the world we live in. Van Krieken believes that "the absolutist state had created a new legitimation problem, because actors could outperform actual kings, and the theatre changed people's perception of authority and social order, making problematic the distinction between the social role and the real human occupying it" (van Krieken 2012, 49). In other words, the nobility's patronage of theater created a new class of persons who appeared to be better nobles than the nobles themselves.

Aware of this the nobles had to adopt stagecraft to remain in power. "Because actors could 'be' kings, apparently often more effectively than real kings, kings also had to become actors" to secure the admiration of their subjects (van Krieken 2012, 115). Political leaders understood that they had to put on a show. Political actors need to engage in a "persuasive political performance" to succeed (Wheeler 2013, 17). It would make sense, then, that the public might very well elect an actor to be the new "king." We are familiar with the expression, "Fake it 'til you make it." Actors are highly skilled fakers. If you can fake doing a good job as a political leader, you might be able to actually do a good job as a political leader. Arnold Schwarzenegger has fictively saved the world numerous times, why not let him try it for real? The current elected officials are not getting it done, he could fake it until he does it. The public imagination had already been primed; this guy can save us from disaster—we have seen it. Television shows like *America's Most Wanted*, *Cops*, and the *Jerry Springer Show* are part of a tabloid television culture that are "part cause, part symptom, and part player in the postmodern process whereby notions of a singular, objective truth give way to a fragmented multiplicity of simulated ones whose imagistic instability establishes the conditions for contestation over a variety of declared truths and even over the nature of truth itself" (Glynn 2000, 45). Americans live in a full-fledged "fantasyland" where there is a blurring of reality and fantasy (Anderson 2017).

For Boorstin, "The American citizen thus lives in a world where fantasy is more real than reality, where the image has more dignity than its original" (Boorstin 1992, 49). Americans create illusions and replace reality with those illusions. "The power to make a reportable event is thus the power to make experience" because the pseudo-event is perceived as real (Boorstin 1992, 22). The world we live in is one where, "Vivid image came to overshadow pale reality" (Boorstin 1992, 25). The ability to create an image and manufacture an event are critical tools in the art of public persuasion—a key element in politics.

Benjamin Franklin, one of America's founders and leading political figures, understood the importance of creating a favorable public image. In his autobiography he says,

> In order to secure my credit and character as a tradesman, I took care not only to be in *reality* industrious and frugal, but to avoid all *appearances* to the contrary. I drest [sic] plainly; I was seen at no places of idle diversion; I never went out a fishing or shooting . . . and to show that I was not above my business, I sometimes brought home the paper I purchased at the stores, through the streets on a wheelbarrow. Thus being esteemed an industrious thriving young man, and paying duly for what I bought, the merchants who imported stationary solicited my custom. (Wright 1989, 87–88)

We can imagine the young Franklin walking through the streets of Philadelphia with his wheelbarrow waving at the shopkeepers as he walked by to show them how hardworking he was. The cultivation of a reputation is now referred to as branding, but Franklin understood that the projection of a positive image of oneself was critical for one's success. He knew appearances matter.

Machiavelli understood this necessity of political leadership. Leaders must appear to have various virtues but in reality defy them for the benefit of the nation.

A prince, then, must be very careful not to say a word which does not seem inspired by the five qualities I mentioned earlier. . . . He should appear a man of compassion, a man of good faith, a man of integrity, a kind and religious man. . . . Everyone sees what you appear to be, few experience what you really are. . . . The common people are always impressed by appearances. (Machiavelli 1995, 56)

For Machiavelli, the appearance is more important than the reality because appearances can subdue the people and frighten enemies.

Successful politicians are keenly aware of the importance of project-ing the right image and image management is now a critical feature of the contemporary American political campaign. Wheeler argues that "celebrity politicians (CP1s) have incorporated matters of performance, personalization, branding and public relations into the heart of their political representation" (Wheeler 2013, 70). Street believes that "As with any profession, politicians have to acquire appropriate skills. . . . Skills of performance are skills in self-presentation" (Street 2003, 95). Turner says,

The management of public personae has become a core activity for contem-porary politics. Politics is now overwhelmingly about the management of the media representation of individuals, of specific areas of debate, or of the party's "message" of the moment. The strategies employed are overwhelmingly derived from, on the one hand, public relations' models of crisis management and, on the other hand, from the celebrity industry's methods for building the public identities of the celebrity-commodity. (Turner 2014, 152)

When modern analysts like Street, Wheeler, and Turner discuss the perfor-mance or image of a politician, they are simply discussing a fact of social and political life that Benjamin Franklin understood well. Putting on a show to develop a favorable reputation among the public is a long-standing strat-egy in politics. Democratization and the mass media have merely increased its importance.

Catherine Needham argues that Bill Clinton and Tony Blair were success-ful because they "sought to sustain their relationships with their winning coalitions of voters through projecting aspects of leadership which are analo-gous to branding. Both leaders strived to develop simple, reassuring and cred-ible messages, which distinguished them from their opponents and resonated with the aspirations and values of voters" (Needham 2005, 355). The talent for projecting the right image of oneself is critical to the labor market success for celebrities, politicians, and everyday Americans.

Joe Kennedy purchased a Hollywood production company in 1919. Eventually, he purchased a movie studio in 1926. While in the industry he learned the value of image management. Image management can be used to turn a scoundrel into a paragon of virtue. He learned, "the camera can turn a short nobody into a tall hero" (Stanley 2014, 197). The Kennedy's would become masters of image management and maintain close relationships with Hollywood elites in the decades that followed (McDougal 1998; Wray 1999). When JFK was assassinated Lyndon Johnson made sure that Jackie Kennedy was photographed by his side when he took the oath of office, "Johnson insisted that she be in the frame so that Kennedy supporters would acknowledge his legitimacy as the new president. LBJ, too, had come to understand the power of a staged image" (Stanley 2014, 203). Schwarzenegger married into the Kennedy family and was advised by them during his campaign for governor.

The ability to craft a public persona, reputation, or brand, and the ability to garner the attention of the mass public is a transferable skill. "Celebrity in any one field can often be converted to another field: actors become politicians, models become actors, fashion designers become film directors, photographers work as actors and journalists, politicians host radio shows" (van Krieken 2012, 67). This is possible because these occupations require the same set of skills. Actors can become politicians (Ronald Reagan and Arnold Schwarzenegger) and politicians can become actors (Fred Thompson and Sarah Palin) because social status is acquired through the performance of stagecraft in a celebritized society and celebrities are good at it.

When transitioning from entertainment to politics these "famed nonpoliticos" have advantages "because they gained acclaim outside of the political realm they are used to being in the public spotlight and dealing with the accoutrements of celebrityhood—media coverage, adoring fans, gossip columnists, and intrusions into their private lives" (West and Orman 2003, 4). They are already familiar with the publicity industry and are capable of enduring and profiting from media exposure. Indeed, they have developed a skill that most others have not acquired.

In the 1980s, "the importance of consultants, joke writers, speech writers, pollsters, image advisors, ad makers, spin doctors, sound bite writers and delivery coaches in America became institutionalized" (West and Orman 2003, 10). Political parties on both sides of the Atlantic have full time communication staffs to craft and to hone messages that promote the party agenda (Franklin 2004; Stanyer 2007). This means the job of the politician is simply to deliver the pre-crafted message. Actors have the professional skills to accomplish this task most effectively.

Van Krieken suggests that "Celebrity and politics are Siamese twins, for the simple reason that both are about visibility, recognition and esteem" (Van Krieken 2012, 123). Wheeler agrees that "Celebrity politicians have appropriated image-making techniques taken from packaged campaigns to blur the lines between politics and entertainment" (Wheeler 2013, 82). This interchangeability is precisely what defines celebrity politics, "It is when the celebrities from the entertainment world cross over into the political system, and when the celebrities from the world of politics cross over into the world of entertainment, that the celebrity political system is generated" (West and Orman 2003, 117). It is possible because entertainers and politicians rely on the same set of skills, they have particular talents that propel them to success.

FAME

Name recognition impacts candidate support. Candidates whose names are recognized gain more support than candidates whose names are not recognized by voters. This is because known candidates are perceived to be more viable and legitimate (Stokes and Miller 1962; Kam and Zechmeister 2013). Celebrities, by definition, are known to the mass public. This by itself is a tremendous electoral advantage (Wright 2019). If the celebrity is running against an unknown candidate, name recognition alone would be enough to win, absent any other information about the candidates.

Members of Congress are divided into two camps, work horses who draft legislation, and show horses who seek media attention (Tacheron and Udall 1966; Payne 1980). As show horses par excellence celebrities are masters of the public domain. In Congressional elections, Herrnson has found that media attention helps both incumbents and challengers (Herrnson 2008). Additional media attention, for those candidates that acquire it, increases vote totals. This is consistent with the name recognition hypothesis. Celebrities can expect to get more votes simply because of the tremendous media attention they receive.

Celebrities become well known because of their talent at gaining the public's attention. This is a very important type of social capital. Van Krieken believes there is "another kind of capital, 'attention,' and that understanding the economics of attention—the accumulation, distribution and circulation of the abstract form of capital that is attention—is central to understanding how celebrity and celebrity society works" (van Krieken 2012, 24). We have no shortage of information in today's society; the internet has created a super abundance of information and knowledge. The issue becomes selecting which information to access.

We are then able to think through what underpins all celebrity—the management of attention—and how important attention has become in an information or knowledge society. Economics is about the management of scarce resources; when there is a surplus of information, data and knowledge, the scarce resource becomes attention, and it is the capacity of celebrities to function as "bundles of attention-capital" that is the key to understanding how all forms of celebrity operate. (van Krieken 2012, 26)

Celebrities can direct the public's attention to things that matter or to things that are trivial. They play a critical role because they attract the public's attention. Attentional capital itself can "be transformed into other kinds of 'capital'—esteem, status, wealth, influence, perhaps even power" (van Krieken 2012, 18). The modern celebrity is highly esteemed (or derided), wealthy, influential, and increasingly politically powerful.

The change in America's media environment has caused a change in the process of American government. "The rise of gossip journalism and the talk show, for instance, as well as satiric news commentary programmes such as *The Daily Show* and *The Colbert Report*, has challenged traditional sources of news and thus influenced how the process of mass-mediated political presentation must be organized" (Turner 2014, 150). Carl Bernstein (1992) called changes in how the media covers news "infotainment" because it attempts to blend information with entertainment and transform the trivial into something important. This brand of market driven journalism focuses on stories that capture the attention of the public, usually because the story is titillating or sensational, rather than "hard news" on matters that should be of serious concern. This change has transformed how politics is covered in America. West and Orman argue that "the line between Hollywood and Washington has virtually disappeared as politicians are covered as scandal-plagued celebrities" (West and Orman 2003, 18).

Bill Moyers was upset because CBS News, "yielded to the encroachment of entertainment values from within. Not only were those values invited in, they were also exalted. The line between entertainment and news was steadily blurred. Our center of gravity shifted from the standards and practices of the news business to show business" (Alter 1986, 53). If the news is now showbusiness, then entertainers will make the news more readily than other types of people. In this media environment, celebrities have a clear advantage over traditional politicians. Because they have achieved fame in the entertainment sector, they can more easily transition into the new politics as entertainment regime of celebritized politics.

Marshall argues that "Celebrity status also confers on the person a certain discursive power: within society, the celebrity is a voice above others, a voice that is channeled into the media systems as being legitimately significant"

(Marshall 1997, xlviii). They will get the attention that others do not get. This will increase their name recognition and give them a platform that other candidates do not have. Celebrities more easily acquire earned media; they get free publicity from the press. Whereas other political actors might have to pay for advertising, paid media, to get their message delivered to the public, celebrities can deliver their message for free. This means that Americans face greater exposure to the views and ideas propagated by celebrities than the views and ideas held by other types of individuals. Entertainers have a structural advantage in the American political system. It makes sense that we would hire celebrities to be America's spokespeople by electing them to public office.

RESOURCES

Celebrities have money and they have friends with money. This makes fund-raising much easier. The 100 top celebrities earned over five billion dollars in 2017. Sean "P. Diddy" Combs, the highest grossing celebrity in 2017, earned $130 million (Robehmed 2017). Even dead celebrities can rake in the cash. The top earning dead celebrities of 2017 included Michael Jackson ($75 mil.), Elvis Presley ($35 mil.), Bob Marley ($23 mil.), and Elizabeth Taylor ($8 mil.), whose image is still used to sell diamonds (Greenburg 2017). In 2011, the estate of Marylin Monroe brought in $27 million (Pomerantz 2011). Even after his death, Paul Newman's charity continues to earn revenue from the sale of branded products and uses that money for philanthropic endeavors (Raphael 2017). This ability to generate wealth gives celebrities economic power that can seep into other areas.

By bringing attention to a product, celebrities can have dramatic effects on the marketplace. In the twelve weeks before being included in Oprah Winfrey's Book Club just over 11,000 copies of *Anna Karenina* were sold. More than 640,000 copies were sold in the twelve weeks after Oprah's endorsement. During the mad cow scare Oprah indicated on her daily talk show that she no longer ate hamburgers due to her fears and cattle futures declined by 10 percent the following day. They can have equally important effects with respect to political candidates. Oprah's endorsement of Barack Obama increased voter turnout and added approximately one million additional votes for Obama in 2008 (Garthwaite and Moore 2008). When the singer Rihanna criticized Snapchat for an ad "making a game of domestic violence that featured photographs of her and Chris Brown" the stock value of Snapchat dropped precipitously (Held 2018). Advertisers employ celebrity endorsements because the words and image of the celebrity makes the advertisements more memorable in the minds of consumers who may see hundreds of ads in a given week. It is a technique used to get through the clutter that media saturated consumers experience (Zipporah and Mberia 2014). People pay more attention, and are thus more likely to be influenced, when a celebrity is speaking.

Celebrities have resources that other citizens don't have. "In an era where politics is expensive and cash is king, celebrities bring distinctive advantages to the task of political fundraising. They have high voter recognition, favorable public images, access to financial resources, and the ability to attract positive press coverage" (West and Orman 2003, 37). They can use these financial resources to support a political cause or candidate.

Presidential candidates have a long history of courting Hollywood elites for campaign contributions. FDR utilized support from the film industry in his 1944 victory. In the 1960s, the Kennedys had a solid relationship with Hollywood celebrities. In 1972, Warren Beatty was one of George McGovern's top advisors and organized multi-million-dollar fundraisers by reaching out to other celebrities. In 1976, Ronald Reagan, Jimmy Carter, and Jerry Brown all had the support of various Hollywood A-listers. In 1980, Hollywood was able to get one of their own elected to the presidency. By the 1990s, Bill Clinton was able to acquire nearly $2 million at a single Hollywood fundraiser that was attended by the most prominent names in the entertainment industry, including Jack Nicholson, Dustin Hoffman, Michelle Pfeiffer, Danny DeVito, Steven Spielberg, and Barbara Streisand. Barbara Streisand, herself, hosted a $10 million fundraiser for the Clinton Presidential Library in 2000. In 2008, Oprah Winfrey raised more than $3 million dollars for Barack Obama's presidential campaign. Bill Maher and Morgan Freeman each donated $1 million to Obama's super-PAC (political action committee). An Obama fundraiser with Sarah Jessica Parker and Anna Wintour not only brought in cash, those two celebrities were used to reach out to a key demographic—young single women. The overall support from Hollywood is now in the tens of millions of dollars each election cycle. While contemporary Hollywood tends to support Democrats because of their more progressive posture on social issues, Republicans have their fair share of more conservative entertainers, including Chuck Norris and Tom Selleck. Candidates from both parties now regularly call on Hollywood in their search for campaign cash (West and Orman 2003; Ross 2011; Wheeler 2013; Cashmore 2014; Stanley 2014).

Campaign contributions provide large donors with access, if not policy influence. Large donors receive phone calls from elected officials and invitations to dinners with them. The ability for Hollywood elites to make large contributions makes them more influential than everyday citizens. Hollywood professionals could seek favorable policies by attempting to influence elected officials or they could follow the more direct approach of electing one of their own to public office. Clint Eastwood used his tremendous wealth to self-finance his campaign. Ronald Reagan's and Al Franken's list of campaign contributors include large dollar donations from their many celebrity friends. Celebrities are wealthy people with wealthy friends, and this is helpful for fundraising purposes. They have the money to succeed, giving them yet another structural advantage over other candidates.

POLITICAL ENVIRONMENT

The political environment has a lot to do with whether, or not, a celebrity candidate will win the office they seek. In many ways the celebrity politician has to face the same problems any other candidate would face. A minority party candidate running in a one party dominated district has very little chance of winning no matter how rich and famous they are. Candidates who take positions that are too far outside of the political mainstream to seem credible will still lose even if they have the megaphone of celebrity. The case studies of celebrities that lost elections demonstrate that something more than the power trifecta is decisive.

On the other hand, sometimes incumbents make serious errors, are involved in controversy, or seem ineffective at solving the problems that voters are concerned with. Celebrity challengers can take advantage of the problems facing the incumbent. Weakened incumbents are easier to beat for any challenger, but the celebrity challenger has the increased ability to draw attention to the defects the incumbent may have—making an upset win more likely for celebrity challengers.

Sometimes new issues arise that open the door for new candidates and new ideas. For example, the war in Iraq had strong public support that was reflected by strong support by politicians on both sides of the aisle. Ten years later when the war was unpopular incumbents had to defend a choice that the public did not like. Someone without a recorded position on the issue can say they opposed the war from the beginning, giving the challenger an advantage. Taking that position ten years prior would have been unpopular. Sometimes the time is right for a particular message, but a new messenger is also necessary because it is difficult for an incumbent to change their position on an issue and remain credible.

Polling indicates that Americans are open to the idea of voting for celebrities. A consumer research firm found that a majority of Americans thought that Hollywood stars could make good politicians if they had the aptitude for it and had the right team in place. Only 13 percent believed that Hollywood stars should "stick to acting" while a plurality believed they are "free to do what they want." The poll found significant support for Dwayne Johnson and Matthew McConaughey as political candidates. A 46 percent plurality supported Johnson for president and a 41 percent plurality supported McConaughey for Texas governor. A poll conducted by The University of Texas at Tyler found that 45 percent of Texas registered voters would vote for McConaughey, while 33 percent would vote for the incumbent governor, Greg Abbott, and 22 percent would vote for someone else (Garrett and Jeffers 2021). A double-digit lead over an incumbent governor by a celebrity who decided not to seek the office suggests that there is some popular support for celebrity politicians. It is likely that fans of the actor registered support for him because of his public persona.

TEXTBOX 2.1

Hollywood Stars as Politicians

Do you think Hollywood stars can make good politicians?[1]

Yes, if they have the political aptitude	39%
Yes, if they have the right team in place	24%
No, just being famous is not enough	13%
No, their lives are way too different	12%
Not sure	12%

What is your opinion about Hollywood stars running for political posts?[2]

They are free to what they want	45%
Anyone can join politics these days	19%
They must just stick to acting	13%
They must stick to political activism at the most	12%
Not sure	11%

Actors Matthew McConaughey and Dwayne "The Rock" Johnson have lately shown keen interest in running for Texas governor and the US presidency, respectively. Would you like to see both or either of them run for political office?[3]

Matthew McConaughey	12%
Dwayne "The Rock" Johnson	17%
Both McConaughey and Johnson	29%
No	21%
Not sure	21%

Source: 1–3 Piplsay, April 2–April 4, 2021, April 6, 2021, https://piplsay.com/hollywood-celebs-as -politicians-what-do-americans-think-of-it/.

Candidates without prior political experience are a tabula rasa for political consultants. Messages, issue positions, style, and other items can all be invented to suit the political environment of the moment. Well known celebrities who are apolitical can be molded and crafted to take advantage of the current political climate. In addition, celebrities can take unpopular positions on issues that will with time become popular. Ronald Reagan was a celebrity supporter of Goldwater who held conservative views at a time when liberal ideas were more popular. Social unrest and economic troubles opened the door for Reagan's new brand of conservatism. For him, timing was everything. His previously unpopular ideas were gaining in popularity and would eventually become very popular.

Political professionals seek out opportunities to get onboard with a winning campaign. This sometimes means that they will harness the allure of celebrity to achieve their own political aims. What seems to the public like a new political face may in reality be a carefully crafted image by political insiders who are tapping into public sentiment in their own effort to gain power. When the political environment changes professional political operatives can back candidates that can capture the new mood of the public and carry them to victory.

Celebrities also benefit from *celebrity slack*. Celebrity slack is when the public is willing to forgive or overlook behavior that would typically be considered unacceptable. Celebrities often engage in behavior that is outrageous, deviant, or norm breaking. They engage in this behavior to draw attention to themselves. For an ordinary person, such behaviors would lead to social sanctions, ranging from ridicule to ostracization to criminal charges, but for the celebrity the behavior is very often rewarded with increased media exposure and sometimes praise. People understand this behavior as a "publicity stunt" and dismiss it for what it is, deliberate attention seeking.

In the case of deviant behaviors that are not intentionally attention seeking, there is a second explanation. Celebrity candidates run as political outsiders. Because of this, mistakes, blunders, and accusations, even serious ones, are viewed as further evidence of the celebrity's outsider status. Celebrity candidates say, "I'm not a politician," which insulates them from critique. A "real politician" would not brag about his exploits with prostitutes, as Jesse Ventura did on the campaign trail. The breaking of political norms simply adds to the narrative that celebrity politicians are agents of change attempting to break log jams and provide new and potentially more effective leadership.

The mistakes are viewed as proof that the celebrity candidate is more genuine than practiced and polished political veterans. Celebrities do not play by the same rules and this ability to break with convention gives celebrities tools that other people do not have.

Celebrity slack does not mean that celebrities are totally immune from sanction. An employer who employs a celebrity can fire the celebrity for making controversial comments or after serious allegations, Roseanne Barr and Kevin Spacey. Celebrities that engage in criminal conduct can be prosecuted by legal authorities, Lori Loughlin and O.J. Simpson. Celebrity slack means that in the context of American elections the voting public is far more permissive of deviant conduct or outrageous statements when it is a celebrity politician that does it. Each of the celebrities profiled in this book made statements or engaged in behaviors that likely could have ended the careers of non-celebrity politicians. As the case study chapters will demonstrate, the celebrity politicians who won elected office were able to survive scandals.

HARNESSING THE POWER TRIFECTA

Celebrities have the talent, fame, and resources to be successful political candidates. They are skilled performers who can memorize and read scripts in a manner that is convincing to an audience. They are skilled at creating a personal brand that resonates with audiences. They understand the importance of image management and media relations. Often, they benefit from the "halo effect" of physical attractiveness. They are skilled at drawing attention to themselves, a vital tool in any celebrity's or politician's toolkit. The ability to garner media attention gives them high levels of name recognition and large amounts of earned media; they can deliver a message to the public for free. This gives them an enormous advantage over other candidates. They are millionaires who are networked with other millionaires, their personal contact list is full of people that can help finance a viable political campaign. These three items give celebrities a power that ordinary citizens do not have. Of course, the political environment also plays a role in whether, or not, a celebrity will succeed in politics. Part of this environment is that they benefit from *celebrity slack*, the public seems to easily forgive social transgressions committed by celebrity candidates that are not so easily dismissed when committed by non-celebrity candidates. Party leaders should realize, if they have not already, that celebrity candidates have built in advantages over other candidates. Rather than fighting the talent, fame, and resources of the celebrity candidate party leaders can harness the power of the celebrity candidate to promote their agenda.

Political realists must realize that contemporary American society has been celebritized. Celebrities play an important role in organizing a society where image management and inter-personal performances guide our lives. Transformations in the mass media elevate those who are skilled at manufacturing publicity. They are the highest status individuals. To succeed politicians must adapt to this new social reality. Traditional politicians must become celebrities, or celebrities must become politicians. The latter is easier because celebrities already possess *the power trifecta*. Unless one plans to disrupt the entire social order, and this does not happen overnight, the best strategy is for politicians to join forces with the celebrities. Celebrities can be utilized for social and political ends. Recent history has shown how effective this strategy is. Starting as celebrities, Ronald Reagan, Clint Eastwood, Fred Grandy, Sonny Bono, Jesse Ventura, Arnold Schwarzenegger, Al Franken, and Donald Trump used *the power trifecta* to achieve electoral victories. Starting as politicians, Fred Thompson, Sarah Palin, and Jerry Springer became TV stars. This happens because entertainers and politicians rely on the same skill set to be successful. These skills can be used in either industry making transitions between the two nearly seamless. In a society where politics and entertainment have converged *polebrities* will be the leaders.

This book leaves out activist athletes for two reasons. There is already an extensive literature on sports stars who engage in political activism. Also, by this author's count, there are at least twelve professional athletes that have won elected office in the United States. For the sake of brevity, they were excluded. They could be fertile ground for a follow up book to this one. This book remains focused on entertainment celebrities. The case study chapters that follow are organized chronologically by date of election.

Chapter 3

Ronald Reagan

Ronald Reagan often commented on the similarities between politics and show business. He once told Warren Beatty, "I don't know how anybody can serve in public office without being an actor" (IMDb "Ronald Reagan"). Prior to leaving office for the last time journalist David Brinkley asked if his career as an actor was useful as president, Reagan said, "There have been times in this office when I've wondered how you could do the job if you hadn't been an actor" (Cannon 2000, 31–32). He told Stu Spencer, his campaign manager, "Politics is just like show business. You have a hell of an opening, coast for a while, and then have a hell of a close" (Stanley 2014, 181). The skills needed to be a good actor are the same skills that are needed to be a good politician. Reagan said, "There's a thing about being in front of an audience that's called an actor's instinct and it's really based on attempting to understand human beings. An actor's whole stock in trade is his ability to put himself in some-one else's shoes, in someone else's frame of mind" (Duscha 1967, 296). This ability allows candidates to connect with people and to convey messages to an audience in a way that they will find agreeable.

His three decades of experience as a professional actor allowed him to develop a persona that the American people admired. He was typecast as the charming, nice guy and the patriotic hero. He had "the look" and "the voice" to make him a star. The studios helped Reagan create this persona because he was a good fit for those roles, they knew where his talent lay. While some of this was based on the experience of directors and producers, it was also based on polling of movie audiences. Studio executives were figuring out how to sell movies with scientific precision and the polling showed them how to best sell Ronald Reagan movies. This persona, developed over many years of professional acting, helped Reagan win elections. "Did America perhaps consciously choose to be governed by an archetype rather than someone who could have reflected the realities of her many problems? Apparently so, for in 1984 they reelected the Gipper by a 59–41 percent margin" (Stanley 2014,

187). Once a positive public persona gets developed that persona could be used to sell movies or to sell public policies.

Reagan often drew on his Hollywood career during his presidency. He gave a commencement address at Notre Dame where he told the students, "to go out and win one for the Gipper!" referring to his role in *Knute Rockne*. "Reagan channeled not just the character of the Gipper but the values associated with that character, too: self-reliance and determination" (Stanley 2014, 187). Ronald Reagan was not just a man; he was a character from a movie. Because most Americans never personally meet their elected officials, they are just voting for media characters they are familiar with. For many Americans there really was not a clear distinction between Ronald Reagan the man and George Gipp the character. If they like the character, they will vote for the man. This is the nature of public personas.

Reagan especially benefited from a political environment that cast doubt on professional politicians' ability to lead the country. Race riots, the Vietnam War, crime, and monetary inflation could be blamed on the Establishment. As an outsider, Reagan could blame the incumbents for America's woes and represent an alternative. After all, he is an actor not a politician and it was the politicians who were responsible for the mess. This outsider status allowed Reagan to be, "Dubbed the 'Teflon President,' Reagan was not held accountable for unpopular policies, was impervious to scandal, and, until Bitburg and Iran Contra, was beyond blame for mismanaged political events" (Raphael 2009, 118). The American public gives more slack to celebrity politicians than they do to career politicians. This allows them to remain popular in instances where other public officials would likely lose popularity.

TALENT

Ronald Reagan began his acting career as a young boy performing skits and readings at his mother's church. He continued in high school where he acted in the drama program's plays. In college, he was lauded for his individual performance when his troupe earned a third-place finish at a competition at Northwestern University (Brands 2015; Wills 2017). After college he secured a job as a radio sportscaster where he honed his story telling skills. He would call the play-by-play for baseball games by reading coded telegraph messages. His listeners in Iowa might not know that Reagan was not at the game in Chicago. Dallek says,

> His voice would soon become a staple of Midwestern play-by-play. Proving himself a major broadcast talent who possessed a deep and engaging voice and a flair for the melodramatic, Reagan became a master of invention in his craft,

enlivening games that he neither saw nor heard with elaborate descriptions of ball parks and fans. (Dallek 2000, 30)

It was through his job as a sports announcer that Reagan learned how to capture an audience.

> The voice of the sports announcer is part of the cultural conditioning of most American boys, and the voice speaks as much *to* a fantasy life as *from* an external world of verifiable events. It was Reagan's first professional discipline to reach that life of fantasy with his voice, to create the suspense and drama of a "real" game from laconic code messages he received over the telegraph wire. In fact, his games were often more exciting than the ones being played far away, a fact that people not only mentioned but admired. (Wills 2017, 159)

Of course, they knew he was not there and, "They gloried in the fact. His skill at 'visualizing' was praised in the papers. People were invited to the Crystal Palace at the Iowa Fair Grounds to watch him as he invented the game from scraps of paper" (Wills 2017, 159).

His goal had always been to pursue an acting career and he quit his stable radio job to test his luck in Hollywood. At the time theaters would present movies in a double feature so that audiences would feel that they were getting their money's worth. The second film of the double feature was the "B movie." Often these were lower budget films with less promising scripts, but Reagan's charm, good looks, and practiced voice secured him leading roles in these films (Brands 2015). "Reagan's rise in Hollywood would be as rapid as his ascent in radio. In his first year as a movie actor, Reagan acted in eight films, gaining a reputation among directors as a solid performer well suited for lead roles in B movies" (Dallek 2000, 30).

Reagan's good looks propelled him to stardom as he moved beyond his B movie beginnings. "By 1940 Reagan had established himself as a bona fide Hollywood movie star. He starred in a string of successful blockbusters, winning considerable attention from film directors impressed with his good looks and from a public smitten with his Midwestern screen persona" (Dallek 2000, 30–31). Polls of moviegoers taken by Warner Brothers showed that he was more liked by women than men, giving credence to the "halo effect" that good looking people benefit from (Stanley 2014; Wills 2017). Indeed, he was "most popular with women in the twelve-to-seventeen age bracket (an important audience at the box office). He was the bobbysoxers' hero" (Wills 2017, 222). Like John F. Kennedy, Reagan's looks contributed to his success. Reagan established a fan base that would not forget their first celebrity crush as adolescents.

The studios were extremely important in Ronald Reagan's political development. "In the same way that they 'handled' his evolution from poor boy to matinee idol, they stage-managed his evolution from faded actor to global statesman" (Stanley 2014, 179). They called upon him to represent the industry during Congressional hearings into communist infiltration because they knew he could be a capable spokesperson (Brownstein 1990; Vaughn 1994). "It is remarkable to consider that the image Reagan carried around with him for life—even into the White House—was the product of polling done in the 1940s" (Stanley 2014, 176). The movie studios helped Reagan develop a persona that would help them sell movie tickets, later this persona would help Reagan sell himself to voters. Training as a professional actor develops skills that are useful in the political arena.

His relationship with voters

> was an extension of the bond he had forged with movie and television audiences during his long career. On screen and in person Reagan came across as virile and midwestern, expressing patriotic certitudes and old-fashioned values that were somehow softened by his smile. He was tall and handsome, with a commanding bearing, but his manner was self-deprecating and lacking in conceit. (Cannon 2000, 23)

The practiced Reagan persona that was developed for the screen became the Reagan persona that he used in everyday interactions with others, "He had practiced acting as a vocation and allowed it to become his principal mode of behavior. He had learned to play himself on screen, and he had also learned to remain on camera when the shooting stopped" (Cannon 2000, 32). He was acting even in real life and appealing to a mass audience.

Reagan's detractors might suggest that he was a second-rate actor, but he still played the leading role in his movies and was talented enough to be one of the most highly paid actors in Hollywood. Many aspiring actors never succeed and support themselves with menial service work while waiting for their big break. Reagan made it in Hollywood and was a national celebrity; he was rich and famous. This occurred because he was, in fact, a very good actor.

After World War II, Reagan had difficulty securing roles that he desired because he desired roles that did not fit his on-screen persona. "Reagan did not mind being typed. In fact, he wanted it. But he felt he was being mistyped. He wanted to be an action-adventure hero. They wanted him in light comedy roles" (Wills 2017, 221). He was excellent at playing the nice guy and was not gritty enough to be the hero in the westerns that Reagan wanted to be in. The tween audience that the studios felt Reagan was suited for because of their polling was not interested in westerns. But by this time Reagan had made it to the A-list films and was able to demand films of his choosing, including westerns. Unfortunately, "Reagan proved that the studio had been right all along. He is too light and likeable to have the menace needed for such roles" (Wills 2017, 226). His acting career began to wane.

It was then that he became the spokesperson for General Electric and the announcer for General Electric Theater, a weekly television program sponsored by the company (Brands 2015). His skill on television was integral to his political success. Reagan

> keenly appreciated that his career had given him a head start in politics. He knew how to make a speech and how to deliver a punchline. He knew that it was necessary to look directly into the television camera without bobbing his head, and he knew how to give a concise answer that compressed easily into a fifteen-second sound bite. (Cannon 2000, 22)

Brownstein notes that, "Reagan pointedly demonstrated the enormous practical value of an actor's training in an era when television dominated politics. As if by flicking a switch, Reagan could convey sincerity, conviction, anger, humility, sadness, pride. Other politicians weathered under the camera's insistent eye; Reagan reveled in it" (Brownstein 1990, 275). As a TV personality he was more prepared for the television age than your typical politician.

Jesse Unruh, the Democratic Speaker of the California General Assembly in 1967, noted that Reagan was a threat in the 1968 presidential election because, "he has no record to speak of, nothing too specific for people to shoot at, and look at the way he comes over on television" (Duscha 1967, 296). His campaign invented new ways to communicate through the media that would utilize Reagan's talent.

> In preparing voters for the tax increases and in arguing for legislative approval of them, Reagan developed a technique best described as the televised press release. With private funds contributed by some of his supporters, Reagan filmed 90-second and 15-minute statements about the state's financial situation which were then made available to all of California's television stations, and most of the stations used them exactly as they were received. (Duscha 1967, 296)

According to political reporters who covered Reagan when he was the governor of California, "The Governor is one of the few public figures who looks and sounds better on television than in person" (Duscha 1967, 296). The low resolution of TV images of the time, compared to the high definition of today, covered up flaws like small wrinkles or blotchiness. Through the filter of TV some people became better looking. Reagan was keenly aware that he looked better on TV and became visibly tense when still photographers were in the room because photos made him look older. Indeed, he tried to avoid still photographers as much as he could (Brands 2015). The skills that he learned filming movies enhanced his TV presence, "Reagan looks the camera in the eye, never fidgets and comes through on film dripping sincerity" (Duscha 1967, 296). He had a certain panache that worked on TV.

Reagan himself was aware that the skills that led to his success as a Hollywood actor would be helpful in a political career. Indeed, he saw himself as playing the role of a politician and acted accordingly.

> Asked what kind of governor he would be, Reagan quipped, "I don't know, I've never played a governor." And when he left the White House twenty-three years later and came home to California he told Landon Parvin, "Some of my critics over the years have said that I became president because I was an actor who knew how to give a good speech. I suppose that's not too far wrong. Because an actor knows two important things—to be honest in what he's doing and to be in touch with the audience. That's not bad advice for a politician either. My actor's instinct simply told me to speak the truth as I saw it and felt it." (Cannon 2000, 20)

It is this interchangeability of the skill set that allows good actors to be good politicians.

As the General Electric (GE) spokesperson Reagan would travel to GE factories and give speeches to the workers (Stanley 2014). It was here that he honed his skills as an orator. When he finally decided to run for political office, "Reagan used his presentational skills not only to propagate his right-wing values within the Sunshine State but to further his appeal to the US electorate on the national scene" (Wheeler 2013, 92). His speeches at GE would emphasize what would later become his political message: self-reliance, hard work, individualism, and the virtues of the free market. He criticized the government for wasteful spending but was forced to back off when his superior at GE told Reagan that GE has many government contracts and benefits from federal largesse (Brands 2015).

More than just a skilled performer, Reagan had political talent. He represented his class as a freshman when staffing disputes at his college led to a student strike (Wills 2017). By his senior year at Eureka College, he was elected class president (Brands 2015). Later, in Hollywood, he would join and be elected president of the Screen Actors Guild, a union for professional actors (Vaughn 1994; Cannon 2000; Dallek 2000; Stanley 2014). At the time, two competing unions were vying for the right to represent the actors and Reagan used his personal charm and political acumen to negotiate a settlement between the competing unions and the studios (Vaughn 1994). The ability to balance competing claims from multiple groups and interests is a genuine and useful leadership skill.

Reagan became a celebrity supporter of the Goldwater presidential campaign and gave speeches on Goldwater's behalf. GOP fundraisers Henry Salvatori and Holmes Tuttle asked Reagan to speak at a Goldwater fundraiser and the audience was so impressed that several suggested to them that Reagan should give that speech on TV. On the eve of the 1964 election, Reagan gave a televised speech supporting Goldwater that was hailed in Republican circles as one of the greatest speeches espousing conservative principles they had ever heard. His "time for choosing" speech propelled Reagan onto the national political stage. Wealthy Republican donors and campaign professionals were ready to support Reagan after Goldwater's loss (Dallek 2000; Wills 2017).

Reagan knew when he did not know things and was willing to listen to experts, this is both a skill and matter of temperament. Reagan hired professional political consultants, like Stu Spencer and Bill Roberts, and he heeded their advice (Cannon 2000; Dallek 2000; Wills 2017). Professional political operatives love working with candidates who listen to them because it means the campaign will have a greater chance of success. When aspiring politicians do not listen to sound political advice, they lose and everyone working for and supporting the campaign also lose.

> Reagan submitted to a tutoring that would have been insulting to most people of even ordinary pride. He was told to avoid subjects that would reveal his ignorance. He was spoon-fed knowledge in five-by-eight baby spoons. He was told by personality constructors that he had to invent a "total concept" of himself. He took it all with equanimity, and not only because he was a political novice. He would continue to take such handling through his political life. (Wills 2017, 368)

Reagan embraced his role; he was the spokesperson for the allied groups of the conservative cause. "Reagan was the first candidate to be engineered by professionals" (Wills 2017, 367). His advisors knew how to create a winning political coalition, all Reagan needed to do was deliver the correct message.

Reagan's White House advisors behaved like stage managers. They knew, "that Reagan preferred the comfort of the cue cards, and they saw no reason to take chances" (Cannon 2000, 34). Throughout the day he would take the cue cards his advisors had prepared into meetings, but the trait that endeared him to his advisors irritated his fellow politicians.

> In meetings with outsiders he usually stuck to the script that had been scribbled down on his cards, once provoking a furious outburst from House Speaker Thomas P. (Tip) O'Neill, who was angry that Reagan read to him from his notes rather than speaking extemporaneously on subjects they had discussed many times before. (Cannon 2000, 18)

Reagan, "was always willing to place a call to a wavering congressman if provided with the script of what he ought to say. What animated Reagan was a public performance" (Cannon 2000, 36). Reagan viewed himself as an actor/ spokesman and allowed others to be the directors and screenwriters.

Reagan's effectiveness at creating a personal brand combined with his ability to create a fan base with his on-screen charm and practiced sincerity, helped him weather political storms.

> One of the most important assets Reagan acquired during his years with General Electric was the capacity to use television to promote a wide variety of products through the magical properties of a fully dramatized brand image. One measure of the power of the Reagan brand was his administration's ability to deploy it to generate consent for Reagan's presidency in lieu of a popular mandate for his policies. The remarkable disparity in polling figures between public approval for Reagan (for large stretches of his presidency in the range of 60 to 70 percent) and approval of his policies (rarely higher than the low 40th percentile) has been downplayed by political scientists. (Raphael 2009, 117)

This gap can be identified as celebrity slack and is attributed to the popularity of the Reagan brand; a brand that had been fifty years in the making. Through his skill at developing a TV persona he was able to get Americans to focus on the image of Reagan. Reagan as a TV personality was great, Americans liked him. Reagan, as a human being making policy decisions, was not great; indeed many people, including conservatives, did not like what he was doing. But they loved the guy on TV; Reagan had fans. These fans supported him, even if they did not like his policies. They were his political base, his unwavering supporters.

Reagan was not an independent thinker, but he knew what his role was in the campaign, and he was likable. "[H]e used his fame, oratory skills and personality to construct an effective right-wing identity which could be sold to the American electorate" (Wheeler 2013, 92). Ronald Reagan was able to handle criticism, "Because he was very, very nice. He was, by all accounts, the actor's actor, and in conversation he deflected controversy with quips and anecdotes" (Stanley 2014, 263). When campaigns have clearly defined roles for those in it and people are skilled in their respective roles there is a greater probability of success. Reagan was the type of candidate that political professionals love to work with because he was the spokesperson, not the decision maker. He followed the advice of people who knew what they were doing.

His skills in stagecraft transferred easily into the political arena, literally. When Reagan was scheduling a presidential debate with George H. W. Bush there was some disagreement between the campaigns. The Bush team wanted a one on one with Reagan, Reagan preferred to include additional candidates John Anderson, Howard Baker, Phil Crane, and Bob Dole. They agreed to the one-on-one debate, but Reagan asked the other candidates to attend and to walk on stage before the debate. Reagan then asked that the other candidates be allowed to address the audience, but the Bush team scoffed at the suggestion and an argument ensued in full view of the audience (Brands 2015). Reagan looked magnanimous while Bush looked like he was afraid of minor competition. It was this type of stagecraft, his ability to play the audience to his favor, and to develop a public persona, that led to his political success. Reagan, "understood that presence mattered more to television viewers, the audience he cared about, than the details of his answers" (Brands 2015, 319). As an actor, he understood optics; and optics are critically important in politics.

FAME

Reagan became well known in the Davenport, Iowa area through his sports-casting job at WOC before moving to the larger market of Des Moines when WOC merged with WHO to become WOC-WHO (Brands 2015; Wills 2017). "By this time—September 4, 1936—Reagan was a celebrity himself, not only his voice but his face familiar to everyone in Des Moines. He was a frequent speaker at civic occasions, an attraction at the State Fair, a man valued by the sponsors of his baseball broadcasts, and the sports columnist of the Des Moines *Dispatch*" (Wills 2017, 147). Being a local celebrity was not enough for Reagan whose true passion was acting, so he headed to Hollywood to pursue his dreams.

Reagan became a well-known figure in America by appearing in sixty-nine films over a twenty-seven-year time span between 1937 and 1964. These included *Knute Rockne: All American, Murder in the Air, Santa Fe Trail, Million Dollar Baby,* and *Kings Row* (Ronald Reagan Presidential Library "Ronald Reagan Filmography"). Beginning in 1939, he played Brass Bancroft, a crime fighting federal agent, in a series of movies for Warner Brothers (Vaughn 1994; Brands 2015; Wills 2017). During World War II Reagan joined the Army Signal Corps and starred in propaganda films designed to recruit young men into the armed forces and glorify the war effort. He was in movies such as *Rear Gunner, For God and Country, Beyond the Line of Duty,* and *This is the Army* (Vaughn 1994; Dallek 2000; Wills 2017). It was in these films that Reagan gained a reputation as a hero. The public would come to know him as a patriotic soldier fighting the good fight and saving America (Vaughn 1994; Brands 2015).

General Electric Theater placed Reagan inside millions of homes where he became a kind of weekly houseguest for many Americans. He acted in thirty-five episodes of GE Theater. It was the third highest rated television show in 1956–1957 (Brooks and Marsh 2007), and "It was regularly the number one show in its desirable prime-time slot" (Wills 2017, 332). At the end of his acting career, he appeared in eight episodes of *Death Valley Days*. In all, Reagan appeared in sixty-four television episodes between 1950 and 1965 (IMDb "Ronald Reagan"). There is power in these "para-social" relationships. Americans feel like they have come to know the people they regularly encounter on their television screens. It is a one-way bond between viewer and TV personality that easily translates into political capital.

Most voters never actually meet their elected representatives; but may come to know them through the media and will loyally support their favorite candidates. The future president would switch to television just as the medium was gaining popularity.

> In 1947 there were only about 14,000 television sets in the United States. . . . By 1954, the year Reagan began as host, the number of televisions had more than doubled to almost 32 million. By the time Reagan left the show in 1962, television was in 90 percent of American homes, the average American watched five hours of television per day, and TV had replaced movies as American's dominant leisure-time activity. (Raphael 2009, 127)

While Reagan might have believed that acting on television was a step down from appearing in films, it was this transition that led to his future political success. It increased his exposure to larger and larger audiences, and he increased his name recognition nationally.

By the time he decided to run for governor of California in 1966, 75 percent of Americans knew who he was. Interestingly, however, only 14 percent wanted to see him become president. Fifty-one percent did not want to see him as president one day. Even after being elected governor, a majority of Americans believed that his background as an actor did not give him "the kind of experience needed to become president." What could have convinced a skeptical public about Ronald Reagan's fitness for office? Sixty-two percent believed he was doing a good job as governor and 58 percent believed "he represents a new approach to politics, different from the usual politicians." Sixty-five percent of Americans thought that Reagan was "very attractive, charming, [and] sincere." Despite initial skepticism, there were selling points that suggested Reagan had a political future beyond California.

TEXTBOX 3.1

Ronald Reagan

Can you tell me who Ronald Reagan is or what he does?[1]
    Yes, respondent correctly identified Reagan
    (Candidate for governor of California or movie actor)   75%
    Yes, respondent incorrectly identified Reagan   2%
    Don't Know   22%

Would you like to see him (Ronald Reagan) become president some day?[2]
    (Subpopulation: Those who know who Reagan is or what he does [75%])
    Yes   14%
    No   51%
    Don't know   35%

I want to read you some things that have been said about Governor Ronald Reagan of California. For each, I wish you would tell me if you tend to agree or disagree. His background as an actor is not the kind of experience needed to become president.[3]
    Agree   51%
    Disagree   31%
    Not sure   18%

I want to read you some things that have been said about Governor Ronald Reagan of California. For each, I wish you would tell me if you tend to agree or disagree. He represents a new approach to politics, different from the usual politicians.[4]
    Agree   58%
    Disagree   12%
    Not sure   30%

I want to read you some things that have been said about Governor Ronald Reagan of California. For each, I wish you would tell me if you tend to agree or disagree. He has been doing a good job as governor of California.[5]
    Agree   62%

| Disagree | 14% |
| Not sure | 24% |

Do you agree or disagree with the following statements about Ronald Reagan? He's very attractive, charming, sincere.[6]

Agree	65%
Disagree	17%
Not sure	18%

Sources: 1–2Gallup Organization, October 21–October 26, 1966, retrieved June 27, 2018 from the iPOLL Databank, The Roper Center for Public Opinion Research, University of Connecticut;3–5 Louis Harris & Associates, September 1967, retrieved June 27, 2018 from the iPOLL Databank, The Roper Center for Public Opinion Research, University of Connecticut; 6 Louis Harris & Associates, December 1967, retrieved June 27, 2018 from the iPOLL

On the strength of his voice, Reagan returned to radio as a political commentator after stepping down as the governor of California (Wills 2017). This kept his persona alive in the public imagination while he planned his bid for the presidency. Later, politicians like Mike Huckabee would use their media shows, his on Fox, to set the groundwork for future political runs. Jesse Ventura also hosted a politically oriented talk radio show before running for governor of Minnesota. It is better than free advertising, they get paid to express their opinions and gain, or retain, national name recognition.

RESOURCES

Reagan was a very well-paid actor. Indeed, his earnings were on par with other Hollywood elites. Reagan secured a million-dollar contract from Warner Brothers, which is a large sum today and an even larger sum in 1942 dollars when he earned it (Wills 2017). In 1946, Reagan "earned . . . just a little less than Errol Flynn, and more than Rita Hayworth," two of the most recognized movie stars of their time (Wills 2017, 193). After that, Reagan earned $125,000 a year as the spokesperson for General Electric, today that would be over a million dollars yearly adjusted for inflation (Dallek 2000).

Before running for governor of California political donors helped Reagan sell his Santa Monica Ranch to 20th Century Fox for $8,000 an acre. Reagan had paid $293 an acre when he bought it 15 years prior. Reagan earned a nearly $2 million profit from the sale of the ranch. "In 1966, Reagan ran for governor of California with financial support from MCA executives" and won because of their help (Stanley 2014, 180). Fox then sold the land to the State of California, while Reagan was governor, for $1,800 an acre—taking a major loss on the property (Wills 2017). His next real estate deal in Riverside County was just as lucrative.

> As a down payment on this purchase, the trustees used fifty-four acres of land left over from the 20th Century-Fox sale, which was accepted by the sellers at five times its assessed value. The partners doing the selling-which included Kaiser Aluminum-were were in a mood to be generous to the governor. . . . Eventually, when Reagan was running for the presidency, he sold his Riverside ranch for well over twice its purchase price, in a secret deal with a developer. (Wills 2017, 333)

Through schemes such as these the film studios and other California industries made Reagan personally wealthy and curried political favor with him. As governor, he signed a bill giving film studios multi-million-dollar tax breaks (Wills 2017).

Reagan used his Hollywood celebrity connections to raise money for his political campaigns. One of his most prominent celebrity supporters was Frank Sinatra who raised more than $6 million for Reagan's presidential bids (Davis 1980; Kittle and Murphy 1980; Adler et al. 1981). Hollywood producer Jack Wrather and theater producer Alfred Bloomingdale, heir to the Bloomingdale's Department Store fortune and founder of Diner's Club credit card, were Reagan supporters (Bumiller 1980; Mansfield 1981). Satellite TV pioneer Charles Wick was a longtime friend of Reagan's, a major fund-raiser for his campaigns, and co-chaired Reagan's inaugural committee (Bumiller 1980; Mansfield 1981). The actors and actresses that supported Reagan were among the most prominent names in show business at one time. The names included June Allyson, Susan Anton, Desi Arnaz, Ray Bolger, Irene Dunne, Clint Eastwood, Zsa Zsa Gabor, Charlton Heston, Bob Hope, Victor Jory, Dorothy Lamour, Michael Landon, Piper Laurie, Fred MacMurray, Dean Martin, Margaret O'Brien, Roy Rogers, Robert Stack, James Stewart, Gloria Swanson, and Efrem Zimbalist Jr. (Davis 1980; Sanoff 1980; Magnuson 1982; Walsh 1987). Singers Pat Boone, Glenn Campbell, Merle Haggard, Wayne Newton, Donny and Marie Osmond, and Tanya Tucker made appearances at Reagan fundraisers (Davis 1980; Sanoff 1980). Kay Gable, Clark Gable's widow, and Buddy Young, the widower of Mary Pickford, were other supporters (Davis 1980). Elizabeth Taylor was a "longtime friend of Nancy Reagan's" who was at one time married to Republican US Senator John Warner (Bumiller 1980).

These Hollywood friends helped Reagan directly and indirectly. Being wealthy themselves they could provide Reagan with financial support, but they also used their celebrity to attract other donors who would pay a premium to mingle with the stars at a Reagan fundraiser. Reagan used "His stardom [and] attracted donors whose funds allowed him to buy airtime for spot-ads and press coverage" (Wheeler 2013, 93). In the 1980 primary, Reagan was able to raise nearly 14 million in direct contributions and acquired another 7.3 million in federal matching funds from the presidential public finance system (Campaign Finance Institute n.d.). Reagan's campaign rallies included many of his celebrity friends (*Los Angeles Times* October 20, 1966, 189). The chance to see so many celebrities acted as a draw to increase public attendance at Reagan's campaign events.

POLITICAL ENVIRONMENT

The political environment of the 1960s, 1970s, and 1980s was ideal for a candidate like Ronald Reagan. Though they benefit from the power trifecta of talent, fame, and resources it is the political environment that is decisive for celebrity candidates. William Winter, a 1950s broadcaster, said that news broadcasts are shallow and trivial, the anchor's only job is to read the teleprompter pleasantly. Americans became accustomed to TV news as their source for political information during the 1950s, so it made sense that the country would elect Ronald Reagan who was a great "anchor" on TV (West and Orman 2003, 10). Politicians who could deliver a message with a nice face and good voice were perfect for this era. "He arrived in politics when it was absorbing show-business technique and personnel at an increasing rate" (Wills 2017, 227).

Reagan came to political prominence during a time of social upheaval. He was elected governor of California in 1966 by arguing that the Watts riots and protests at the University of California, Berkeley were a result of poor political leadership. The incumbent, Pat Brown, made several mistakes that cost him the election. He happened to be on vacation when the Watts riots occurred and was not there to deal with the situation. The Brown campaign leaked a story to the press that would undermine Reagan's primary opponent, mistakenly believing that Reagan would be easier to beat. Brown also stated that an actor killed Lincoln to cause public distrust of actors, or perhaps as an ill-received joke, but in Los Angeles County thousands of people work in the film industry. This would be like criticizing steelworkers in Pennsylvania or autoworkers in Michigan. It did not help when the sitting US Senator, George Murphy, who had himself been a movie star before taking public office, criticized Brown for his comments (Longoria 2022). Reagan took advantage of Brown's blunders and capitalized on anti-establishment sentiment (Cannon 2000; Dallek 2000).

Reagan said that his biggest asset during the campaign was Gov. Brown himself. He criticized Brown's "unmet promises" and when asked about race riots in San Francisco Reagan said, "anything that upsets the people will tend to create dissatisfaction with those in power" (Bergholz September 30, 1966, 3). Brown, on the other hand, criticized Reagan's background as an actor and said that Reagan lacked the political knowledge to govern effectively. He also said that white backlash from racial unrest was helping Reagan (*Los Angeles Times* June 17, 1966, 3). Brown's unpopularity combined with social turmoil created an anti-status quo mood in the electorate. By criticizing Reagan's lack of experience Brown simply reinforced Reagan's outsider persona. Reagan earned 3,639,609 (57 percent) votes, while Brown garnered 2,690,391 (43 percent) votes (Bergholz November 10, 1966, 1).

Reagan employed what could be called an "inside-out" strategy. Reagan was an outsider who never previously held elected office, but his campaign team was full of political insiders who were adept at the art of campaigning. Reagan's staff included fundraisers, managers, strategists, media relations experts, pollsters, and others. Highly skilled political professionals understood that the turmoil of the 1960s created an opening for a change-oriented candidate. When there are social problems that the current set of political leaders seem unable to resolve, the political establishment can front a new candidate without any political experience as a remedy, while still managing the entire effort behind the scenes. The insiders back an outsider to give the public what it wants, but also to secure their own place in the new political environment.

Reagan campaigned like an ideologue but governed like a pragmatist. On the campaign trail he derided government, promised to reduce spending, and praised free market business interests. But as governor of California, he supported the largest tax hike of California's history and supported environmental protection efforts. He also relied on executive branch bureaucrats to draft legislation, thus relying on the expertise of professional administrators to govern effectively (Putnam 2006). How did Reagan manage to abandon his conservative principles and still be idolized by conservative voters?

There are a number of possible answers to this question, but the most important is the power of television. With an actor's skill, he manipulated that medium's Orwellian capability to dull thought and stimulate emotion, to abjure ideas and emphasize images, to strengthen slogans and weaken reasoned discourse, and to anesthetize memory and convert citizens into political amnesiacs. While pushing through his budget and tax increases of 1967, Reagan simultaneously proclaimed to TV audiences and in public speeches that his administration had constantly effectuated numerous economies in his ongoing policy of "squeeze, cut, and trim." (Putnam 2006, 33)

As president he increased government spending and ballooned the national debt, policies that should have outraged conservatives. He also supported amnesty for undocumented immigrants, another conservative trigger. Both as governor and as president he had to deal with Democratic controlled legislatures and managed to enact legislation by abandoning his ideological principles. Yet, his skill at espousing conservative principles on TV largely shielded him from widespread condemnation by the conservatives he was abandoning.

By the time the 1980 election came around the nation was facing several major problems and Americans wanted a change of direction.

> As the months rolled by, the nation was wracked by high inflation and unemployment, gasoline shortages, and a hostage crisis in Iran in which more than 50 Americans were held captive by radical Muslims. Carter seemed weak and powerless, and voters felt down on their luck and deeply worried about the future. Reagan proved to be the antidote. He urged Americans to believe in themselves again and declared that the United States was a "shining city on a hill" whose best days were still ahead. Many people thought that he was too extreme and simplistic, but opposition to the status quo ran so deep that the electorate decided to give the former movie star a chance in the White House. (Walsh 2008)

The same inside-out strategy that helped Reagan become the governor of California helped propel him to the presidency. Mostly, however, he was the beneficiary of a public mood that was tired of politics as usual and who felt that the current government was ineffective at solving problems.

CONCLUSIONS

Politically, Reagan elevated style and image over substance. This is a defining characteristic of celebrity politics. As president he manipulated the media to avoid responsibility for failures. He incorporated movie lines into his speeches, including "Win one for the Gipper" from his movie *Knute Rockne* (Brands 2015). He also quoted lines from *Mr. Deeds Goes to Town*, "as a representation of his own philosophy and principles" (Scott 2011, 58). He was the "quintessential media president" and used his celebrity to engage the public (West and Orman 2003, 48).

Reagan's biographer recalls an interview he had with Reagan about the connection between being a Hollywood actor and being a political figure.

> He said that being an actor had taught him to understand the feelings and motivations of others. He said being an actor had "the practical side" of preparing people to face batteries of cameras and questions from the press. He also claimed that bad reviews and "undeserved criticism" prepared an actor for the

rough exchanges of politics, although Reagan could be as thin-skinned and sensitive to criticism as any novice politician. Most important, he said, actors find themselves being called upon to perform on the spot at public gatherings. (Cannon 2000, 32–33)

Hollywood actors and politicians rely on the same skill set to succeed. Reagan was able to harness his acting skills for political advantage.

Democrats were flummoxed by Reagan and understood that his success was a result of his acting ability. *New York Times* reporter Julius Duscha found a frustrated Democrat who said, "I can't find the real man. Reagan is always playing a part. He is an actor and he is acting out the role of Governor. He says all the clichés but he doesn't do anything. And that, I guess is what the people want—a guy who looks good and sounds sincere and competent, but doesn't actually do anything" (Duscha 1967, 296).

Reagan was the most compelling communicator in American politics since Franklin Roosevelt, and he knew it. His mastery of the rhetorical art reflected his long experience as an actor and public speaker. His years with General Electric taught him to read a room; his time before the camera trained him to see an audience beyond the camera. He mixed humor and pathos, philosophy and anecdote. (Brands 2005, 309)

Ronald Reagan was a talented actor who connected with audiences. He developed a public persona—that of a nice guy and military hero—that resonated with voters. Because he was a movie star and because he had spent several years on a popular prime time television program, he had enormous national name recognition when he first began pursuing a political career in California. The movie studios supported Reagan financially and his celebrity friends attracted large crowds and additional media attention. He also had genuine political talent, rising to the head of a labor union, and he listened to political experts to succeed. Reagan benefited from celebrity slack, he violated conservative principles with impunity and remained popular with his supporters. Crucially, the political environment favored an outsider who had never held elected office before because of the social turmoil of the era.

Chapter 4

Clint Eastwood

Clint Eastwood is one of America's premier actors whose career has spanned more than half a century. Born in 1930 his family moved frequently as his father searched for work in Depression Era California. As a young boy he lived in Pacific Palisades and Hollywood before moving to Oakland as a teenager. His poor grades in high school caused his parents to send him to vocational school. He had a series of labor-intensive low wage jobs before being drafted into the Army for the Korean War. That is when he had a stroke of good luck. He had indicated that swimming was one of his skills in his entry form. Rather than being sent off to war, he was assigned to be a lifeguard/swim instructor for the Special Services.

Occasionally, a celebrity would be drafted, but rather than run the risk of a high-profile death, the military would assign the celebrities to the Special Services unit which provided PR for the military during the war. Mostly, the celebrities would spend time at the base pool during the day and visit local night clubs in the evenings (Schickel 1996; Eliot 2009). According to Schickel, "The pool became a kind of informal social center. Among those dropping by to improve their tans were a number of actors who had been drafted, including three who would ultimately gain fame as television series leads: Richard Long (*77 Sunset Strip*, *The Big Valley*), Martin Milner (*Route 66*), and David Janssen (*The Fugitive*)" (Schickel 1996, 60). Eastwood became friends with these celebrities and, after his tour was over, he moved to Los Angeles to be near his new buddies and to marry his first wife (Eliot 2009).

In the 1950s, Universal Studios was attempting to get into TV production. However, most movie actors of the era believed that TV roles were a step down. The studio set up Universal Training School (UTS) to discover and train new talent to appear in their TV programs or movies. One of his friends, who was a cameraman for Universal, recommended him to one of the directors and Eastwood was interviewed. At this stage, the studios were primarily selecting the most physically attractive men and women, the acting coaches would handle the rest. He passed muster and UTS hired Eastwood to train as an actor. He acquired small roles in a few movies while at UTS. For example, he would be a lab technician who enters the room and says, "Here are the X-rays." Aspiring actors were usually incredibly happy to get a few minutes in a feature film. Of course, not all UTS recruits were deemed talented enough to make it. UTS dismissed Eastwood, and his classmate Burt Reynolds, because they were not impressed with their onscreen performances (Schickel 1996; Eliot 2009).

Eastwood continued to land bit roles in several movies, but these one day only roles would not pay enough to support himself and his new wife. He worked as a laborer during the week and as a janitor on the weekends, while taking the occasional role offered to him. His big break occurred when he auditioned for and received the co-star role in TV's *Rawhide*. It was this role that propelled Eastwood into global stardom (Schickel 1996; Eliot 2009).

Over the course of a career spanning more than sixty years Eastwood came to embody the quintessential American tough guy. He had a starring role in *A Fistful of Dollars, For a Few Dollars More, The Good, the Bad and the Ugly, Dirty Harry, Magnum Force, The Outlaw Josey Wales, The Bridges of Madison County, Unforgiven, Million Dollar Baby, and Gran Torino*. His talent goes beyond acting into producing and directing. He has won critical acclaim and his movies have earned billions of dollars.

Although Eastwood never aspired to major office, he was elected mayor of Carmel-by-the-Sea, California and was appointed to two California state commissions and one national council. He has been active in Republican Party politics and his talent, fame, and resources allow him to move in elite circles. His sexual appetites caused him to father several children with women who were not his wife. His infidelity was overlooked by the residents of Carmel, demonstrating that the power of celebrity slack is effective in small electorates. His win could be attributed to three important factors. He far outspent his opponent, he had tremendous name recognition, and he received a significant amount of earned media coverage.

TALENT

Clint Eastwood was forced into acting in grade school. Clint was extremely shy. So much so that his teachers were worried that he was not developing the social skills that would allow him to succeed in life. To remedy the problem, he was cast in the lead role for a school play. The idea was to make the kid swim by throwing him in the water. The young Eastwood did not want to do it and made several mistakes on stage, it was simply not a pursuit Eastwood had in mind (Schickel 1996; Eliot 2009).

After serving in the military and moving to Los Angeles he met George Shdanoff, an acting instructor who followed the method developed by Michael Chekhov. Eastwood's understanding of Chekhov was that acting was about, "certain instincts that you already have and the question is just to channel all that stuff into some sort of visual image" (Schickel 1996, 73). Acting, for Eastwood, was about projecting the right image. As it turns out, politics is also about projecting the right image—what is called "optics." Thus, Eastwood's acting instruction also taught him a skill useful in politics.

He did attend UTS, but only because it paid more than pumping gas. He trained as an actor more out of economic necessity than any real ambition. Mostly, he was being encouraged by friends who believed he had "the look" and he did not find any harm in trying. Still, he did learn the craft through the instruction he was given and was as excited as the other students when Hollywood stars would drop by to give their advice to the apprentice actors. He would carefully observe other actors' performances, study their techniques and attempt to replicate what worked well (Schickel 1996; Eliot 2009).

A large part of Eastwood's appeal was due to his appearance. He had, "strong, broad shoulders, rugged good looks, and seductive half-closed eyes. He had a finely shaped, aristocratically turned-up nose and a thick bush of brown hair that fell in a curly dip over his forehead. The look was tough" (Eliot 2009, 22). Indeed, Eastwood's look can be described as that of the quintessential American tough guy, he exudes masculinity. It was a look that comports well with perhaps his most famous movie line, "Go ahead, make my day."

Critics were unimpressed with Eastwood's early work for likely the same reasons that caused his UTS instructors to recommend him for dismissal, but his popularity among the movie going public eventually caused the critics to reconsider.

> This was a well-established pattern. Clint was not the first star (and not the last) to have been at first dismissed by the critics for his lack of obvious theatrical training and credentials, put down as a lunky, hunky Hollywood phenomenon, then reconsidered as his popularity with the people proved irresistible. As such performers refine as well as broaden their screen personae—or in some cases merely persist as audience favorites—their "development" gives aid and comfort (and Sunday pieces) to reviewers as they reevaluate. (Schickel 1996, 212)

Eastwood developed three distinct, but overlapping, personas that define his body of work. "The first is the mysterious man without a past who is resolute in his loneness" (Eliot 2009, 10). The second is the renegade lawman Dirty Harry. The third is, "the good-natured redneck, who uses his fists the way a more thoughtful person uses words" (Eliot 2009, 10). According to biographer

Marc Eliot, "it is nearly impossible to separate the off-screen person from the on-screen persona. The two feed off each other so thoroughly, it is often difficult to tell where the lives of the characters in his movies end and the life of the man playing them begins" (Eliot 2009, 10). Americans value the rugged individualism and gritty resolve that Clint Eastwood's characters possess.

Dirty Harry was a blockbuster hit with the public and controversial among critics. "The film sparked reams of literature about whether Harry represented the best or the worst of early 1970s America" (Eliot 2009, 145). On the one hand, Harry had an antiauthoritarian bravado that spoke to an America that was fed up with the Establishment. On the other hand, Harry was an obsessive, sadistic, bully who violated civil rights and tortured his opponents. As a bad cop he represented an out-of-control establishment. The sequel, *Magnum Force*, would pair him with a black partner who would be the voice of reason and caution. That film was also a blockbuster and created a whole new genre in Hollywood movies, the "buddy cop" films that pair races and temperament for cinematic effect.

In many of his movies he portrays an aggrieved white man who is fighting against the injustices he has faced. In *The Outlaw Josey Wales* Eastwood portrays a confederate soldier who returns home to find it burned to the ground and his wife killed by "anti-slavery marauders" (Strickland 2017). Of course, he must use violence to correct the injustices. The film was based on a book written by Bedford Forrest Carter, a Ku Klux Klan leader. It is no surprise then that Eastwood's persona embodies "white supremacist identity politics and white working-class anger at financial and political elites" (Strickland 2017). This mythology of white victimization is a key feature of Republican appeals to working class whites and would be later harnessed by Donald Trump.

Eastwood had taken an interest in directing early in his career. He was given permission to direct a few trailers for *Rawhide*. He would not be able to direct, however, until he owned his own production company. After that, as producer and director, he would have all the control he sought to have over his creative works. He mostly learned by observing others and taking mental notes of what worked and what did not when it came to manage a film's production. It was in these endeavors that Eastwood won the most acclaim. Eastwood won the Academy Award for Best Picture and Best Director twice for *Unforgiven* and *Million Dollar Baby* (IMDb "Clint Eastwood Awards"). He has fourteen Golden Globe nominations with five wins including Best Picture and multiple Best Director victories (Golden Globes "Clint Eastwood"). Although an immensely popular actor with the public, his critical acclaim comes from producing and directing.

FAME

In the late 1950s, western series were immensely popular among television viewers. The studios were looking to follow-up the success they had with *Gunsmoke*. Eastwood was cast as the co-star in the enormously successful *Rawhide*. In 1960, *Rawhide* was the sixth most popular show on television. In its time slot *Rawhide* captured 27.5 percent of all television viewers (Brooks and Marsh 2007). The show was watched by millions of Americans over the course of its seven-year run and Clint Eastwood became a household name. *Rawhide* was so successful that the theme music itself became a top selling song. The show was an international success and Eastwood visited Japan, where the show was also a hit, on a promotional tour for the series. Eastwood recorded an album of cowboy songs and, "Audiences bought it in fairly good numbers, a testament to Clint's popularity rather than to his singing" (Eliot 2009, 62). Clint Eastwood was so popular because of his role in *Rawhide* that he appeared in an episode of *Mr. Ed* as himself, "Only upper-echelon celebrities such as Bob Hope, Jimmy Stewart, John Wayne, and Frank Sinatra could regularly make appearances on programs as themselves" (Eliot 2009, 63).

The importance of the *Mr. Ed* appearance should not be underestimated. Appearing as himself on TV

> gives him a chance to demonstrate that he is just a nice, ordinary guy. This was—for that matter, remains—the standard way of presenting celebrity guest performers on sitcoms. When the show's regular cast gets to know the famous person, he always turns out to be very like the best self he presents in whatever role he plays, but charmingly less impressed with himself than the cast is. It could be said, indeed, that this was a historic occasion: the first public acknowledgment of Clint Eastwood as a celebrity. (Schickel 1996, 136)

Guest appearances like these allow celebrities to promote their brand. They are still in persona when acting as themselves. The lines between being a character and acting in the role of a character become blurred. The public, then, only knows the celebrity as the characters the celebrity portrays and meld the characters with the real person playing them.

By the early 1960s, Eastwood had a become a global star. In fact, the first three films in which Eastwood had a starring role were European productions. *A Fistful of Dollars*, *For a Few Dollars More*, and *The Good, the Bad and the Ugly* would only later make their way to the United States, "He had become such a movie star in Europe that he could no longer walk down the street without hordes of people, mostly women, running after him" (Eliot 2009, 78). He went on to star in *Dirty Harry*, *The Outlaw Josey Wales*, *Unforgiven*, *Million Dollar Baby*, and *Gran Torino*, among others.

Eastwood is enormously popular with Americans. A plurality believe that Eastwood is the quintessential leading male actor of all-time. When asked which celebrity they would most like to see as president, a plurality of Americans select Clint Eastwood. Eastwood even bests Arnold Schwarzenegger, who succeeded in being elected the governor of California. His brand of American tough guy has come to embody no nonsense ruggedness and individuality, values Americans admire. It is this fan base that provides an initial voter base to build upon. Those supportive of an Eastwood presidency would likely support him for mayor as well.

TEXTBOX 4.1

Clint Eastwood

Which one of the following comes closest to your ideal of the quintessential leading male actor of all-time? Cary Grant, Jack Nicholson, Steve McQueen, George Clooney, Humphrey Bogart, Denzel Washington, Clint Eastwood.[1]

Cary Grant	12%
Jack Nicholson	9%
Steve McQueen	3%
George Clooney	9%
Humphrey Bogart	8%
Denzel Washington	23%
Clint Eastwood	28%
Don't Know	8%

Many celebrities from the entertainment world have spoken out about political issues, and some have even run for office. I'm going to read you a list of names—if these were the only people running, who would you most like to see elected president? Clint Eastwood, Oprah Winfrey, Mel Gibson, Angelina Jolie, Sean Penn, Barbra Streisand.[2]

Clint Eastwood	32%
Oprah Winfrey	30%
Mel Gibson	9%
Angelina Jolie	4%
Sean Penn	3%
Barbra Streisand	2%
None of these	16%
Don't Know	6%

Which one of the following movie stars do you think would make the best president? Do you think Arnold Schwarzenegger, Harrison Ford, Denzel Washington, Robert Redford, Clint Eastwood, Kevin Costner, Susan Sarandon, or Meryl Streep would make the best president?[3]

Arnold Schwarzenegger	8%
Harrison Ford	15%
Denzel Washington	10%
Robert Redford	14%
Clint Eastwood	27%
Kevin Costner	7%
Susan Sarandon	3%
Meryl Streep	5%
Don't Know	13%

Sources:1 *60 Minutes, Vanity Fair*, 60 Minutes/Vanity Fair Poll, December 2012, retrieved May 15, 2019 from the iPOLL Databank, The Roper Center for Public Opinion Research, University of Connecticut; 2FOX News/Opinion Dynamics Poll, January 2007, retrieved May 15, 2019 from the iPOLL Databank, The Roper Center for Public Opinion Research, University of Connecticut; 3 *Newsweek, PSRA/Newsweek Poll*, October 1995, retrieved May 15, 2019 from the iPOLL Databank, The Roper Center for Public Opinion Research, University of Connecticut.

When famous actors run for office, the media invokes imagery from the actor's movie career to talk about the campaign. An article titled "Eastwood gunning for votes" in the *San Diego Union-Tribune* said,

Go ahead, vote for the incumbent. Make my day. With magnum force, Clint Eastwood stormed the Carmel by the Sea city offices near here Wednesday and went rapid-fire through a stack of papers. . . . He wants to duel incumbent Charlotte Townsend in the April 8 city election. . . . For a fistful of votes—for a few votes more—he might get a chance to run the political gauntlet. That's the good, the bad and the ugly of it. (Kreidler 1986)

The *Washington Post* reported,

Make My Day, You Lotus Eaters! Actor Clint Eastwood, the steely-eyed bane of all manner of criminal undesirables in the movies, has announced for mayor of Carmel, Calif., and the good citizens of that wealthy, picturesque oceanside community had better shape up if he wins. "Dirty Harry" says his decision to seek the part-time, unsalaried office is the result of "my being supportive of various neighbors" in their dealings with the city. (Dickenson 1986)

The Australian newspaper *The Sunday Mail* declared, "'Dirty Harry' to stand for mayor" (*Sunday Mail* February 2, 1986). In this way there is direct link between the actor's on-screen persona and the information that voters receive. It is as though a heroic cowboy and renegade lawman is running for mayor.

He received worldwide press attention for a small-town election; getting more press coverage than would be necessary to convey a message to the constituency voting for the office. "All 120 slots for a post-election press conference were snapped up days before the first vote was cast; Those signed up represented newspapers and magazines from Finland to France and television stations from Belgium to Brazil. London alone was represented by four tabloids, while Tokyo sent two network television news crews" (Stein April 9, 1986, 38). This extraordinary amount of media coverage only added to his already tremendously high name recognition.

RESOURCES

Clint Eastwood is very wealthy. Adjusted for inflation Clint Eastwood movies have earned more than $5 billion (Box Office Mojo "Clint Eastwood" 2019). His personal net worth is $375 million (Rossi 2018). It started with his role in *Rawhide*, "By the end of the first year his $600-a-week salary was doubled, and by the end of the show's run he was making six figures annually" (Eliot 2009, 57). He earned $250,000 for *The Good, the Bad, and the Ugly* (Schickel 1996). He then figured out how to take a bigger share of his movies' profits. He started his own production company, Malpaso. Malpaso's first movie, *Hang 'Em High*, was made for $1.5 million and in its initial release had earned $7 million. The success of *Hang 'Em High* allowed Eastwood to request a million-dollar acting contract for *Coogan's Bluff*. *Play Misty for Me* was made for less than $1 million and earned $5 million in its initial release (Eliot 2009). Steady profits like these meant that Eastwood was now a success in the movie *business*. With a few exceptions, Eastwood's movies have been revenue behemoths that made the studios and the actor/director/producer a lot of money, even when critics were unimpressed with the product (Schickel 1996). One needs to keep in mind that critically acclaimed movies and top grossing movies are not the same thing.

Because Carmel-by-the-Sea had just over 4,000 registered voters, a campaign for mayor would not be particularly expensive. It also has a surface area of about one square mile, making the whole city exceedingly small geographically. Getting his name on the ballot for the non-partisan election would require only twenty signatures (Associated Press January 31, 1986). He spent more than $40,000 on his self-financed campaign; beating the incumbent mayor who spent $3,000 (*Los Angeles Times* April 8, 1986, 20). Being independently wealthy was an important part of his success.

POLITICAL ENVIRONMENT

Before running for office Clint Eastwood was already friends with some immensely powerful politicians. Clint Eastwood and Ronald Reagan were major TV stars at the same time during the late 1950s and early 1960s. Also, as president of the Screen Actors Guild, it was Reagan's job to know TV's top talent. At a fundraiser hosted by Frank Sinatra for a hospital in Nebraska in December 1985 Ronald Reagan, "told the crowd that, when first elected to the White House, he had fantasized about a 'dream' cabinet, including, among others, John Wayne as secretary of state and Clint Eastwood as secretary of defense" ("People" December 13, 1985). Reagan imagined more celebrities in major positions of authority, including Eastwood specifically.

Clint Eastwood is a Republican, but not of the doctrinaire sort. According to Schickel,

He may vote Republican most of the time, but his political beliefs were then, as they are now, far from the standard right-wing positions: He is mildly in favor of gun control and strongly in favor of abortion rights (and most of the rest of the feminist agenda), he is close to being a First Amendment absolutist, and his hatred of anything that hints at racism is very close to the surface. The best label for him is probably "libertarian," but of a distinctly live-and-let-live kind. (Schickel 1996, 211)

Marc Eliot describes Eastwood's politics in this way:

Although he was a Nixon man, having voted for him in the explosive year of 1968, he rejected the president's constant bombing of Vietnam as unnecessary, both politically and morally. In no way could Clint ever be described as a liberal, but neither was he ever a proselytizing Republican. The best way of describing his politics would be "pragmatic independence." By 1970, after seven years of a blistering war that was going nowhere, he, like many Americans on both sides of the political fence, was simply fed up with it. (Eliot 2009, 121)

It turned out that Richard Nixon was a huge fan of Eastwood perhaps because, "Clint was the one whose screen persona played fastest and loosest with civil rights and the Constitution itself when it came to enforcing law and order" (Eliot 2009, 146). Nixon appointed Eastwood to serve on the National Council on the Arts.

Carmel-by-the-Sea is near the base where Eastwood served during the Korean War. It also is the town that Eastwood decided to live in as soon he earned enough from his acting jobs to afford better living conditions. In 1986, he decided to run for mayor for two reasons. First, the city had denied his permit to build an addition to his restaurant in Carmel, The Hog's Breath Inn. Second, the city had an ordinance against the selling of ice cream cones. Both issues spoke to the dominant political cleavage in the small town. Some residents wanted Carmel to be an exclusive residential community and did not like the idea of tourists coming and going through their town. Other residents understood that the tax revenues that tourists bring to the scenic community paid for much of the city's operations (Schickel 1996; Eliot 2009).

The city of Carmel-by-the-Sea was hostile to business interests (*San Francisco Examiner* April 16, 1986, 11). The conflict began in 1929 when the city passed an ordinance to preserve the residential character of the municipality. Carmel-by-the-Sea then systematically created a town that was actively hostile to tourists. The city banned the selling of ice cream cones, electric signage, the wearing of high heal shoes, the playing of frisbee and sitting on the grass in public parks, and it required every building permit to be approved by the city council itself. In a notorious incident, "one irate city official, fed up with out-of-towners, jumped aboard a tour bus and ordered the shocked tourists to vamoose" (Conklin 1985). The mayor, Charlotte Townsend, said, "The local people feel like they've been driven out of their own town. . . . It's like being a salmon going upstream trying to drive up Ocean Avenue" (Conklin 1985).

Meanwhile, local business owners lamented the heavy-handed city administration. Taxes on local businesses accounted for more than half of the city's operating budget. The city was able to maintain exceptionally low property taxes because of the high revenues from tourist related businesses. These businesses relied on the thousands of tourists that visit the city for its beaches and other attractions. One business owner said, "They have no compassion. They're against any change. I mean, they have only two public toilets in the whole city. They just don't care about tourists" (Conklin 1985). Business owners displayed signs in support of Eastwood. (Flinn April 9, 1986, 1). When the city council denied business owner Clint Eastwood a permit to expand his restaurant the stage was set for a showdown that would receive international attention. To rectify the building permit and ice cream issues Eastwood ran for mayor (United Press International January 30, 1986).

He began by contacting a Republican consultant named Eileen Padberg who conducted a poll of the local electorate to determine if Eastwood had a chance of winning. Padberg then suggested that Sue Hutchinson be hired has Eastwood's campaign manager (Schickel 1996). Marc Eliot writes,

Almost immediately campaign posters with his picture that looked like a cross between Ronald Reagan and Dirty Harry began to appear on the sides of buildings and streetlamps. Bumper stickers bore the slogan "Go ahead, make me mayor!" With Ronald Reagan's improbable leap from movies to the White House still fresh in everyone's minds, the news that Clint had "entered politics" filled the front pages of newspapers around the world. (Eliot 2009, 132)

In this way, Eastwood's bid for public office followed a template that is used by other celebrity candidates. He used imagery evoking his onscreen persona. In his case, Dirty Harry. Eastwood said, "Dirty Harry is always fighting bureaucracy, and I guess that's what I'm doing here, too" (Flinn April 9, 1986, 1). He capitalized on his movie fame by using his most famous line in his campaign. Voters knew that America's favorite tough guy wanted to be their mayor.

Eastwood also benefited from celebrity slack. The actor has seven children. Of the seven, two were with is first wife and one was with his second wife. Four were born to women he was not married to. Eastwood had a tremendous amount of sex appeal, and his promiscuous lifestyle did not change even after being married. His friends and family have noted that Clint attracted female admirers without any effort, his physical appearance alone was enough to get women's attention.

> A friend of his recalls sharing a hotel elevator after a banquet in his honor in Paris, and a grinning Clint pulling three room keys out of his pockets; all had been placed there by women he had met at the dinner. We are perhaps in the realm of evolutionary psychology here. As its great explicator Robert Wright tells us, prominent males, like dominant primates, are designed to capitalize sexually on their status. Fame, power and riches draw the attention of women, their own neurochemistry urges such men on and all the rest is easy moralizing and/or spiteful envy. (Schickel 1996, 129)

He would often have relationships with the actresses he worked with on set. These dalliances would produce several children, and two abortions, over the course of Eastwood's life (Schickel 1996).

Eastwood felt no remorse, rather he claimed that he and his first wife had come to an understanding about the life Clint was going to live (Eliot 2009). When Eastwood talks about his encounters with women he, "is neither boastful nor regretful. Certainly it appears to be untouched by guilt. The need to have many women was a fact of his life, his nature if you will, and it remains an undeniable fact of his history" (Schickel 1998, 128). His highly publicized extramarital affairs proved to be no barrier to his success in getting elected to be the mayor of a small town. Such philandering is typically viewed as an indication of untrustworthiness and has harmed non-celebrity politicians who cheated on their spouses. While each case is unique in its circumstances, this suggests that celebrity slack is applicable in small- and large-scale political environments.

Eastwood garnered 2,166 (72 percent) votes and handily defeated the incumbent mayor who got 799 (27 percent) votes. There was a whopping 73 percent voter turnout rate in the high-profile election (Stein April 9, 1986, 38). In addition, the media attention paid to the contest caused voter registration to increase by 461 voters, a proportionately large sum in a city the size of Carmel (Marcus 1986). After winning, Eastwood received a call from President Reagan, who asked him, "What's an actor who once appeared with a monkey in a movie doing in politics?" (Stein April 10, 1986, 3). The joke was that Reagan had made *Bedtime for Bonzo* and Eastwood's co-star in *Every Which Way but Loose* was an orangutan. In short order Eastwood got his building expansion permit and reversed the ice cream law (Wilstein 1986). During his term he used his own money to help the city purchase some nearby land to preserve a natural area and avoid development. He also oversaw the expansion of the town's library. Because the Carmel mayoralty was a part-time position, he continued his film career while serving as mayor. And, having accomplished his goals, he did not seek a second term (Schickel 1996; Eliot 2009).

CONCLUSIONS

Clint Eastwood did not aspire to be an actor in his youth. As a young man he befriended people in the entertainment industry who felt he had "the look" to be successful in Hollywood. Indeed, his looks got people's attention and he used his looks for both professional and personal advantage. He trained as an actor out of economic necessity, but he became a global sensation by playing a rugged cowboy and, later, a renegade lawman. These roles, along with his skill in producing and directing, allowed Eastwood to earn hundreds of millions of dollars, vastly more than the amount needed to run a successful campaign for mayor of a small town. The media provided international news coverage for his mayoral bid and often referenced his movie roles while covering the campaign. He handily defeated the incumbent and benefited from celebrity slack when the voters overlooked his marital infidelities. After being elected Eastwood commented that running for mayor was "more difficult than making a movie" (Stein April 10, 1986, 3). He served only one term in office but regained the political spotlight years later with his widely panned speech to an empty chair at the 2012 Republican National Convention (Warnke 2020).

Chapter 5

Fred Grandy

Fred Grandy is best known for his role as "Gopher" on television's *The Love Boat*. Grandy was originally from Sioux City, Iowa. However, both his parents died when he was young. His father died of a heart attack when Fred was twelve, and his mother died of an aneurysm the next year. Orphaned and in the custody of his mother's best friend he was sent to the elite prep school Phillips Academy Exeter. While there his roommate was David Eisenhower, the grandson of former president Dwight Eisenhower. He later served as best man when David married Julie Nixon, President Richard Nixon's daughter. After Exeter, Grandy went to Harvard University where he majored in English literature. It was at Harvard where he discovered his passion for acting. He joined "The Proposition" improvisational group where he began to learn his skills as an entertainer (Kunen 1985; Norman November 5, 1986, 12).

After college he worked on the congressional staff of congressman Wiley Mayne in Iowa. Mayne was defeated by Berkley Bedell in 1974. Disappointed, Grandy reconnected with his Harvard friends and decided to pursue a career in show business appearing in improvisational comedy groups in New York in 1975. He was discovered by one of Norman Lear's scouts and spent a year performing on the television show *Maude*. He was soon cast in *The Love Boat* and became a celebrity (Kunen 1985; Norman November 5, 1986, 12).

After nine seasons on *The Love Boat* Grandy decided to seek Mayne's former seat in Congress. He would have to persuade voters he was not the inept "Gopher" from the show. But his fame was a definite advantage during the campaign. He harnessed the talent, fame, and resources he had as a celebrity to run a successful campaign. The political environment was also a decisive factor in his victory. The retirement of Bedell meant that Grandy would not face a popular incumbent in the open seat election.

TALENT

Fred Grandy was a talented comedian. Unlike Al Franken, however, he chose not to use his humor on the campaign trail. On television he played the bumbling and inept purser of *The Love Boat* "Gopher" Smith. Gopher was a "love sick clown in white knee shorts" Grandy said, "There is that hard core there that assumes I'm a flake the way he was" (Kamin 1986, 1). He also said his campaign began as a "cartoon candidacy," saying, "It took a long time for people to take me seriously. You've got to convince people that you're for real. That took most of the campaign, I was running against me" (Norman and Hyde 1986, 1). He had to build credibility throughout the campaign. He said, "There is a Gopher gap that I have to bridge. I have to make people understand that there is a long pants version of Fred Grandy, not just Gopher Smith in short pants" (Witosky 1986, 18). The image that he had cultivated as "Gopher" for nearly a decade was not one that could be taken seriously. By his own admission "Gopher" was a clown. It was necessary for Grandy to rebrand himself, while still using his celebrity to his advantage.

Grandy said the low expectations often worked in his favor. The Exeter and Harvard graduate quickly impressed people who realized he "isn't as dumb as 'Gopher'" (Kamin 1986, 1). Voters who encountered him while he was campaigning figured out that Grandy was intelligent and articulate. He was not a bumbling fool; he was supremely educated and sincere in his desire to hold a position of public responsibility.

The television debate was a crucial turning point. Grandy and his general election opponent, Clayton Hodgson, were tied in polling before the debate. Grandy, of course, was a skilled performer in front of the cameras and new polling indicated that undecided voters broke in Grandy's direction after the debate (Norman October 27, 1986, 1). At the debate, Grandy praised Reagan's "Star Wars" initiative while Hodgson criticized it as insufficient and too expensive (Hoeschen October 18, 1986, 24). Both candidates agreed that the Farm Credit System needed action to be saved but disagreed on the best approach. They sparred on whether additional regulations or loan restructuring would solve the issues (Norman October 18, 1986, 2). Grandy's practiced skill in front of the cameras put him at ease, while his opponent seemed out of place in the spotlight.

It was not until after he won that he permitted his humor to shine through. Asked his assessment of the campaign, he said, "There isn't one thing I'd change in the campaign except for maybe the liver and onion dinner I had the other night at Spirit Lake" (*Des Moines Register* December 8, 1986, 15). After his swearing in he joked about his treatment, "I get no respect. Whenever I get on the elevator, the guy asks, 'Speaker's Lobby or lido deck?'" (*Des Moines Register* February 1, 1987, 20). His humor was contagious. Washington insiders joked that he might seek a seat on the House Merchant Marine and Fisheries Committee (*Des Moines Register* November 30, 1986, 20). He re-branded himself as a serious problem solver during the campaign, but he was really the "funny man" people enjoyed.

FAME

Grandy was on *The Love Boat* during its entire nine-year run on television. In the 1980 to 1981 season *The Love Boat* was the fifth highest rated show on television with a 24.3 rating. That means nearly 25 percent of television viewers in that time slot were watching *The Love Boat* (Brooks and Marsh 2007). Polling indicated that Grandy entered the race with 85 percent name recognition. (Kamin 1986, 1). Typical first-time candidates must spend enormous sums in advertising to gain name recognition. Polebrities enter their races with important advantages.

Although his "Gopher" persona was a hurdle, it was also an advantage. He said, "If nobody even knows you it's lower than ground zero" (Norman November 5, 1986, 12). In discussing the state of the race reporters said, "Grandy also has been the only person to draw any kind of crowds. Many of them, however, apparently attend because they want to see a celebrity, not because they are particularly interested in Grandy's political views" (Witosky 1986, 18). Grandy was prepared for voters requesting autographs during campaign events. He had photographs, and markers to sign them with, ready for anyone who asked for his autograph (Norman October 27, 1986, 1). Like the other polebrities in this volume he capitalized on his fame to lure voters. They came for an autograph and got reasons to vote for him.

Grandy's fame became an issue during the primary campaign. Terry Jobst, his opponent, requested equal time on local television stations that were airing *The Love Boat*. When the stations announced that they would cancel airing the program rather than comply Jobst faced a public backlash and withdrew his request. Approximately 60,000 district residents watched *The Love Boat* weekly and were upset that they would miss the final season of the show due to Jobst's request (Hoeschen April 9, 1986, 1). Fans of *The Love Boat*, and by extension Grandy, directly intervened in the campaign. Their defense of the program hurt Grandy's competitor. Gopher's silliness was a direct contrast to Jobst's perceived mean spiritedness. Jobst had not requested cancelation, only equal time, but the damage was done.

RESOURCES

Fred Grandy was a wealthy man. Financial disclosure statements showed that in 1985 he earned $832,900. In 1984, he earned $743,200. His disclosed assets made him a millionaire (Norman May 9, 1986, 19). Some of his wealth was used for his campaign. He loaned his campaign $97,000 (Norman November 5, 1986, 12). Early fundraising totals showed that Grandy had a sizeable advantage over Hodgson. In July 1986, Grandy reported raising $177,752.86 compared to $66,351 for Hodgson (*Sioux City Journal* July 17, 1986, 1). Grandy raised more than Hodgson from traditional political sources. Grandy received $123,957 from PAC contributions, while Hodgson raised $108,540 from PACs (Westphal 1986). In total, Grandy spent $610,837 and Hodgson $404,002 (*Sioux City Journal* December 11, 1986, 1).

Grandy raised $36,000 from "actor friends" (Beeman 1986, 11). Celebrities that donated to Grandy included Ed Begley Jr., John Davidson, Phyllis Diller, Brad Dillman, David Doyle, Linda Evans, Jamie Farr, Anne Francis, Robert and Donna Guillaume, Helen Hayes, Harvey Korman, Mary Ann Mobley, Bill Macy, John Ritter, Andrew Stevens, Gale Storm, and Gavin MacLeod, who portrayed the captain of *The Love Boat*. He also received a donation from David Eisenhower (Hyde April 26, 1986, 3; Kamin 1986, 1). Polebrities are wealthy people with wealthy friends, and this provides an additional source of campaign funds that are difficult for opponents to compete with.

POLITICAL ENVIRONMENT

The incumbent, Berkley Bedell, retired from Congress rather than seek a seventh term. The reason quickly became a tale of political folklore in Iowa. Bedell was bitten by a wood tick while on a fishing trip and was gravely ill with Lyme disease. He was hospitalized and sapped of strength. Unable to campaign, he decided not to run. Grandy admitted that he could not have defeated the popular incumbent, but the open seat made it possible for him to win (*Des Moines Register* November 6, 1986, 1).

Grandy's two primary opponents entered the race late. It was assumed that Grandy would be an "also ran" candidate facing a popular incumbent. When Bedell unexpectedly announced he would not seek re-election two challengers to Grandy hastily attempted to seek the office themselves. Grandy had tremendous name recognition, had already been campaigning for months, and received most of the media attention during the short-lived primary battle (Witosky 1986, 18). Grandy easily won receiving 19,390 (68 percent) votes.

Moriarty received 5,219 (18 percent) votes and Jobst received 4,052 (14 percent) votes (*Des Moines Register* June 4, 1986, 1).

In the general election he faced Clayton Hodgson who was Bedell's congressional aide (*Des Moines Register* November 6, 1986, 1). Joe Biden campaigned on behalf of Clayton Hodgson, saying, "If you send a guy whose claim to fame is that he was on 'Love Boat' back to Washington, D.C., I want to tell you—and I'm not exaggerating—you will send a very loud and clear message, the loud and clear message is that agriculture isn't as bad off as it really is" (Norman October 24, 1986, 3). The claim was that "Gopher" was not a serious candidate.

A poll showed that 58 percent of voters thought that Grandy's *Love Boat* role made no difference in their vote choice, despite the media's, and his opponents' focus on it (Pins October 22, 1986, 1). The biggest issue was whether Grandy was a carpetbagger.

> The candidacy of former television actor Fred Grandy in the 6th District has turned the northwest Iowa race into a genuine political oddity. It is a one issue race, and the issue is Grandy. Grandy, a Republican, is the focus of virtually every television and radio commercial - both his own and those of his Democratic opponent, Clayton Hodgson - and the strategies of both candidates are geared exclusively around the question of his legitimacy. (Hyde November 1, 1986, 1)

Grandy's campaign responded with advertisements that discussed his "deep Iowa roots" and informed voters that his grandfather had settled in Iowa in 1882 (Norman and Hyde 1986, 1). Grandy highlighted his service to the district during his time as a staffer to Wiley Mayne. With Reagan in the White House during the campaign it is probable that most voters saw parallels between the two Republican former actors. It was not a bizarre leap to think that a television actor could be a political leader (Norman October 27, 1986, 1).

Grandy won the endorsement of the *Sioux City Journal* which said that Hodgson had created a "phony issue" by questioning Grandy's Iowa bona fides (*Sioux City Journal* October 30, 1986, 4). The *Des Moines Register* endorsed Grandy arguing that "The Harvard-educated actor is very polished. He has done his homework and presents his case well." They said his opponent, "whose ability to convey and defend his views is limited" had farm policy views that were "astonishingly shallow and ill thought-through" (*Des Moines Register* October 19, 1986, 21). The local press, it seemed, were convinced that Fred Grandy would be a capable leader.

The election was close. Fred Grandy earned 81,861 (51 percent) votes. While Clayton Hodgson garnered 78,807 (49 percent) votes (*Des Moines*

Register December 12, 1986, 3). It was a race Republicans had expected to lose but Grandy's debate performance and his national media attention allowed them to squeak out a victory.

Fred Grandy had made some statements that could be considered sexist or chauvinistic, "Back in the days when he played 'Gopher on ABC's 'The Love Boat,' Iowa congressman-elect Fred Grandy remarked: 'Every year I visit the world's most romantic ports and make love to beautiful women, and when I'm finished I get money'" (*Des Moines Register* November 9, 1986, 24). Fortunately for Grandy, the criticism was not leveled at him until after the election. It could be a case of celebrity slack that the issue did not come up during the election. It could also be a case of poor opposition research on the part of his opponents in the primary and general elections. In either case, his campaign was free from any major scandal.

CONCLUSIONS

Fred Grandy was the focus of every news story about the election. The media focused on him, and his opponents focused on him. He received national attention and was by far the most well-known candidate in the race. He was also able to outspend his opponents during the campaign. Indeed, Fred Grandy was the issue of the campaign for everyone involved. Most importantly, Grandy did not have to face a popular incumbent because of the fortuitous wood tick bite.

After Grandy's victory, some commentators lamented the celebritization of politics, "Politics was once a passion; now it is entertainment, something to do between roles. Charlton Heston has the choice between running for the U.S. Senate or starring in 'The Colbys.' After 'The Love Boat' was cancelled, Fred Grandy ('Gopher') ran for Congress from Iowa and won, while Gerald Ford and Henry Kissinger, after retiring from rather respected offices, made appearances on 'Dynasty'" (*Des Moines Register* November 26, 1986, 11). For some, the election of "Gopher" was a signal that Americans did not take politics as seriously as they should. Grandy would go on to get re-elected three times before losing a primary contest for Iowa governor.

Grandy remarked that Washington and Hollywood are remarkably similar, "They're both one-industry towns fueled by gossip. Washington is Hollywood with higher ceilings" (*Des Moines Register* February 1, 1987, 20). Thus, Grandy saw the interchangeability of his roles. He went from actor to congressmen and then back to actor. After retiring from politics he made appearances on *Law & Order*, *The Mindy Project*, *General Hospital*, *Fresh Off the Boat*, *Fuller House*, *Moonbase 8*, and *Side Hustle* (IMDb "Fred Grandy").

Chapter 6

Sonny Bono

Sonny Bono knew he wanted to be in show business as a young boy. He says, "In grammar school I made up skits, acted out sword fights and told jokes, anything to get a reaction—usually a laugh. . . . And by high school, my peers accepted me in the role of the entertainer" (Bono 1991, 31). At the age of seventeen Bono appeared on a TV talent show and performed a song that he wrote. He won the competition, and that song was recorded; it would be his first single release as a solo artist. Having gained some exposure Bono worked as a producer and song writer and many of his songs were recorded by more prominent singers in the late 1950s. By the 1960s Bono was writing songs for *The Righteous Brothers* and *The Rolling Stones*. When Sonny was twenty-seven, he met sixteen-year-old Cherilyn Sarkisian LaPierre and they quickly became romantically involved. Sonny and Cher worked as background singers for many popular musical groups in the early 1960s. They were two of the background singers for The Righteous Brothers number one hit single "You've Lost That Lovin' Feelin'" and The Crystals' hit song "Da Doo Ron Ron." At that time Sonny and Cher made a living on the margins of the recording industry (Bono 1991).

Using a combination of wacky outfits and publicity stunts Sonny and Cher became international pop superstars when "I Got You Babe" became the number one single in the UK and in the United States. Sonny Bono was highly skilled at developing and maintaining a public persona. Despite financial and personal problems, Bono maintained a public façade that would allow him to remain a star. Sonny and Cher would eventually split with Cher continuing her own successful career as a singer and actress. Sonny would go on to appear in several movies. These included *Escape to Athena* (1979), *Airplane 2: The Sequel* (1982), *Troll* (1986), *Dirty Laundry* (1987), and *Hairspray* (1988). He was elected the mayor of Palm Springs, California in 1988. He lost a bid for the US Senate in 1992 but was elected to the US House of Representatives in 1994. His unorthodox lifestyle was no barrier to his political success.

TALENT

Sonny Bono understood the concept of developing a public persona and he hired people in the industry who knew how the game was played. The rumor is that Sonny and Cher's manager and publicist orchestrated a publicity stunt. Sonny and Cher were kicked out of Manhattan's Americana Hotel because, according to the hotel manager, "We serve a certain class of people" (Bono 1991, 116). Sonny and Cher represented all the beatnik hippies who were mocked and ridiculed for their way of life. They became a symbol for a generation of youngsters who were determined to forge their own path and go against traditional social conventions. This scene was repeated at the London Hilton so that the couple would personify "undesirables" the world over. It embodied the struggle between the upper-class establishment and the riff raff hippies who disdained the status quo.

Bono learned how to get people's attention by emulating Phil Spector, a big shot music promoter that Bono befriended. Bono describes Spector, "He even practiced the coolest way to sit in his car, studying the various angles. He would put one arm on the window, try steering with one finger, all sorts of different poses. Then he would have me stand outside the car and ask how he looked" (Bono 1991, 75). Bono quickly learned the importance of showmanship, "There was value in that, I realized, especially for someone like me, who wanted to absorb every aspect of Spector's tremendous power to turn heads. Of course, both Jack Nitzsche and I began imitating our guru. We grew out our hair, donned shades indoors and out, and attempted to dress as weirdly as possible" (Bono 1991, 76). Long before Lady Gaga came on the scene artists understood that one way to get people's attention was to don weird clothing.

Why did people pay attention to Sonny and Cher? According to Bono, wearing outrageous costumes helped them draw attention. Evoking the imagery of an old-time carnival Bono described what happened to them after "I Got You Babe" hit number one on the charts, "A rabid, screaming, hysterical mob greeted us at Kennedy International airport. People stared at us, in our jeans, fur-lined vests and boots, and long hair, as if we were sideshow freaks" (Bono 1991, 115). Bono writes, "Our look was so costumey that we were outraging people," even Nancy Sinatra called them clowns (Bono 1991, 119). People pay attention to things that are bizarre and outlandish because their peculiarity makes them interesting and out of the ordinary. Bono understood this human predilection and used it to garner the public's attention. The couple also utilized cosmetic surgery to improve their physical appearances, with Sonny reducing the size of his nose (Bono 1991).

The marriage of Sonny and Cher began and ended as a fabricated public persona. Sonny was still married to his first wife when Sonny and Cher began performing as a couple. Bono writes, "For image's sake, I downplayed my past. . . . Cher and I fabricated a romantic tale that had us eloping to Mexico. People believed us and the story became part of the Sonny and Cher lore. It wasn't true, though" (Bono 1991, 99–100). They maintained that falsehood for five years before they did eventually marry in a secret ceremony designed to maintain their original hoax.

The couple spent the entirety of their early fortune on producing *Chasity*. They even had to pawn off their furniture to complete the film. Like many other athletes and entertainers that come into their fortune suddenly and in their youth, they squandered it and had nothing in the bank. But Bono understood that he had to maintain Sonny and Cher's public persona, "In Hollywood image counts for everything, and I'd be damned if I was going to be perceived as desperate as I really was. I hatched a plan. For five thousand dollars I bought an old Rolls-Royce, an immense, black gas guzzler, and hired a chauffeur. If we went to a studio we made sure everybody knew that we were arriving in a chauffeur-driven Rolls" (Bono 1991, 164). He writes, "a performer has to be part con artist" (Bono 1991, 178). He understood that his success rested on maintaining an illusion.

Bono was a successful singer, actor, and comedian. While performing their concerts Sonny and Cher, "gradually developed a humorous and fairly sophisticated repartee. . . . We kept the jokes that worked and pretty soon we had a comedy routine to punctuate our musical act" (Bono 1991, 174). *The Sonny and Cher Comedy Hour*, which aired from 1971 to 1974, was a precursor to *Saturday Night Live*, which began in 1975. Both shows are primarily sketch comedy programs that include musical guests. The show was popular because of "Sonny's ebullient enthusiasm and Cher's sardonic wit and continual put-downs of her husband" (Brooks and Marsh 2007, 1271). According to Bono, they were, "the bickering Romeo and Juliet of prime-time television" (Bono 1991, 174). Among the popular sketches there "was a 'Vamp' segment in which Cher would portray several of the more notorious women throughout history; a 'Sonny's Pizza' segment featuring Sonny as the dumb owner of a pizzeria and Cher as his sexy, beautiful waitress Rosa" (Brooks and Marsh 2007, 1271). The show also spoofed news headlines and television commercials. The program allowed Sonny Bono to develop an affable persona among America's television viewing public.

Even after the couple's relationship soured, they maintained their happy couple façade for the sake of their television show. The couple was earning 4 million dollars a year and had purchased a fifty-four-room 30,000 square foot mansion. To maintain their lifestyle and continue their livelihoods they continued to live together. However, Sonny's new girlfriend and Cher's new boyfriend lived in the mansion with them along with their daughter. There was plenty of space for them to never see each other at home, they only interacted in public. Sonny writes, "The romance that worked so well on television was, in fact, exactly what we'd sold to television, and exactly what television had sold to advertisers—a commodity" (Bono 1991, 195). Of the public deception Bono says, "It was a big put-on that should've won us an acting award long before Cher did *Moonstruck*" (Bono 1991, 206).

In his bid for Congress Bono resorted to his stage act to entertain crowds. "Observers say it was 'color and movement' which did it for him, something which Bono acknowledges and makes no apology for. In one of his last public meetings, Bono spent the first five minutes of his speech entertaining the audience with one-liners about Cher" (Burke 1994). In other words, he resorted to his past in sketch comedy and concert performances to gain audience approval. He was a likable funny man that voters were willing to support. The years he spent developing and maintaining a fabricated public persona allowed him to develop his "con artist" performance skills to make sure he was perceived favorably by the public.

FAME

Sonny and Cher's debut album, *Look at Us*, sold 3 million copies and was number 2 on the Billboard music charts for eight weeks. It included "I Got You Babe," a number one hit single, 4 other songs that reached the top 20, and 2 more in the top 100. The album was a smashing success globally, including in Europe and Australia. The couple appeared on television programs, *The Ed Sullivan Show,* and others, to promote their music. Sonny and Cher were globally recognized celebrities (Wheway 2017).

They filmed the movie *Good Times* in 1967 because they were both interested in acting careers in addition to their music. In 1968, they starred in a film called *Chastity*, which they wrote and produced themselves. They also performed as guest actors in several television programs including, *The Man from U.N.C.L.E.*, *Love, American Style*, and *The New Scooby-Doo Movies*. They were becoming an entertainment power couple and they used their success to secure their own television show. The *Sonny and Cher Comedy Hour*, a variety show featuring the couple, was a huge success. The show received twelve Emmy Award nominations, with one win, and was watched by millions of Americans in the early 1970s (Television Academy "The Sonny and Cher Comedy Hour"). Because they would perform their new songs, and their greatest hits, on the show their album sales would surge after their TV performances of their music. They were simultaneously television and music superstars (Wheway 2017).

The Sonny and Cher Comedy Hour was tied with *Kojak* as the seventh most popular television show in 1973 with nearly a quarter of all television viewers watching it in its respective time slot (Brooks and Marsh 2007). That year the show had over 15 million viewers (Wheway 2017). *The Sonny Comedy Revue* was a short-lived television series that attempted to feature Sonny without Cher after the couple's divorce. While still appearing on television, Sonny was not able to generate the same popularity without his ex-wife (Brooks and Marsh 2007). The couple reunited in 1976 and 1977 for *The Sonny and Cher Show*, an attempted revival of their *Comedy Hour*. The show did not work as well in part because Cher's put downs of Sonny did not seem as playful now that the couple was divorced (Bono 1991). Nevertheless, the show allowed Sonny to remain in the public eye more than a decade after "I Got You Babe" was the number one single. In 1979, he portrayed Deacon Dark, a character modeled after K.I.S.S. and Alice Cooper, in an episode of *The Love Boat* where he shared the screen with Fred Grandy.

Sonny appeared in several movies during the 1980s. These included *Escape to Athena* (1979), *Airplane 2: The Sequel* (1982), *Troll* (1986), *Dirty Laundry* (1987), and *Hairspray* (1988). In discussing why he went into acting Bono writes, "I was a fly-by-the-seat-of-my-pants kind of guy, and what is acting besides faking it? Although financially sound, I looked on acting as a way of keeping my name in the public mind" (Bono 1991, 232). *Hairspray* was released a month before his mayoral election and the entertainment sections of most newspapers carried reviews of the film (Lipper 1988). Sonny Bono was being talked about for non-political reasons nationally. This has the effect of reinforcing his already high name recognition without alienating any potential voters with political views they might disagree with.

As luck would have it, Cher was promoting her new movie, *Moonstruck*, and the release of her new album, while Sonny was running for mayor. The producers of *The David Letterman Show* called Sonny Bono and asked if he would like to appear with Cher. They were sure to mention that the exposure would be good for his campaign. Sonny did not turn down the earned media and appeared on the show. Letterman said, "You have, temporarily at least, left the world of showbusiness. Although politics is not that far removed from show business, but you're running for mayor in Palm Springs" (Letterman 1987). Bono then went on to explain that the city had forbade him to put up signage at the opening of his new restaurant in town and that the neighboring towns were growing economically while Palm Springs had laws that made it difficult for business owners like himself. He claimed that the long serving incumbent mayor was "dictatorial" and that he wanted to do what he could to change the city's antiquated policies (Letterman 1987). The show received massive ratings because Sonny and Cher reunited to sing, *I Got You Babe* for the final time. Bono knew, "I'd be grabbing some national visibility while helping to draw attention to Cher and her new record. It was the kind of fabricated event television lives on" (Bono 1991, 9). Bono received national media attention, while his opponents did not.

Bono continued to receive national and international media attention when he decided to run for the House of Representatives in 1994. He cruised to victory in the primary and general election by substantial margins. After winning his congressional race he was mocked by TV's *Murphy Brown*, a show known to wade into political controversies, and appeared on *The Tonight Show with Jay Leno* where he was given the chance to reply to Cher's comments that politicians are "one step below used-car salesmen" (*San Jose Mercury News* November 19, 1994; *USA Today* December 12, 1994). Celebrities use feuds with other celebrities to keep themselves in the news. It was a tactic Bono was aware of and used to his advantage.

RESOURCES

During his mayoral bid Sonny Bono capitalized on his fame to assist his fundraising efforts. His campaign was "financed almost entirely from the sale of Sonny Bono T-shirts to winter tourists" (Van Deerlin 1988). Bono spent $52,479 compared to the $24,486 of Eli Birer, his closest competitor. His largest source of funding was $36,986 from the sale of T-shirts, buttons, and bumper stickers (Farah 1988; Mecum April 1, 1988). In his run for the US Senate, Bono's celebrity did not help his fundraising efforts. Establishment favorite, Republican Congressman Tom Campbell, raised more than $5 million and was the preferred candidate of PACs. The winner, Bruce Herschensohn, raised $3.5 million. Bono raised a paltry $344,781 (California Journal's Election Weekly August 31, 1992).

When Bono ran for the US House in 1994, he received the backing of the Republican Party establishment and drew on his personal wealth to succeed. Bono received $377,119 in donations and loaned his campaign an additional $228,000 from his own pocket. In total Bono spent $592,789, far more than his Democratic opponent who only managed $297,448 in donations. Bono received support from the National Republican Congressional Committee, Republican affiliated PACs, and party leaders such as Newt Gingrich and Dick Armey (Roberson 1994). His initial fundraising success was because of his fame, but his later success relied on traditional methods and his personal wealth.

POLITICAL ENVIRONMENT

Bono was not a typical Republican, he campaigned for Bobby Kennedy. After Kennedy's assassination he supported Hubert Humphrey and appeared at several Humphrey rallies as a celebrity endorser. As such he met many of the more prominent politicos of that era and he stated in his diary, "The more I see of politics, the less I like it. It seems like a lesser stage of show business and very phony" (Bono 1991, 169). The irony is palpable. Bono had fabricated a phony marriage and pretended to be fabulously rich to maintain his public persona as a pop star. That he would deride the phoniness of politicians suggests that he saw how the two industries were similar.

Like Eastwood, Bono decided to run for mayor because of a building permit dispute. Bono claims that the City of Palm Springs was inconsistent in its permitting process. At the time he was attempting to remodel his home and to put up signage for his restaurant. He was told it was against city ordinance to add a second floor to his home, yet other homes had two stories. He was told he would not be allowed to put up a sign for his restaurant, yet other businesses had signs (Bono 1991).

Before getting started with his campaign for mayor Sonny Bono called Clint Eastwood for advice. Eastwood was not in town, but he was able to reach Sue Hutchinson, Eastwood's campaign manager. Bono and Eastwood had known each other for years. When Eastwood was planning to sing his album of cowboy songs to capitalize on his *Rawhide* fame, Bono was one of the music producers that he spoke with (Bono 1991). Bono said, "Clint did it, and I went, 'Yeah, I can do it too!'" (Picardie 1988). Still, he tried to downplay the celebrity comparison, "I think the only comparison to Clint is not the fact we're both celebrities, but . . . that he went into a community, invested as a businessman and found a lot of antiquated laws and conflicting codes and rules. From that standpoint, his awareness is the same as mine" (United Press International February 1, 1988). Still, Bono's celebrity network coincided with his political network.

Palm Springs, California has less than 40,000 residents and was home to many celebrities. Bob Hope, Frank Sinatra, Dinah Shore, Red Skelton, Victoria Principal, Harry Glassman, Mary Martin, Kirk and Anne Douglas, Cary Grant, Bing Crosby, Jack Benny, Liberace, Alan Ladd, Edward G. Robinson, Jean Harlow, Clark Gable, Dorothy Lamour, Zsa Zsa Gabor, Jim and Tammy Bakker, Debbie Reynolds, Trini Lopez, Donald O'Connor, and Dean Martin all resided in Palm Springs. In addition, former President Gerald Ford and former US Ambassador to Britain Walter Annenberg lived in the city. Near Sonny Bono's restaurant Sidney Chaplin, the son of Charlie Chaplin, operated his own restaurant (Cullen 1987; Young 1988). Because of this, it would seem perfectly natural for a celebrity to be the mayor of a town full of celebrities.

The previous mayor, Frank Bogert, who was mayor from 1945 to 1970 and again from 1981 to 1988, decided not to seek re-election (Associated Press February 6, 1987; Cullen 1987). Bono's announcement that he would run for mayor was covered in national news broadcasts and newspapers as far away as Australia publicized it (ABC News Transcripts April 8, 1987; Advertiser February 9, 1987). One of the first questions Bono received from reporters had to do with Clint Eastwood's successful mayoral bid the year before. "Sonny Bono says his decision to run for mayor of Palm Springs, Calif., has nothing to do with Clint Eastwood being elected mayor of Carmel, Calif. 'But it's nice to know if you're a celebrity, it can be done, because he did it,' Bono said" (Trott February 20, 1987). Soon after Bono received his first celebrity endorsement from his neighbor Suzanne Somers who believed that Bono would be a good mayor (Trott April 6, 1987).

Except for the extra-ordinary amounts of earned media, Sonny Bono's campaign was just like that of any other political amateur.

> Mine was strictly a grass-roots campaign, staffed by friends and volunteers and plotted by Mary [his wife at the time]. The coffers were filled by selling T-shirts, buttons, and bumper stickers; the campaign was fueled, as are all campaigns, by gallons of coffee and tens of thousands of calories' worth of doughnuts. I shook thousands of hands, gave out as many autographs, and kissed more babies than I'd ever seen in my life. (Bono 1991, 263)

Bono tapped Greg McDonald, a music promoter, to be his campaign manager. McDonald knew that Bono's celebrity would be a big help to the campaign, "Sonny did a press conference a few weeks ago, and it got picked up by the BBC. The opponents did a press conference, and it didn't get in the Indio paper" (Braun 1987). Like other celebrities turned politicians, Bono would run as an outsider, "I'm a non-politician. The way I see it, a politician should be like a doctor, looking for the overall good of the community" (Picardie 1988).

Celebrities are skilled at gaining attention. With just over a week to go before the election Bono was scheduled to appear on a televised debate with the other candidates. Unfortunately, his wife Mary, who was due to give birth just a few days after the election, was rushed to the hospital on the day of the debate. Bono told the organizers that he could not attend the debate and provided his reason. As the debate aired Bono was watching from his wife's hospital room and became alarmed when the moderator simply stated that Bono had other business to attend to, implying that Bono did not believe the debate was important. Bono called the station and asked them to make an announcement as to why he was not there. They did not. Enraged, Bono drove to the auditorium where the debate was being held and stormed the stage as he began berating the moderator for not explaining to the audience what had happened. At one point he threatens the moderator, "If anything happens to her, you'll have to answer to me." The moderator said he could participate just like the other candidates, but that he would have to sit down and follow the rules. He again said that he could not participate because his wife was in the hospital. He threw down his microphone in disgust and stormed off the stage as the audience cheered him on. Although this very public "flip out" was not planned, he began receiving praise for prioritizing his ailing wife over his political ambitions. While not participating in the debate, he was the top headline from that debate. Newspaper coverage of the debate focused exclusively on Bono's raging outburst, nothing any of the other candidates said was reported. He created a spectacle on live television that has become a part of the Sonny Bono legend and it demonstrates how celebrities can dominate the news coverage to the detriment of political rivals (Sonny Bono Debate 1988; Van Deerlin 1988; Associated Press March 31, 1988, April 3, 1988; Bono 1991).

With just two days to go before the election Bono was once again on the national ABC News broadcast promoting his candidacy, "I think from my show business background I'll have a tremendous ability to promote the town nationally and internationally and we need that desperately." Brian Rooney, the ABC correspondent said, "Bono is considered the leader in a seven way race, but his opponents say he has an unfair advantage in name recognition." Then his opponent, Eli Birer, is shown saying, "It seems like Sonny blows his nose and the media shows up from all over the place that he's got a cold" (ABC News Transcripts April 10, 1988). If that was not enough, on the eve of the election Cher won an Oscar for her role in *Moonstruck*, and Sonny and Cher were in the news together (Farah 1988; Associated Press April 12, 1988).

Bono was one of seven candidates running for Bogert's vacated office. The most prominent was vice mayor Eli Birer, a local real estate broker (Van Deerlin 1988). Bono received 4,842 votes. It accounted for 44 percent of the total. His next closest rival Lloyd Maryanov received 2,498 votes (Associated Press April 13, 1988). Turnout soared, "An election in this community of 38,000 residents usually draws about 6,000 of its 18,000 registered voters" (Farah 1988). But "City Clerk Judith Sumich reported that 10,933 or about 60 percent turned out this year and there were waiting lines at the polls" (Seager 1988). As mayor Bono was responsible for improving the city's economy by adding, "a marathon, a vintage-car race, a Grand Prix bicycle race, and the Palm Springs Film Festival" (Bono 1991, 273).

Like other politicians Sonny Bono could be criticized for his sexual behavior. When he was a teenager, he had an incestual relationship with one of his cousins (Bono 1991). When he began his relationship with Cher, she was still underage. Sonny was twenty-seven and Cher was sixteen and, although Cher had lied to him and claimed to be nineteen, he did not reject her after finding out about her real age (Letterman 1987). When Sonny and Cher's relationship soured, they publicly maintained the happy couple facade because their careers depended on it. However, Sonny's new girlfriend moved in to live with Sonny, Cher, and their daughter Chastity (Wheway 2017). When he ran for mayor at age fifty-two, his fourth wife was twenty-six (Picardie 1988). These unusual, and potentially criminal, actions were no barrier to Bono's later political success.

He ran for the US Senate in 1992 but lost in the primary to Bruce Herschensohn. Part of the reason for the loss was that Herschensohn was a celebrity himself. He started in Hollywood as a director, producer, and writer. Later, he became a political commentator for KABC's radio and television stations in Los Angeles. Given the size of the Los Angeles media market, Herschensohn was already very well known to a sizable portion of the California electorate having spent more than a decade on the air (Reinhold 1992; California Journal's Election Weekly June 8, 1992).

The primary reason for Bono's loss had to do with the policy positions of the three candidates running. Both Congressman Tom Campbell and Mayor Sonny Bono took liberal positions on many issues, both were pro-choice on the issue of abortion. Herschensohn presented more traditionally conservative views. He wanted to ban abortion, privatize Social Security, increase defense spending, increase oil drilling, and abolish the EPA, the Department of Energy, and the Federal Reserve Bank. Despite Campbell's fundraising advantage, the vote totals were Herschensohn 38 percent, Campbell 36 percent, and Bono 17 percent. Analysts argued that Bono was a spoiler for Campbell's presumed victory (Braun 1992; Cannon 1992; "Feinstein, Boxer Win California Senate Nominations; Seymour, Herschensohn Get GOP Bids"; Reinhold 1992).

To say that Sonny Bono was running in a very favorable political environment when he ran for the House of Representatives would be an understatement. Bono was a Republican running in a Republican district in a year that saw the Republican party flip fifty-four congressional seats to gain a majority in the House of Representatives for the first time in forty years. The incumbent, Republican Al McCandless, retired after 6 terms in the House. Steve Clute, Bono's Democratic opponent, was a state assemblyman with little chance of winning the heavily Republican district (Minzesheimer 1994). Bono received 56 percent of the vote, while Clute managed 38 percent. Unsurprised observers noted, "this is California, home of the celebpolitik tradition of Ronald Reagan and former mayor Clint Eastwood, so Mr. Bono's four consecutive wives and regular acting appearances on the television soaps *Love Boat* and *Fantasy Island* are perfect qualifications for the job" (Muir 1994).

CONCLUSIONS

Sonny Bono's celebrity helped him sell T-shirts and people showed up to his events to get his autograph. However, it was Bono's extremely high levels of earned media, receiving national and international coverage for a mayoral race that was the decisive factor. One is hard pressed to find statements by the other candidates that were covered by the media. Bono was also skilled at presenting a public persona, much of it fabricated for the sake of maintaining a desired public image. Rather than disqualifying him, his enraged berating of a debate moderator won him accolades. He was the top story from a debate he did not even participate in. His competitors, who presumably had policy positions on city issues, did not receive press coverage. Bono's sordid sexual history was no barrier to his success, celebrities like Bono seem to be given a pass for unorthodox behavior. When Bono lost his bid for the US Senate it was to a local celebrity whose positions more closely aligned with the conservative views of Republican primary voters. Bono again received national and international media attention with his bid for the US House, but this time Bono was the establishment candidate. He coasted to victory because he was a Republican running in a Republican dominated district.

Chapter 7

Jesse Ventura

Jesse "The Body" Ventura was a WWF star who used his talent and fame to become a Hollywood actor and a talk radio host. He had a bad guy persona that resonated with disaffected citizens. He was elected mayor of Brooklyn Park, Minnesota before successfully running for governor of Minnesota (Hauser 2002). Ventura "had great credibility with a public (especially young people) that mistrusted conventional politicians. Using anti-establishment ads and shining in campaign debates, Ventura demonstrated that sports politicos could transfer fame to the political process" (West and Orman 2003, 11). During the gubernatorial debates Ventura would allow the Democratic and Republican candidates to engage in petty bickering before interjecting, "I'm embarrassed as a United States citizen and as a veteran to what both of these two premier parties, the Democrats and Republicans, are sinking to today" (Hauser 2002, 13). He represented everyone who was disgusted with conventional politics. Ventura had the talent, fame, and resources to succeed in the political ring. Minnesota's progressive voting laws with their same day voter registration and publicly financed campaigns helped Ventura get elected. In addition, the public overlooked his boastfulness and bullying behaviors. Lastly, because it was a three-way race for governor, he only needed a small plurality of the vote to win. This circumstance of the political environment was a critical component of his victory.

TALENT

Professional wrestling is where Ventura learned the skills he would later use to run for office. "Asked about the biggest legacy from his wrestling career, Ventura says it was 'learning to perform'" (von Sternberg 1998b, 21A). Professional wrestling requires at least a modicum of acting ability.

The cinema was a great friend to wrestling during the Depression era. The simple morality play of wrestling's good guy versus bad guy adapted well to motion pictures (and pulp magazines). Wrestling films represented a significant aspect of Hollywood's sports-related melodramas. . . . Motion pictures also provided additional income for many wrestlers. As large men already trained in the ways of making fake fights look legitimate, wrestlers were ideally suited to work as stuntmen or actors in action sequences. (Beekman 2006, 66)

The switch from live audiences to largely televised audiences in the 1950s caused professional wrestlers "to adopt elaborate characters and to develop successful microphone skills" (Beekman 2006, ix). Hulk Hogan made appearances in movies and had his own reality TV show. Both Dwayne Johnson and Jesse Ventura were able to take their acting abilities to the next level to become Hollywood actors. Both starred in action movies that are not known for their fabulous dialogue. Rather, they used their muscle man persona and skills at fake fighting to make a living in a very profitable movie genre.

According to Ringham, voters "liked the audacity of a candidate who would quote his own lines from action films ('It's payback time!')" (Ringham 1998, 33A). When a celebrity candidate uses a memorable quote from their past in entertainment, the voters immediately recall the character they were playing at the time they said it. They remember the persona, they remember the fictional character, and they do not draw much of a distinction between the character and the actual person. Afterall, most people experience political figures only through their TV images. Real politicians are as much characters as other characters they see on TV or in the movies. If they remember liking the character, the celebrity politician has now garnered an affinity from that voter. The celebrity's fans can provide a base of support. It is a useful ploy that non-movie star politicians do not have at their disposal.

Professional wrestling recruits from the body building circuit. Not just any body builder will make the cut, however. The body builder must be sufficiently attractive or ugly to portray a good guy or bad guy. Appearances matter greatly. Like the carnival "freaks" of yesteryear, the goliath men in wrestling capture the public's attention. And getting the public's attention is a crucial step in a successful political campaign. After securing the Reform Party nomination, Ventura crashed "a candidate forum, dressed in combat fatigues, boots, and a camouflage Australian-outback hat he once wore in the movie *Predator*" (Hauser 2002, 8). Although only the Democratic and Republican nominees were invited to the forum, Roger Moe, the Democratic nominee for governor, yielded a portion of his time to Ventura as a gesture of good sportsmanship (Hauser 2002). This was a critical mistake because the attention-grabbing Ventura began the process of drawing voters' and journalists' eyes to his candidacy. When Ventura attended the National Governors

Association he wore "his fringed leather jacket, a white golf shirt, and cowboy boots" rather than the traditional business suit worn by conventional politicians (Hauser 2002, 56). Consistent with a strategy employed by other celebrities, Ventura used crazy costumes to get people's attention.

The Jesse Ventura television campaign advertisements were unusual and memorable. One mimics a toy advertisement aimed at children. It features two boys playing with action figures. One was a Jesse Ventura figure, and the other was Special Interest Man. The boy with the Ventura action figure says, "I don't want your stupid money!" to Special Interest Man and "This bill wastes taxpayer money. Redraft it!" while pounding the action figure's fist into a toy desk (North Woods Advertising 2009a). Another has Ventura posing as Rodin's *The Thinker* wearing only shorts. In large letters "The Body" transitions to "The Mind" and a narrator outlines Ventura's plan to lower property and income taxes and to reduce class sizes in public schools (North Woods Advertising 2009b).

Jesse Ventura, who was born James Janos, was able to develop his own brand as a wrestler. As Jesse "The Body" Ventura he played a particular type of bad guy. His character was vain and self-absorbed. He admired his own physique and called on others to admire it as well. He belittled his opponents, mocked them, and flouted his superiority. Some people root for the villain because it is fun, remember the bad guys sometimes win in professional wrestling. That is part of the show. Ventura acknowledged as much when confronted by a voter who did not like his manner. Ventura said, "People need to remember I was a villain in the world of pro wrestling for fifteen years, and as a villain your job was to offend people. Your job was to be outspoken, bombastic. And it's very difficult to get away from that persona when you did it for so many years. As a villain in wrestling you're forced to be confrontational. That's how you make your money" (Hauser 2002, 400–401).

Rather than re-brand himself Ventura used this bad guy persona in his political campaign and as governor. A conservative talk radio host who dubbed himself "Mr. Right" said Ventura could not win. After winning Ventura said, "I'm renaming you Mr. Minnesota Wrong. . . . Well, Mr. Wrong, stick it where the sun don't shine!" (Hauser 2002, 45). Darrell McKigney, the president of the Taxpayers League of Minnesota, was referred to as "McIdiot," "fat load," and "Lumpy Rutherford" by Ventura (Hauser 2002, 193). After a row with Reform Party leaders over the location of the party convention Ventura referred to party chair Russell Verney as "Russ Varmint" and "Russ Vermin" (Hauser 2002, 291). Shortly before the publication of his book, *Do I Stand Alone?: Going to the Mat Against Political Pawns and Media Jackals*, he created new press credentials for reporters covering the governor's mansion. Their new badges read "Official Jackal" and warned that their pass could be revoked for any reason. An editor for a local newspaper noted that as mayor

Ventura tended to lose his temper at city council meetings, and he sought to settle disputes using physical intimidation (Hauser 2002). The "bad guy" act was part of a deliberate strategy to gain attention and lure voters.

This type of boorish behavior would later be emulated by Donald Trump. In fact, Ventura supported the idea that Trump should run for president under the Reform Party label in 2000. Trump visited Minnesota and attended a Ventura fundraiser amid media speculation about his own political aspirations (Hauser 2002). Trump observed that obnoxiously ridiculing opponents was a winning political strategy. Sometimes the voters want the bad guy to win. In those cases, being the unapologetic bad guy curries favor with the public.

Ventura did not arrive at politics as a complete novice. Worried about pay and workplace safety Ventura led an effort to unionize WWF wrestlers. He was a labor organizer fighting for workers' rights (Jenkins 2005b). Given the serious injuries that professional wrestlers fall victim to, and the long-term physical damage caused by the stunt work it made sense that the employees would seek better protections. Like NFL players, wrestlers were worried about the long-term consequences of their occupation.

Perhaps this early attempt at organizing workers proved useful when developing a strategy to win the governor's race. He knew that he would be unable to peel off enough Democratic and Republican voters to win, so Ventura's strategy was to target unlikely voters. He would need 20–24 percent of likely voters plus a boost from first-time and unlikely voters to secure the 34 percent he needed to win in a three-way race. He knew he would need to go outside of the traditional bounds of politics to succeed (Hauser 2002). As a political strategist Ventura was not inept, he made calculated maneuvers designed to garner attention and support.

FAME

Professional wrestling in America has millions of devoted fans. Eight of the 51 most watched pay per view events in American history were professional wrestling events. These events averaged more than 1 million pay per view purchases each (Dawson 2017). In 1983, Vince McMahon launched *All-American Wrestling* on the USA network. By 1984, the USA network was available to 24 million households, "and this national coverage turned the WWF into the most-watched wrestling federation in the nation" (Beekman 2006, 121).

Ventura was a professional wrestler from 1975 to 1985. At the peak of his wrestling career, he fought Hulk Hogan for the WWF Championship title in three consecutive matches. After 1985, he remained in the wrestling business as a commentator and co-host of WWF events. This platform made

Jesse Ventura a celebrity and he was able to use his celebrity to work in other industries. He became an announcer for the Tampa Bay Buccaneers while he was running for mayor of Brooklyn Park. He was also running for mayor when his movie *Thunderground* hit the theaters (Mabery 1989). His multiple commentator jobs and his movie meant he had national media exposure while running for mayor.

Dwayne Johnson, another WWF wrestler, has appeared in 40 movies and 13 television programs. Jesse Ventura, though not as successful in Hollywood, appeared in 14 movies and several television series. In three of these movies, he appeared with Arnold Schwarzenegger; these were *Predator*, *The Running Man*, and *Batman & Robin*. Schwarzenegger and Ventura became good friends (Winegar 1989) and Arnold attended Jesse's inauguration. Ventura appeared in episodes of *The X-Files*, *The Young and the Restless*, and *Teenage Mutant Ninja Turtles*. In the three years before running for governor he was also the host of a talk radio program in Minneapolis that he used to express his political views (Hauser 2002). After his political career he returned to television by hosting *Conspiracy Theory with Jesse Ventura* on TruTV for three seasons in 2009–12. The first episode of *Conspiracy Theory* had 1.6 million viewers (Seidman 2009).

The key to Ventura's political success lies in professional wrestling's appeal to specific demographic groups. "The very young, the very old, blue-collar workers, and minorities became wrestling's core audience" starting in the 1970s (Beekman 2006, 105). As a television program it appealed to "law-and-order blue-collar Americans willing to embrace wrestling's simple good versus evil dichotomy" (Beekman 2006, 107). As a form of low-brow entertainment professional wrestling had a male working-class fan base that is often overlooked by political operatives.

> WWF wrestling adopts the personal, social, and moral conflicts that characterized nineteenth-century theatrical melodrama and enacts them in terms of physical combat between male athletes. In doing so, it foregrounds aspects of masculine mythology which have a particular significance for its predominantly working-class male audience—the experience of vulnerability, the possibilities of male trust and intimacy, and the populist myth of the national community. (Jenkins 2005a, 39)

Disaffected working-class men may feel as though the political system is not looking out for their interests. Jesse Ventura's persona as a blunt aggressive dominant male appealed to a group that does not feel empowered in today's society (Hauser 2002). WWF *Smackdown* was geared toward those who loathe political correctness.

> *Smackdown* was consciously designed to appeal to a demographic segment
> of the population excluded from (or hostile to) the tidy accommodating
> living-room and workplace life of most prime-time narratives. . . . *Smackdown*
> was more than simply sexual and violent; it was intentionally hostile to family
> values. (Sammand 2005b, 142)

Far from being unique, professional wrestling's subversive themes are part of
a long tradition in American performance art. "Some of its ancestors include
burlesque, minstrelsy, vaudeville, jazz, rock 'n' roll, and punk" (Sammond
2005b, 153). Professional wrestling appeals to those with anti-establishment
proclivities. As a demographic group that typically has very low rates of
political engagement, they are available to be activated during an election.
Ventura pulled in many new or infrequent voters by engaging them on their
own terms, "Minnesota attracted the largest voter participation of any state in
the country" (Jenkins 2005b). "He energized young people and other politically apathetic segments of the population to go to the polls" (Hauser 2002,
xii). Ventura was popular with this demographic group precisely because of
his crude and convention breaking style. People who are upset with the status
quo look for candidates that cut against the grain.

TEXTBOX 7.1

Jesse Ventura

I'd like to get your overall opinion of some people who were in the
news this year. As I read each name, please say if you have a favorable
or unfavorable opinion of this person, or if you have never heard of him
or her. . . . Minnesota Governor-elect, Jesse Ventura?[1]

Favorable	53%
Unfavorable	14%
No opinion	33%

I'm going to read you a list of some people who have been in the news
lately. Not everyone will have heard of them. For each one that I name,
please tell me whether or not you have heard of this person. . . . Jesse
Ventura Have you heard of this person or not?[2]

Have heard of	79%
Have not heard of	20%
Don't know/refused	1%

I'm going to read you a list of some people who have been in the news
lately. Not everyone will have heard of them. For each one that I name,

please tell me whether or not you have heard of this person. . . . Jesse Ventura Have you heard of this person or not?[3]

Have heard of	83%
Have not heard of	17%
Don't know/refused	<1%

We'd like to get your overall opinion of some people in the news. As I read each name, please say if you have a favorable or unfavorable opinion of this person—or if you have never heard of him or her. How about . . . Minnesota Governor, Jesse Ventura?[4]

Favorable	51%
Unfavorable	25%
Never heard of	12%
No opinion	12%

Sources:1 *Gallup Poll*, December 1998. Retrieved February 24, 2019 from the iPOLL Databank, The Roper Center for Public Opinion Research, University of Connecticut;2 Pew Research Center for the People & the Press. Pew News Interest Index Poll, July 1999. Retrieved February 24, 2019 from the iPOLL Databank, The Roper Center for Public Opinion Research, University of Connecticut;3 Pew Research Center for the People & the Press. Pew Research Center for the People & the Press Typology Survey, July 1999. Retrieved February 24, 2019 from the iPOLL Databank, The Roper Center for Public Opinion Research, University of Connecticut; 4 Gallup Poll, September 1999. Retrieved February 24, 2019 from the iPOLL Databank, The Roper Center for Public Opinion Research, University of Connecticut.

It is unnecessary to pay for advertising when you are the biggest political story in America. Celebrities can exploit their attention capital to gain large amounts of earned media. Jesse Ventura had tremendous name recognition when he decided to run for governor in 1998. The race for governor of Minnesota became national news. Ventura was given attention by news magazines, broadcast news, cable news, and late-night talk shows. At the time of Ventura's election at least 67 percent of Americans had heard of him and 53 percent had a favorable opinion of him. In July of 1999 two Pew polls found that between 79 percent and 83 percent of Americans had heard of Governor Ventura. Furthermore, a majority of Americans had a favorable opinion of him. This favorable opinion is based on his work as an entertainer. This is how a celebrity's fans can become potential voters. The night of his election as mayor of Brooklyn Park radio political reporter Eric Eskola said, "That was a great kick. I'm a big pro wrestling fan, and my one hope out of this whole thing is that I get one of Jesse Ventura's campaign buttons" (Holston 1990). Fame and national media attention allow celebrity politicians to campaign without having to spend enormous sums of money on advertising aimed at increasing name recognition. The media covers the campaign for free and the candidate can distribute his or her message to voters without expense. Ventura's campaign for governor put a national spotlight on him for a state level contest, giving him more attention than is necessary to win a governor's race.

RESOURCES

Jesse Ventura's campaign for governor is remarkable for its lack of resources. According to Dean Barkley the campaign's chairperson, "The campaign had only $12,000 [in July]. We had to raise $35,000 in $50 contributions by the end of August to be eligible for the $327,000 of public money. Jesse finally turns the corner on fund-raising and brings himself to begin actively soliciting money. We do our first direct mail piece and between Jesse's fund-raising at small events and direct mail work, we raise over $50,000 in August to qualify for the money" (Smith and Barkley 1998, 1A). Public financing would be a key component of Ventura's success.

The campaign did not air a single TV advertisement until one week before the election. That was because only $17,000 of the public finance money was distributed prior to the election. By state law the remaining $310,000 is not distributed to the campaigns until after the election. A loan could not be secured until it seemed certain that Ventura would get the 5 percent vote total to qualify for public financing. Banks are prohibited from seeking collateral for campaign loans in Minnesota and the public finance money would be used to repay the loan (Baden 1998; De Fiebre October 27, 1998; Smith and Barkley 1998). Prior to the loan the Ventura campaign had just $96,305 cash on hand, which is why several banks denied the Ventura campaign's loan requests for several months prior to the election (De Fiebre October 27, 1998; Smith and Barkley 1998).

The campaign did finally receive a $305,000 loan and successfully solicited $258,847 in contributions (De Fiebre 1998 October 27, 1998; Gordon 1998). Even though Ventura's social network includes the likes of Arnold Schwarzenegger only $28,132 came from large individual donors. Small individual donors accounted for $170,795 of his campaign receipts (De Fiebre October 27, 1998).

> But only the 128 who gave more than $100 are listed by name on the report, as state law requires. They range from Darryl Jorgenson, an Elk River rubbish hauler who gave $120, to Hubbard Broadcasting chairman Stanley S. Hubbard, the only person who gave Ventura the legal limit of $2,000. In between are a mix of blue-collar and government workers, small entrepreneurs, farmers and retirees. Nearly absent are the lawyers, lobbyists, big businessmen and interest-group types who dominate many politicians' financial disclosures.

. . . Ventura formerly worked for Hubbard as a talk-show host on KSTP Radio. (De Fiebre December 7, 1998)

Ventura simply did not like the idea of begging people for money and was not enthusiastic about fundraising. Lacking money, the campaign did not have a headquarters, the top campaign staff simply used their mobile phones to coordinate with each other and with the campaign's volunteers (Smith and Barkley 1998).

Ventura was able to win despite being outspent by his opponents by large sums. "Ventura spent just $626,067 to get elected, or about $.81 per vote. Coleman spent $2,168,393, or $3.02 per vote. Humphrey spent $2,125,465, or $3.62 per vote" (Hauser 2002, 40). After winning, Ventura's campaign did not have sufficient funds for the transition. The legislature only provides $50,000 for "the transition's tasks—screening job applicants, establishing an administration, planning a budget, paying staff salaries and paying for postage, telephones and fax machines" (Whereatt 1998, 1A). They had to continue fundraising just to set up the next administration.

While in office he raised funds from the sale of Jesse Ventura action figures. After seeing the ad mimicking a toy advertisement people really wanted the toy and the campaign team began the process of producing one (Levy 1998). They produced several with the action figures wearing different outfits. Having learned how to earn money from branded items during his time as a WWF wrestler Ventura simply used the techniques he was already familiar with.

It is unclear just how wealthy Jesse Ventura is, but he has certainly earned millions of dollars for his work. He was an important part of the very profitable WWF before being cast in several big budget Hollywood films. During his tenure as mayor of Brooklyn Park, Minnesota, Ventura agreed to a million-dollar contract with World Championship Wrestling, a WWF competitor, to serve as an announcer. In 1999, as governor, he earned between 1 million and 1.5 million dollars to referee a match in that year's WWF "Summer Slam" event. Ventura served as an announcer for the ill-fated XFL (an enterprise co-owned by NBC and the WWE). He earned another half a million for his autobiography, also released while in office. Critics argued that Ventura was profiting from the office of governor, but it is difficult to prove that Ventura would not have been asked to perform these functions independent from his status as governor. He was, after all, already a celebrity with the necessary skills prior to being elected (Hauser 2002). He continued to author books and appear on television programs after his political career. In other words, he simply re-entered the entertainment industry that he was already a part of.

POLITICAL ENVIRONMENT

Ventura ran for mayor of Brooklyn Park, Minnesota because he wanted to preserve a wetlands area near his home (Barreiro 1990). He campaigned door to door and voters were often shocked because they immediately recognized him from his professional wrestling and movie roles. He would tell them his goals as mayor would be to preserve the local wetlands, treat citizens with respect, and pass a proposal for mayoral term limits. He won by 5,300 votes and won every precinct in the city beating an eighteen-year incumbent, Jim Krautkremer (McEnroe 1990). Krautkremer blamed his loss on name recognition, "When somebody has a name it's difficult to do anything about it" (*Star Tribune* November 7, 1990, 26). In the previous election only about 2,500 people voted so Ventura won by more than double the previous election's total vote count (Winegar 1989). In a small local election, name recognition and additional media attention is more than enough to garner victory.

The political environment in Minnesota was critically important for Ventura's gubernatorial victory. First, Minnesota has a history of electing celebrities. In 1970, they elected Olympic hockey player Wendell Anderson as governor of their state (McAuliffe 1998). Later, in 2008, they would elect *Saturday Night Live* comedian Al Franken to the US Senate. Jesse Ventura was able to win because, "He is the embodiment of a culture that consumes sports, movies, and talk radio in mass quantities" (Hauser 2002, xii). The Minnesota electorate has a history of being open to unconventional candidates.

Many Americans are dissatisfied with the political system and have been for some time. In Minnesota, "Voters turned to Ventura as a protest candidate, as a way of thumbing their noses at the system" (Jenkins 2005b, 312).

> Much as the *luchadores* have used wrestling as a platform for political activism and social critique in Latin America, Ventura draws on the populist rhetoric of professional wrestling as a basis for his own critique of the American political system. Ventura tapped a deep-rooted dissatisfaction with the options on offer from the major political parties and a growing distrust of the political system itself, presenting himself as the champion of the common man against party machines and special interests. (Jenkins 2005b, 310)

He was, according to Hauser, "the antidote to all that voters perceived to be wrong with 'career politicians'" (Hauser 2002, xii). He capitalized on the outsider status that polebrities bring to the table when they run for office.

In a close three-way race, a third-party candidate can win without gaining majority support. This is precisely what Jesse Ventura was able to do. "When all the votes are counted, Ventura wins with 37 percent (773,713 votes); Coleman has 34 percent (717,350) and Humphrey 28 percent (587,528)"

(Hauser 2002, 40). In a plurality wins-system the bar for victory is lowered as more candidates enter the field. Ventura's small plurality win was only possible because the race had three candidates all hovering around 33 percent support. It is uncertain what would have happened if Minnesota had mandatory run-off elections between the top two vote getters, as some states do. In addition, the previous incumbent Arne Carlson, decided not to seek re-election even though Minnesota does not have term limits for its governors. Open seat races are easier to win for challengers because they don't have to compete with the resources and popular support that incumbents have in re-election bids.

In the weeks leading up to election day Ventura was behind in the polls. The campaign needed first time and unlikely voters to vote for Ventura. Ventura's campaign decided to exploit a peculiar voting regulation in Minnesota; it is one of only a few states that offer same day voter registration on election day. They spent the final days of the campaign telling non-voters how to register and vote on election day itself through campaign stops and television advertising. It was this surge of typically non-voters that put Ventura over the top in a close three-way race. He was able to activate what Dahl calls "slack resources" in the political sphere (Dahl 1961, 309). Because there are unused political resources a newcomer can tap into these resources to oust an established political elite. In Ventura's case these resources were potential voters who typically do not vote. Non-voters are more likely to be younger and less well-educated people, a group that overlaps with professional wrestling's core audience. Indeed, exit polling showed that Ventura did very well with younger blue-collar workers. Surprisingly, he did equally well with men and women (Bentley and Hogan 1998). One in eight voters in Minnesota said they would not have voted if Ventura was not on the ballot. Nearly all the irregular or first-time voters voted for Ventura (von Sternberg 1998a). "Ventura pinned his long-shot hopes on getting first-time voters to the polls, and a whopping 332,720 voters registered on election day" (Hauser 2002, 40). People who would normally be shut out of the political process came out in support of Ventura by utilizing a populist element in Minnesota's election laws. Critics might argue that Ventura won because people who do not plan ahead of time were overwhelmed by the zeitgeist of the moment, it was a win for people who like to wing it from day to day.

In 1994 and 1996, Dean Barkley was the Reform Party nominee for US Senate in Minnesota. He was able to secure enough votes in these statewide elections to earn the Reform Party major party status and thus access to public financing. In 1997, Barkley was able to convince Ventura to run for governor and volunteered to be his campaign manager. More than half of Ventura's campaign money came from public financing (Smith and Barkley 1998). Public financing makes it easier for non-traditional candidates to seek office and Ventura was here again the beneficiary of Minnesota's particular election process.

Throughout the campaign Ventura made iconoclastic remarks. He called religion a sham and ridiculed overweight people. He said legalized prostitution should be considered because legalized vice is easier to regulate and noted that this approach appeared effective in Nevada and Amsterdam. Governor Christine Whitman of New Jersey seemed jealous of Ventura's ability to violate social and political norms. She said, "He has a freedom of expression that many other politicians don't enjoy to the same degree" (Hauser 2002, 107). Ventura survived, and possibly benefited from, saying, and doing things that would ruin a traditional politician's career. Minnesota journalist Tom Hauser discusses one of Ventura's boasts,

> "I'm probably one of the only human beings standing on the face of the earth today that's gone to a Nevada ranch and been paid!" The crowd roars with laughter and applause while Nixon probably rolls over in his nearby grave. It's not every day a politician of any rank, let alone a governor, stands before you and brags about an exploit with a hooker. He points out that prostitution is legal in Nevada and that he was unmarried at the time. Ventura knows that will make the story somewhat palatable for the few prudes that might be in the audience. "When I got into the ranch, the particular girl looked at me and said, 'I want that belt!'" he says, referring to a belt of spent machine-gun shells he was wearing. "I said, 'Make me an offer.'" The Nixon Library has never rocked with so much laughter in anticipation of the punch line. "And she said, 'How 'bout a trick and ten dollars?'" The crowd is now clapping and rollicking while Ventura stands onstage with a big smile on his face, spreads his arms out wide, bends backward, looks to the heavens, shrugs, and yells, "I did it!" (Hauser 2002, 173–74)

Like other celebrity politicians, Ventra seems to have benefited from celebrity slack. When a typical governor gets caught with prostitutes, that is the end of their political career. But Ventura won while bragging about his escapades with prostitutes on the campaign trail. The public seems to give celebrities a free pass on gaffes and misbehavior that would most likely end the careers of non-celebrity politicians.

CONCLUSIONS

Showmanship is an integral part of professional wrestling. It is a very profitable industry that entertains millions of Americans. It consists of dramatic conflict between good guys and bad guys, much like many Hollywood movies. Indeed, several professional wrestlers have become big time movie actors. Jesse Ventura was able to develop an effective and popular bad guy role. He was vain, conceited, rude, and obnoxious as a character. As it turns out, these qualities are not a disqualifier for political office.

Villains have a cultural appeal. There are bad guys that Americans root for. The Joker, the Terminator, and Darth Vader are villainous movie characters that have their own following. Villains break social norms and are an integral part of morality tales. Darth Vader must kill Obi Wan Kenobi for Luke Skywalker to avenge his teacher's death. Machiavelli's philosophy states that evil can be used in the service of good. Darth Vader killed helpless children, a bad thing, to free the slaves, a good thing. Sometimes a good outcome requires a bad guy to get the job done. Jesse Ventra, Donald Trump, and Arnold Schwarzenegger used villainous personas to their political advantage. Ventura, however, also wanted to make clear that much of the persona was an act,

> My critics said I was a bad role model for children because I'd been in movies where there was violence and I'd made tongue-in-cheek comments in a Penthouse (magazine) article. . . . My answer to the critics was that I was on the board of the Make a Wish Foundation for seven years and I asked if they'd ever been asked to be seen by a dying child? That brings you to reality real quick and makes you humble. That's how it's going to be in the mayor's office. (McEnroe 1990)

Thus, despite the negative persona, he wanted to make clear that he was capable of charity and kindness. It is also a testament to his popularity as a wrestler that dying children would make meeting him their final wish.

Ventura was known by a majority of Americans and was the biggest political story of 1998. The enormous media coverage allowed him to convey his message to voters with a limited campaign fund. His outrageous outfits and his boastful crassness drew attention. Minnesota's political culture and election rules made Jesse Ventura's victory possible. Minnesotans are open to unconventional candidates. The state has a plurality wins system with public financing and same day voter registration. These three factors were of decisive importance in Ventura's gubernatorial victory. Ventura's election broke records for same day registration because he was able to draw non-voters' attention to his candidacy. This is the power that celebrities have; they can get people to focus on them. Once the media's eyes are drawn the message can be communicated. In Ventura's case that message was, "Register to vote on election day and vote for me!"

Chapter 8

Arnold Schwarzenegger

Arnold Schwarzenegger is, "one of the greatest show-business creations of our time" (Andrews 2003, 255). His real life could be a fictional Horatio Alger story. Starting as a poor rural villager Arnold, through his hard work and determination, became an international athlete, a movie star, and a political leader. With talent and gumption, he overcame obstacles and achieved the American dream. He became rich and famous and even married into one of America's most prominent families. The real Arnold Schwarzenegger could be a fictional character himself.

As a teenager Schwarzenegger became interested in body building. Bodybuilding is different from weightlifting. Weightlifting is a sport where the person who lifts the heaviest weight wins. Bodybuilding is a performance where the goal is to appear strong. According to Schwarzenegger, "The ideal of bodybuilding is visual perfection, like an ancient Greek statue come to life. You sculpt your body the way an artist chisels stone" (Schwarzenegger 2013, 102). Bodybuilding requires weightlifting to build muscle, but also a very regimented diet to reduce body fat. Extremely low body fat is necessary so that veins and individual muscles are visible to judges and audiences in bodybuilding contests.

Arnold's rise to prominence is even more remarkable because muscular bodies, historically, were associated with low social standing.

It was not always the case in American culture that a muscular body was considered the best kind of body a man could have. Until the end of the nineteenth century, a muscled body indicated that a man was a laborer, someone whose body showed the evidence of his economic status. Men who worked in offices or who supervised laborers did not develop muscles and visible strength. (Krasniewicz and Blitz 2006, 30)

Thus, Schwarzenegger's physique is an advantage only because of serendipitous historical circumstances. In another era, his body would be the hallmarks of shame and failure, not wonder and awe.

Even as a young boy Schwarzenegger wanted to leave Austria and go to America. When he saw Reg Park, the reigning Mr. Universe, in the movie *Hercules* the teenage Arnold hatched his plan. Bodybuilding would get him to America where he could be in movies (Andrews 2003; Krasniewicz and Blitz 2006). These muscle man movies have a long legacy in Hollywood. Schwarzenegger would star in *Conan the Barbarian* and other films that would show off his body. The genre continues today with stars like Dwayne Johnson and Jason Momoa. The idealized woman has its counterpart in the idealized man.

As a celebrity Schwarzenegger was invited to celebrity events, including a celebrity tennis tournament sponsored by the Kennedy's where he met his future wife Maria Shriver, the daughter of Eunice Kennedy and Sargent Shriver, and niece to John, Robert, and Ted Kennedy. The Kennedy family has a very real and salient commitment to public service and would subtly, and not so subtly, urge Arnold to become more involved in philanthropic work. Schwarzenegger agreed and became involved with the Special Olympics for children with disabilities. The Kennedy's, despite being Democrats, offered Schwarzenegger political advice that helped him in his campaign for governor. Eunice donated money to Arnold's campaign (Andrews 2003; Schwarzenegger 2013).

He campaigned for George H.W. Bush and attended his nominating convention. As a celebrity endorser, his job was to help increase the crowd size and the media attention. Schwarzenegger was aware that celebrities are used in that way by political campaigns, but he was happy to oblige because of his Republican affiliation. Arnold supported Republicans because he felt they were more strongly anti-communist. He was acutely aware of Soviet influences in eastern Europe from his own childhood and was drawn to the free market ideology of Milton Friedman. He met Ronald Reagan, a fellow Hollywood actor, and saw the possibility. For Schwarzenegger, "it was not far-fetched that someone from Hollywood would run for governor. Ronald Reagan had already blazed the trail" (Schwarzenegger 2013, 473).

George H.W. Bush appointed Schwarzenegger to head the President's Council on Physical Fitness and Sports. Schwarzenegger toured the country to promote physical fitness. This provided valuable experience for his eventual gubernatorial run,

> Later on, I realized that it had a lot in common with a campaign trip. You're on a tight schedule, you have to be there at a certain time, do the speech, pump everyone up. The school bands welcome you, and the local politicians come out

and drum up a storm of support. After being the fitness czar, running for governor of California felt like déjà vu. (Schwarzenegger 2013, 403)

Schwarzenegger developed a good friendship with George H.W. Bush and other top Republicans. Arnold credits Richard Nixon with giving him the idea for running for governor of California.

Schwarzenegger had a good sense of the perils and possibilities of this idea because he was familiar with what his friend Jesse Ventura had accomplished in Minnesota. Arnold and Jesse maintained a friendship and were connected from the movie business. They were both in *Predator*, *The Running Man*, and *Batman & Robin* movies. He was also particularly good friends with Clint Eastwood. They would often discuss movies, acting, and politics. After Clint was elected Mayor of Carmel, California, Arnold thought he could also seek public office. Arnold saw that his fame gave him an easy platform to get people's attention, but also that his lack of experience could cause missteps and controversies.

Schwarzenegger believed that being a movie star was remarkably similar to being a governor. Being governor is, "very much like being leading man in a movie. You get blamed for everything, and you get credit for everything. It's high risk, high reward" (Schwarzenegger 2013, 474). He credits his celebrity status for his political success and has discussed how certain skills are transferable and can lead to success in multiple occupations.

TALENT

Arnold Schwarzenegger's success can be attributed to his development of several important skills. He focused on his appearance through weightlifting and dieting. He learned to engage in outrageous behavior to get people's attention. He learned to be friendly and likeable, the soft skill of being personable was not a trait he was born with, but it is a skill he acquired. The studios wanted Arnold in their movies because of his superior physique so they hired acting coaches to train Arnold for his roles in front of the camera. They developed the product because they knew it would sell and Schwarzenegger learned the acting skills that he needed to succeed. As a movie star he developed the persona of person with steadfast determination and single-minded focus, traits that are admired by many Americans. As an entrepreneur in different industries, he prided himself in developing intensive marketing campaigns to promote his products. The press tours associated with promoting a movie are virtually identical to the press tours associated with a political campaign. These skills were practiced throughout a lifetime of extraordinary achievement.

During Schwarzenegger's very first bodybuilding competition in 1965 he realized that he performed better with a cheering audience. Just as many athletes gain extra energy from a roaring crowd, Schwarzenegger needed the approbation of spectators. He was able to lift thirty-five pounds more than his previous personal best because the crowed was cheering him on (Schwarzenegger 2013). This early success drove Schwarzenegger to feel the need for more and more attention. Bigger crowds meant better performances.

After coming in second in his first Mr. Universe contest, Schwarzenegger realized he needed to make improvements. In particular, he needed to improve his posing routine, "To hypnotize and carry away an audience, you need the poses to flow. . . . to slow down and make it like ballet" (Schwarzenegger 2013, 69). In New York, Schwarzenegger hired a ballet instructor to assist him in developing graceful movements on stage. Arnold learned to choreograph his routines focusing on smooth transitions between poses, body alignments, and posture. He was already big and strong, he needed to focus on the performance aspect of bodybuilding competitions. Even minor items, like getting a suntan, were aspects of elite bodybuilding that Schwarzenegger needed to learn (Schwarzenegger 2013). Schwarzenegger began to focus on even the minute details of the image of himself that he was projecting to audiences. Even very subtle differences can influence audience perceptions.

He also worked as a trainer at a gym in Munich, but the gym was special because it was the gym where the professional wrestlers would train when they came to town. Much like American professional wrestling of the era, the wrestlers would travel as a troupe and perform their matches in different cities. Schwarzenegger trained with the wrestlers during the day and went to their matches at night. One of the wrestlers was Harold Sakata, a former US Olympic weightlifter who co-starred in the James Bond film *Goldfinger* (Schwarzenegger 2013). It is likely he picked up some advice regarding showmanship during these encounters, certainly he was exposed to stagecraft and saw a path into the movie business.

Gyms require memberships to stay in business, they need people to come in to use the equipment and pay the instructors. The problem according to Arnold was that "No contemporary bodybuilder was enough of a showman to make training really catch on" (Schwarzenegger 2013, 78). Schwarzenegger engaged in several publicity stunts to increase the gym's membership. In the dead of winter in the freezing cold he posed in his briefs in the town square. Newspapers sent photographers to see Mr. Universe walking around the city in his competition briefs (Schwarzenegger 2013). In the same way that Benjamin Franklin walked around Philadelphia to show the shop keepers how hard working he was, Schwarzenegger walked around Munich to show the residents how big his muscles were. He made a spectacle of himself to get media attention.

Schwarzenegger admitted that he was a brute in these early stages of his career, but Dianne Bennett, the wife of Wag Bennett, a Mr. Universe judge and UK gym owner, helped Arnold with his people skills. She told him how important it was to please the fans that attended his competitions. Skills at dealing with people are useful in most professions, but they are especially useful for people who want to be famous. If a person wants to have hordes of adoring fans, they need to be likable, and Schwarzenegger made it point to "work the crowd" and be personable. He performed at exhibitions across the UK, "Making a name for yourself in bodybuilding is a lot like politics. You go from town to town, hoping word will spread. This grassroots approach worked" (Schwarzenegger 2013, 71). It was with this improved skill set that Schwarzenegger won six consecutive Mr. Olympia titles between 1970 and 1976 (Andrews 2003).

Joe Weider was a publisher of bodybuilding magazines and producer of nutritional supplements. In 1946 he started the International Federation of Body Building and in 1965 began the Mr. Olympia contest. Weider became Schwarzenegger's patron and paid him to stay in America and train for bodybuilding competitions. When Hollywood producers were looking for a bodybuilder to star in a low budget spoof of a sword-and-sandal epic, Weider convinced them to hire Schwarzenegger by lying to them and saying that Schwarzenegger had been a Shakespearean actor in Europe (Andrews 2003; Schwarzenegger 2013).

Hercules in New York was Schwarzenegger's first film. It was produced by Aubrey Wisberg and Lawrence F. Fabian and directed by Arthur A. Seidelman. Because of Arnold's limited English the film was dubbed, and Schwarzenegger's voice was replaced with an American voice. Seidelman wanted to use Arnold's heavily accented voice but was overruled by Wisberg because Wisberg was tired of his editors laughing while cutting the film. Schwarzenegger was voiced over "as a precaution against more unwanted hilarity" (Andrews 2003, 37). The re-released version has Schwarzenegger's original dialogue. He was also given the stage name Arnold Strong because Hollywood executives were still of the mindset that foreign sounding names with too many syllables were a turn off for American audiences. By most accounts, the film was comically bad, but the producers claimed the film was supposed to be that way (Andrews 2003; Krasniewicz and Blitz 2006).

By 1976, Schwarzenegger landed a role in the film *Stay Hungry* featuring Sally Field and Jeff Bridges. By then Schwarzenegger's English was much improved and the studio provided an acting coach to help him prepare. He worked with Eric Morris, Jack Nicholson's acting coach, who apparently was an excellent teacher because Schwarzenegger won the Golden Globe for best new star of the year for his role in the film (Andrews 2003; Schwarzenegger 2013). To get a sense of the achievement, Sylvester Stallone's *Rocky* won the best picture award that year (Krasniewicz and Blitz 2006). Arnold was now in the big leagues of American cinema. And though not every critic would agree, Schwarzenegger proved to be a fairly good actor.

Schwarzenegger decided he needed to use his next film, *Pumping Iron*, as an opportunity to develop a compelling persona. He used Mohamad Ali as his role model. Schwarzenegger says, "Ali was always willing to say and do memorable and outrageous things. But outrageousness means nothing unless you have the substance to back it up—you can't get away with it if you're a loser. It was being a champion combined with outrageousness that made Ali's whole thing work" (Schwarzenegger 2013, 205). Arnold made it a point to make outrageous statements during the filming, the idea was to become the center of attention.

While still a novice in the acting arena, Schwarzenegger continued to exploit his fame as a champion bodybuilder. He said, "I mapped out how to travel from town to town and capture the local press. Then I used that to help secure national magazine covers. I systematically developed a personality that became saleable on television" (Andrews 2003, 55). He was part of a live exhibit at the Whitney Museum in New York where he posed on a rotating pedestal as slides of renown sculptures were displayed in the background. The idea was to draw a connection between Michelangelo's *David*, Rodin's *The Thinker*, and other pieces that idealize the male body. According to Schwarzenegger, "The whole thing was mainly a publicity stunt" (Schwarzenegger 2013, 208). But the event was another example of Schwarzenegger's willingness to draw attention to himself, a key component of celebrity.

Image management was so important to Arnold that he would poll strangers while walking down New York's 5th Avenue. He would ask people, "What do you know me for?" Was it bodybuilding, movies, books, magazines, or television? Did people know him and for what did they know him? How was he perceived by the public? Schwarzenegger needed to make sure that he was crafting the right image and that people knew who he was (Andrews 2003).

This obsessive concern about image management had its intended results,

If Yoda is the Jedi Master, then Arnold is the Image Master. Since the 1960s, he has managed, with unmatched success, to keep positive and flattering images of himself—as the great pumper of iron, as the Terminator, as Conan the Republican, as the Governator, and maybe later as the Prezinator—in the eyes and minds of fans and detractors alike. You could argue that Arnold's showmanship has, for many years, been politically motivated, or you could make the case that Arnold's political career is, first and foremost, showmanship. (Krasniewicz and Blitz 2006, 154)

Celebrity branding requires strict adherence to the public persona. The persona is developed, maintained, and promoted so that one is known as the image that has been constructed. It is this reputation that provides the value for marketers of goods, services, or politics.

Schwarzenegger's distinct accent became part of his persona. Even in his native Austria Arnold's German accent is unusual. Schwarzenegger grew up in a small rural community and when he traveled to the larger city of Graz the urbanites would laugh at his "rural hillbilly dialect" (Andrews 2003, 93). Still, the thing that "helps him to stardom in *Conan* is the very thing he had been told would *stop* him from becoming a star. The accent. No one can listen to this man mangle the English language without falling in love with those discombobulating cadences" (Andrews 2003, 92). The accent was so much a part of the Arnold persona that *Saturday Night Live*'s Dana Carvey and Kevin Nealon mimicked the accent in their own spoof characters of Austrian bodybuilders Hans and Franz.

As an actor, Schwarzenegger developed his own unique brand. He wanted to be an action hero who vanquished bad guys and saved the world. For that reason, he was reluctant to take the role of the Terminator. He told James Cameron, the director, "that being cast as an evil villain wasn't going to help my career. It was something I could do later on, but right now I should keep playing heroes so that people would get used to me being a heroic character and wouldn't get confused" (Schwarzenegger 2013, 311). Cameron replied, "The Terminator is a machine. It's not good, it's not evil. If you play it in an interesting way, you can turn it into a heroic figure that people admire because of what it's capable of" (Schwarzenegger 2013, 311).

The Terminator has several qualities that people admire. It has single-minded focus, it has determination, it has steadfastness of purpose. Granted that the Terminator's purpose is to kill a woman to prevent her from having a baby, but the killer exhibits a kind of gritty resolve and persistence that people admire. *The Terminator* is a damsel in distress movie where some people are rooting for the damsel to get killed. Sometimes people root for the villain because it is entertaining to do so. Krasniewicz and Blitz believe that "Americans had fused together the Terminator with the man who played him" (Krasniewicz and Blitz 2006, 91). As the Terminator, "he is himself Nietzsche's Superman, as human as anyone needs to be, and, in every sense, better than human, the Creator of humanity as well as its Savior" (Indiana 2005, 32). Thus, Arnold Schwarzenegger is perceived to have steadfast determination and an unstoppable will to complete his task of saving the world.

Schwarzenegger was very conscious of the fact that many people objected to the amount of violence that were in his movies. Because of this he wanted to insert comedy into his action films. Before or after killing someone, Schwarzenegger would offer a comedic one liner to offset the violence. He wanted the audience to know it was just for fun and that it was not to be taken seriously. In *The Terminator*, he said, "Hasta la vista, baby" before shooting someone with a shotgun. In *Total Recall* he shoots his wife and says, "Consider that a divorce." In another movie while holding his next victim by the ankle over a cliff he says, "Remember when I said I would kill you last? I lied." When he gets back to the car he's asked, "What happened?" He replies, "I let him go."

Arnold worked with the writers to insert his signature one liners, but often his penchant for comedy ran afoul of the director's vision. A scene in *Commando* called for Schwarzenegger to chop off a man's arm. When the stuntman gave off an unscripted scream Arnold whacked him over the head with his own severed arm and exclaimed, "Shut up!" The director thought the improvisation was too campy to include in the film, so Arnold took the issue to 20th Century Fox executives who told him the idea was sick. The director and producers wanted to make an action movie while Schwarzenegger was trying to make a comedy (Andrews 2003). As soon as Arnold was a big enough star to demand his own films he switched to comedies and starred in *Twins* and *Kindergarten Cop*. While he enjoyed being a tough-guy action hero who saves the world, he also wanted to be perceived as funny and good natured. During his campaign for governor Schwarzenegger hired John Max, who wrote for Jay Leno's *Tonight Show*, to help him with debate preparation. It was important for Schwarzenegger to emphasize his comedic alter-ego to audiences. He's not a big tough guy who wants to be feared, he is a big tough guy who wants to be liked.

After his heart surgery in 1997, he needed people to understand that he was healthy and ready to continue, "The next step was photos: making sure that images of me running on the beach, skiing, and weightlifting made it into newspapers so people would know I was back" (Schwarzenegger 2013, 468). His image as an action hero needed to be reinforced. He could not be perceived as weak, unhealthy, or fragile. His media campaign was deliberately designed to maintain his persona and his next movie, *End of Days*, would be a thrilling action movie. Schwarzenegger, like all celebrities, are in the business of selling their persona. They make great efforts at maintaining their formulated, if not fabricated, public identities. Arnold developed a unique brand of action hero comedian and audiences flocked to see his movies.

Arnold Schwarzenegger was keenly interested in marketing. Whether it was promoting his fitness supplements and equipment, his books, his movies, and later, his policy preferences, he took an active approach to selling (Krasniewicz and Blitz 2006). "I saw myself as a businessman first. Too many actors, writers, and artists think that marketing is beneath them. But no matter what you do in life, selling is part of it" (Schwarzenegger 2013, 189).

He insisted on visiting large numbers of cities, in talking to large numbers of journalists, on making large numbers of appearances, and, in general, meeting as many people as possible to push his latest endeavors. "At the Arnold Classic bodybuilding contest . . . he had his picture taken one by one with almost a thousand people in just over an hour" (Andrews 2003, 170). Creating the product was not good enough. To be successful Arnold knew you had to sell the product.

Schwarzenegger saw that marketing prowess was important in politics too, "People can be great poets, great writers, geniuses in the lab. But you can do the finest work and if people don't know, you have nothing! In politics it's the same: no matter whether you're working on environmental policy or education or economic growth, the most important thing is to make people aware" (Schwarzenegger 2013, 615). The skills that he developed promoting physical fitness, his movies, and his books were just as useful when promoting his favored public policies.

Will Smith, the international television, and film star, recalls an encounter he had with Arnold Schwarzenegger,

I think it was '94 or something like that . . . I found myself in a room with Arnold Schwarzenegger, Bruce Willis, and Sly. I was like, oh my God I got these three guys in a room and I was like, ok, I want to be the biggest movie star in the world and I need you guys to tell me how to do it and Arnold Schwarzenegger, he said, "If your movie is only big in America it doesn't matter. You'll be a movie star only when you're a movie star in every country in the world. You have to travel. You have to go. You have to meet the people. (Smith 2018)

Because of this encounter Will Smith reoriented his career and took the steps that were necessary to accomplish his goal of achieving global stardom. He said,

I've really made my career on press tours. I always thought about the promotional tour as like a political campaign, shaking hands and kissing babies. For me that was always the idea behind the press tour, was less about selling the movie and was more about making friends and connecting with people. (Smith 2018)

The same skill that can turn a fledgling actor into an international movie star can turn a film star into a successful political campaigner. Schwarzenegger knew that he needed to build social capital and his professional network, he needed to garner attention and be well liked, he needed to be known if he wanted to succeed.

FAME

Arnold Schwarzenegger was very well known and very well liked prior to running for office. Between fifty-five and seventy-two percent of Americans had a favorable opinion of him and only one or two percent did not know who he was. Schwarzenegger has, "one of the most recognizable faces in the world. He joins a select group of icons who have achieved such recognition—a handful of people whose faces are not only universally familiar, but have become more or less universally understood as symbols" (Krasniewicz and Blitz 2006, xv). Arnold Schwarzenegger has better name recognition than every US senator in their own states. Even former Senate Majority Leader Mitch McConnell is unknown to nine percent of his constituents in Kentucky (Easly 2017).

Arnold Schwarzenegger has a lot of fans. Seventy-two percent of Americans had a favorable opinion of him when he ran for governor and a large majority liked him as a movie star. Interestingly, pluralities or majorities of Americans would not want Schwarzenegger to be the governor of their state. Yet they think he represents a new kind of politics and believed he would do a good job. Sixty-five percent believed he represents a new kind of politics. Nearly two-thirds of Americans believed Schwarzenegger would be a successful governor following his election. This suggests that despite some hesitation Americans who want to shake things up do not believe that being a celebrity is a disqualifier for public office. His fans begin with a favorable opinion of him and this likely plays a role in public support for the candidate.

TEXTBOX 8.1

Arnold Schwarzenegger

How much do you like Arnold Schwarzenegger as a movie star—a great deal, fair amount, not much, or not at all?[1]

A great deal	25%
Fair amount	49%
Not much	18%
Not at all	5%
Not sure	3%

Next, we'd like to get your overall opinion of some people in the entertainment field. As I read each name, please say if you have a favorable or unfavorable opinion of these people—or if you have never heard of them. How about . . . Arnold Schwarzenegger?[2]

Favorable	72%
Unfavorable	14%
No opinion	12%
Never heard of	2%

I'm going to read the names of some people. Please tell me whether you have a generally favorable or unfavorable opinion of each. If you've never heard of one, please just say so . . . Arnold Schwarzenegger.[3]

Favorable	55%
Unfavorable	23%
Can't say	21%
Never heard of	1%

There has been speculation about actor Arnold Schwarzenegger running for governor of California. If Schwarzenegger were to run for statewide office in your state, do you think you would vote for him?[4]

Yes	28%
No	46%
Not sure	26%

If Arnold Schwarzenegger were to run for governor in your state, do you think you would vote for him?[5]

Yes	31%
No	43%
Not sure	26%

Would you vote for Arnold Schwarzenegger if he were running for governor of your state, or not?[6]

Yes, would	39%
No, would not	55%
No opinion	6%

If you had the chance, would you vote for Arnold Schwarzenegger to be governor of your state or not?[7]

Yes	23%

No   67%
Don't know   10%

Please tell me if you tend to agree or disagree that Arnold Schwarzenegger represents a new approach to politics, different from the usual politicians?[8]
Agree   65%
Disagree   31%
No opinion   4%

Just your best guess, do you think Arnold Schwarzenegger will be successful—or not successful—as governor of California?[9]
Successful   62%
Not successful   33%
No opinion   5%

Just your best guess, do you think Arnold Schwarzenegger will be successful—or not successful—as governor of California?[10]
Successful   61%
Not successful   34%
No opinion   5%

Sources: 1 Harris Interactive. Harris Poll, August 2003, retrieved February 24, 2019 from the iPOLL Databank, The Roper Center for Public Opinion Research, University of Connecticut;2 Gallup/CNN/USA Today Poll, February 2003, retrieved February 24, 2019 from the iPOLL Databank, The Roper Center for Public Opinion Research, University of Connecticut;3 Fox News/ Opinion Dynamics Poll, August 2003, retrieved February 24, 2019 from the iPOLL Databank, The Roper Center for Public Opinion Research, University of Connecticut; 4 *Fox News/Opinion Dynamics Poll*, June 2003, retrieved February 24, 2019 from the iPOLL Databank, The Roper Center for Public Opinion Research, University of Connecticut; 5 *Fox News/Opinion Dynamics Poll*, August 2003, retrieved February 24, 2019 from the iPOLL Databank, The Roper Center for Public Opinion Research, University of Connecticut;6 *Gallup/CNN/USA Today Poll*, October 2003, retrieved February 24, 2019 from the iPOLL Databank, The Roper Center for Public Opinion Research, University of Connecticut; 7 *Quinnipiac University Poll*, October 2003, retrieved February 24, 2019 from the iPOLL Databank, The Roper Center for Public Opinion Research, University of Connecticut;8 *Gallup/CNN/USA Today Poll*, October 2003, retrieved February 24, 2019 from the iPOLL Databank, The Roper Center for Public Opinion Research, University of Connecticut;9 *Gallup/CNN/USA Today Poll*, November 2003, retrieved February 24, 2019 from the iPOLL Databank, The Roper Center for Public Opinion Research, University of Connecticut; 10 Gallup/CNN/USA Today Poll, October 2003. Retrieved February 24, 2019 from the iPOLL Databank, The Roper Center for Public Opinion Research, University of Connecticut.

Fame begets more fame. As Mr. Olympia, Arnold would travel to various locations to promote Joe Weider's enterprises. These included nutritional supplements, exercise equipment, bodybuilding exhibitions, and competitions. As part of the promotional tour he made an appearance on *The Merv Griffin Show*. He demonstrated that he was in fact very funny and likable, he was not just a muscle-bound jock without intellect or personality. As it happened, Lucille Ball watched the appearance on TV and was so impressed that she wanted Arnold to appear in a TV movie she was making. Schwarzenegger excitedly agreed and Ball took it upon herself to promote his acting career. She personally coached him in preparation for the role he would play. She also invited Arnold to parties where he could meet Hollywood's elite producers, directors, actors, and other important folks in the industry (Schwarzenegger 2013).

Any publicity is good publicity. Despite his inglorious debut in *Hercules*, Schwarzenegger was now on the radar of Hollywood producers looking for a muscle man to star in their movies. In *Stay Hungry* he plays a champion bodybuilder whose gym is being purchased by a wealthy scion of privilege. Winning the Golden Globe for that movie put Schwarzenegger in the Hollywood big leagues. His next film, *Pumping Iron*, a documentary about bodybuilding, received the full Hollywood treatment. The studio hosted a premier event chock-full of celebrities. During a pre-premier party, the small party before the big party, Schwarzenegger met Jackie Onassis, who would also attend the Hollywood premier. A few weeks later at the Boston premier Schwarzenegger would meet other members of the Kennedy family and their friend John Kerry (Schwarzenegger 2013). Recall, the Kennedy's were part of the Hollywood scene ever since Joe Kennedy was a studio mogul in the 1920s. Arnold was now moving in the circles that would later contribute to his political success.

After *Pumping Iron*, Arnold notes, "I went to every party I was invited to and was always one of the last to leave" (Schwarzenegger 2013, 220). It was at these parties in Los Angeles, Hollywood, and New York that Schwarzenegger mingled with and befriended America's top entertainers. In California, he met many stars. They included Harry Belafonte, Carol Burnett, Dino De Laurentiis, Peter Falk, Henry Fonda, Deborah Kerr, Jessica Lange, Sophia Loren, Cybill Shepherd, Sylvester Stallone, Jimmy Stewart, Raquel Welch, Henry Winkler, and Shelly Winters. In New York he dined with the cast of *Saturday Night Live*, Dan Aykroyd, John Belushi, Laraine Newman, and Gilda Radner. He was introduced to Robert Altman, Woody Allen, Francis Ford Coppola, Al Pacino, and Andy Warhol (Schwarzenegger 2013). Celebrities are celebrities in part because they associate with other celebrities. They feed off of and share the attention of other celebrities to garner more attention for themselves.

In the 1980s and 1990s Arnold Schwarzenegger was one of the top stars in Hollywood. He has gained worldwide name recognition. Importantly, the media covered his gubernatorial run as if the Terminator himself was running for office. "The Terminator became the framework for Arnold's election. . . . Domestic newspapers, radio programs, Web sites, and television coverage reinforced the idea that it was the Terminator who was running for governor of California, not just a movie star" (Krasniewicz and Blitz 2006, 130). The media helped blur the lines between Schwarzenegger the man and the fictional Terminator character.

Schwarzenegger credits his celebrity and the earned media it garners for not only his electoral victory, but also his ability to push forward his policy agenda. While governor, Schwarzenegger took a trip to Iraq and met with Prime Minister Nouri al-Maliki. They discussed energy policy, the economy, the California university system, and the innovation of Silicon Valley. Schwarzenegger credits his celebrity for making the meeting possible, ordinarily governors of US states don't meet with foreign leaders. Schwarzenegger believes that his being a movie star was politically useful because it made him a more desirable candidate for special consideration (Schwarzenegger 2013). He was given advantages that a non-celebrity governor would not have. It opened doors and gave Schwarzenegger additional opportunities to form political alliances.

RESOURCES

Arnold Schwarzenegger's films have earned $4 billion dollars worldwide for the studios that produce them (Krasniewicz and Blitz 2006). Because of this, Schwarzenegger became one of the highest paid actors in Hollywood. Each new success allowed him to command a higher salary for his subsequent films. He earned $250,000 for *Conan the Barbarian* then increased that amount for *Terminator* ($750,000), *Conan the Destroyer* ($1 million), *Commando* ($1.5 million), *Red Sonja* ($1 million), *Predator* ($3 million), *The Running Man* ($5 million), *Red Heat* ($5 million), *Total Recall* ($10 million), *Terminator 2* ($14 million), and *True Lies* ($15 million). Those salaries do not include royalties from the negotiated percentage of gross receipts which increase his total earnings from the films. With *Twins*, for example, Schwarzenegger earned more than $35 million from net profits. All together Schwarzenegger has earned hundreds of millions of dollars from his films (Andrews 2003; Krasniewicz and Blitz 2006; Schwarzenegger 2013).

He further increased his wealth as a shrewd investor in the real estate market. He earned tens of millions buying and selling real estate properties in southern California. He arrived in California at the beginning of the real estate boom and capitalized on rapidly increasing property values in the 1970s, 1980s, and 1990s (Schwarzenegger 2013). One Santa Monica property was purchased by Schwarzenegger for $450,000 and sold for $2,300,000. He earned a $7 million profit investing in an office building in Nevada (Andrews 2003).

In his first ever fundraising call for Proposition 49 he called tech entrepreneur Paul Folino and secured a million-dollar commitment. His second call was to Univision owner Jerry Perenchio where he secured another million-dollar commitment (Schwarzenegger 2013). Whereas typical first-time politicians start with small donations from friends and family for small local offices, Schwarzenegger had the ability to start with large donations for a statewide campaign. One of the perks of celebrity is access to very wealthy individuals and the kind of name recognition that virtually ensures they will take the call themselves. And, since the call is from another wealthy individual, there is likely an elite camaraderie and greater trust. When Schwarzenegger ran for governor, he raised $21.9 million, Cruz Bustamante raised $12.4 million, and Gray Davis raised $17 million (Morain and Rubin 2003).

POLITICAL ENVIRONMENT

In the early 2000s California was facing some serious challenges. Tech companies in Silicon Valley saw big losses when the tech bubble burst and the country entered a recession. The recession caused state revenues to drop, and California faced a $38 billion deficit. There was an electricity crisis brought about by the Enron fiasco. Fraud and mismanagement at Enron caused the company to become insolvent. To increase revenue, the company caused blackouts to justify an increase in electricity rates. Californians saw electricity prices tripling and dealt with frequent blackouts as the company tried to pump up revenues to avoid bankruptcy.

Gray Davis sought to reduce the state budget deficit by eliminating the vehicle registration tax abatement policy. That move would effectively triple automobile registration fees in a state not known for having walkable cities. Western cities were designed around the automobile and the fee increase would be wildly unpopular with California's motorists. Automobile dealers despised the tax increase and donated almost $800,000 to Schwarzenegger's campaign (Andrews 2003; Morain and Rubin 2003). Although Enron was a Houston based company, Davis was blamed for not taking actions to prevent the price gouging. Californians were upset with the present situation.

Schwarzenegger got advice from Bob White, Pete Wilson's chief of staff, to find seasoned professionals to help with his campaign. He also received advice from George Gorton, another one of Pete Wilson's inner circle, "If I sponsored a ballot initiative, Gorton pointed out, I could get out in front of the people without having to announce right away for governor. I'd have a reason to build an organization, hold fund-raisers, form alliances with important groups, talk to the media, and do TV ads. And if the initiative passed, it would prove that I could win votes across the state" (Schwarzenegger 2013,

478). Schwarzenegger would sponsor a ballot initiative as a trial run for seeking the governor's office. Proposition 49, the After-School Education and Safety Program Act, would be a tryout for Arnold's political acumen. The proposition passed and Republican leaders in California had reason to think that Schwarzenegger was a real contender.

Schwarzenegger's socially liberal policy preferences would be a tough sell to Republican primary voters, but California recall elections do not have a primary. This allowed Schwarzenegger to clear the first hurdle without any effort; instead of winning two elections he would need to only win one. Just like state election laws gave Jesse Ventura some help in Minnesota; state elections laws would help Schwarzenegger in California.

The other advantage was a crowded field of candidates. California requires only a plurality victory, so Schwarzenegger did not need a majority, only more votes than any other single candidate. Again, California election laws helpèd. Anyone could declare themselves a candidate with just sixty-five signatures and a $3,500 filing fee (Krasniewicz and Blitz 2006). The crowded field of 135 candidates included child star Gary Coleman, media mogul Arianna Huffington, adult film actress Mary Carey, adult magazine publisher Larry Flint, MLB commissioner and US Olympic Committee chairman Peter Ueberroth, and the comedian Leo Gallagher. The most prominent rivals for the governorship were Democratic Lieutenant Governor Cruz Bustamante and Republican state senator Tom McClintock.

Schwarzenegger actively used his movie career in his campaign for governor. His campaign tour busses were named the *Running Man* and *Total Recall*. On the stump he said he would "terminate" the car registration tax (Krasniewicz and Blitz 2006). He earned the nickname "The Governator" playing on his fame as "The Terminator." Throughout his political career Schwarzenegger would utilize lines and imagery from his acting career drawing a direct link between the imagined characters he played and the real politician he was (Drake and Higgins 2006). The action hero persona that Schwarzenegger took care to develop over the years was front and center in his campaign.

For "programs" Schwarzenegger's best-known bits of movie dialogue substituted as blocky "messages": The people wanted *action, action, action*. For Gray Davis, the current governor whose removal from or retention in office was the first decision voters had to make on the recall ballot, it was going to be *hasta la vista, baby*. The internal gridlock in the Sacramento legislature, *no problemo*. The budget deficit, the energy crisis, the imminent hike in car registration fees, the high taxes driving businesses out of California would all be *terminated* by Conan the Barbarian himself. This language of coercion, plucked from the fictions that glorified force as the preferred method of problem-solving, formed an intoxicating, vaporous mirage in the sketchy shape of a political "platform." (Indiana 2005, 20)

Schwarzenegger supporters were voting for an action hero to lead them. He saved the world in his movies, now he could save California in real life (Scott 2011). California voters, "felt that the appeal and immediacy of the surface image was more important, even more trustworthy, than any deep consideration of a man's policies" (Andrews 2003, 247). Schwarzenegger won with a 49 pecent plurality. His next closest competitor was Bustamante with 31 percent of the vote (Morain 2003).

While campaigning, and as governor, Schwarzenegger survived scandals that may have ended the careers of other politicians. He was accused of womanizing, groping, harassing, and making lewd comments (Andrews 2003). He denied the charges of groping but did admit that he was on "rowdy movie sets" where he acted "inappropriately" (Schwarzenegger 2013, 520). Alluding to the *Saturday Night Live* characters Hans and Franz he called state assembly members "girlie men" while speaking to a group at a shopping mall (Schwarzenegger 2013, 535). The crowd laughed but Schwarzenegger was accused of being sexist and homophobic because of the comment. He soon apologized because he did not want to antagonize the legislators he would have to work with in the future.

In another incident he called Bonnie Garcia, a state legislator, "very hot" due to her "Black and Latino blood" (Schwarzenegger 2013, 560). Garcia, who was a friend of Schwarzenegger, accepted the apology and later joked, "I wouldn't kick him out of bed" (Schwarzenegger 2013, 560). In this case his masculine good looks helped get him out of trouble. He found some women hot, and they found him hot right back. It is likely that less physically attractive politicians would not be let off the hook as easily. Arnold benefited from "celebrity slack" because Californians overlooked his misdeeds and offensive comments.

CONCLUSIONS

Schwarzenegger's fame was only possible because of his exceptional physique. He parlayed his bodybuilding success to star in Hollywood films. He understood the value of a good publicity stunt. He developed a public persona that is known the world over and was obsessed with how he was being perceived by audiences. He learned how to become a skilled self-promoter to sell his books and movies. He learned that promoting a movie was not all that different from promoting a public policy. As a politician, Schwarzenegger acknowledged that being a celebrity has helped him succeed. It gave him a platform and immediate media attention. Potential donors would take his calls and he could start with large requests. He did not have to waste time slowly climbing up the political ladder. He could start right at the top because celebrities are among the highest status people in society. Schwarzenegger received valuable guidance from America's top entertainers and politicians and survived scandals that could have been career ending for others. The unique circumstances of California politics were crucial. The Enron induced blackouts and price increases, the lack of a primary battle, and a plurality win rule all worked in Schwarzenegger's favor. He transformed his fictional "Terminator" character into a real life "Governator" to lead the state of California.

Chapter 9

Al Franken

Al Franken began his comedic career in his suburban Minneapolis high school. He volunteered with his friend Tom Davis to make the morning announcements. The announcements became a daily stand-up comedy routine that borrowed from famous comics of the time. They also performed their comedy at the pep rallies where they would engage in parodies of high school pep rallies and thereby make a mockery of high school traditions. The duo began to perform at open mic nights at Dudley Riggs's Brave New Workshop, a comedy club in Minneapolis. The club was well known for its variety. It featured stand-up comedy, improvisational acts, sketch comedy, poetry readings, and satirical performances (Royce and Justin 2005). Franken and Davis were soon invited to give regular performances and began getting paid to perform their comedy routines (Franken 2017).

As an undergraduate at Harvard, Franken would travel to Manhattan and perform at the comedy clubs there. He and Tom also traveled to Los Angeles to perform at The Comedy Store where they performed improv "with comedians like Jay Leno, Robert Klein, and Andy Kaufman" (Franken 2017, 18). After graduating he moved to California to perform at L.A. area comedy clubs. It was there that Hollywood executives and talent scouts discovered the pair of talented comedians.

His big break occurred when he and Tom were hired as two of the original writers for *Saturday Night Live* (*SNL*) in 1975. He moved to New York and began his work with comedy legends Chevy Chase, Garrett Morris, Dan Aykroyd, Bill Murray, Gilda Radner, and John Belushi. He worked at *SNL* from 1975 to 1980 and again from 1985 to 1995. During his second stint he worked with future stars Chris Rock, Chris Farley, Ben Stiller, Dana Carvey, Dennis Miller, Mike Meyers, Adam Sandler, and Conan O'Brian (Shales and Miller 2002). As a writer and performer, he invented the character Stuart Smalley, a parody of a 12-step self-help guru, that became a regular part of the *SNL* shows. Unlike other *SNL* cast members who successfully transitioned to films, his movie, *Stuart Saves His Family*, was a box office bomb (Franken 2017).

Saturday Night Live is part of America's political environment. The show's impersonations of political figures are part of the political discourse. "Comedic caricature is about essence, reducing numerous competing narratives to a particularly arresting one. These narratives bestow upon a politician a popular persona" (Jones 2013, 81). Whether it was Chevy Chase's Gerald Ford, Will Ferrell's George W. Bush, Tina Fey's Sarah Palin, or Alec Baldwin's Donald Trump, the caricatures play "a particularly significant role in U.S. political culture by generating a popular interpretation of presidents and presidential aspirants" (Jones 2013, 83). By exaggerating personality traits, the impersonations reveal to the public a key part of their leaders' beings. Although performed for comedic effect, the caricatures create a context for Americans to understand their political world. As one of *SNL*'s writers for many years, Franken was behind the scenes in shaping American political discourse long before entering politics himself.

His career as a political satirist continued when he was hired to be an anchor for Comedy Central's coverage of the 1992 Democratic and Republican National Conventions called *Indecision '92*. He wrote several books attacking what he called "the whack-job right" and became a darling of the liberal activist community (Franken 2017, 41). He became a celebrity endorser and active participant in Paul Wellstone's senate campaigns. Along with Robert Redford, Franken entertained the crowd at Wellstone fundraisers (Baden 1996). He also endorsed Chris Coleman for mayor of St. Paul, bringing his national star power to bear on a local contest (Crosby 2005). To increase his influence in Minnesota politics Franken started his own PAC to support liberal candidates (*Star Tribune* Editorial Board 2005).

Like Jesse Ventura, Al Franken went into radio and was the host of the *Al Franken Show* where he would provide his liberal commentary on the political news of the day. These talk radio programs are better than earned media, where candidates get free coverage, the future candidates get paid to express their political opinions. Celebrities are given platforms that non-celebrities do not have access to.

He hosted the radio program from 2004 to 2007 and quit to declare his candidacy for the US Senate. Franken is a talented comedian who used his comedic skills on the campaign trail to woo potential voters. He was well known nationally as a TV personality, radio host, and author. His contacts in the entertainment community provided financial support for his campaigns. Franken had the talent, fame, and resources to win a US Senate seat in Minnesota. He also survived controversies related to statements he made as a comedian. This suggests that Franken also benefited from celebrity slack, the public was willing to overlook some of Franken's objectionable comedic material.

TALENT

Al Franken is a talented comedian. On *SNL* he was able to both write and perform comedic sketches. *Saturday Night Live* has 252 Emmy nominations, the most for any program in the seventy years of the Emmy Awards (Television Academy "Fact and Figures for 2018 Nominations"). Al Franken himself was nominated for fourteen and has won five Emmy Awards for Outstanding Writing (Television Academy "Al Franken"). Franken's comedic talent has been recognized by the entertainment industry.

Al Franken also has an underlying personality trait that makes him especially suited to a career in politics. He says, "I didn't realize that being an extrovert actually counted as a skill when it came to politics. For a lot of people who run for office, constantly having to talk to people is exhausting. For me, it was energizing. I really liked learning about people's lives. I really liked hearing their stories. I really liked meeting their kids" (Franken 2017, 61). Being an extrovert is useful for anyone pursuing a career in which public performances are part of the job. This is true for politicians, actors, and comedians.

Franken describes a situation at a Native American powwow where he realized that being a strait-laced politician was not going to work for him. A few minutes into a speech about education and healthcare he noticed that his audience was disinterested. He stopped and decided to break into his stand-up comedy routine. The crowd began laughing, smiling, and having a good time. After telling jokes for an hour one of the powwow organizers approached Franken and said, "We've never had a politician here who knows how to read a crowd as well as you" (Franken 2017, 121). Franken harnessed his years of show business experience in front of live audiences to win over voters.

At the state fair Franken, "goofed for the cameras . . . as he did a weather segment on KSTP-TV, Channel 5. Assuming a comic stance in front of a blank green wall (on television, weather images are superimposed), Franken informed viewers that 'hail as big as watermelons' was heading for Marshall" (Lopez 2007). A fairgoer remarked, "He's hilarious, I appreciate a sense of humor in a candidate" (Lopez 2007). A reporter noted just how popular Franken was at the fair, "Every time the former 'Saturday Night Live' comedian, author and radio talker showed up—which happened daily, for long hours—a queue formed for photos and autographs. Old political hands likened his appeal to that of 1998 fair phenom Jesse Ventura—a portentous comparison" (Sturdevant 2007). His decades worth of experience at improvisational and sketch comedy helped him get attention and win over crowds on the campaign trail. If a political speech was starting to go badly, he was talented enough to turn it into a comedy routine and get the crowd laughing and hollering.

FAME

Saturday Night Live is America's premier sketch comedy show on broadcast television. It "has consistently and intentionally debated the politics, pop culture, and social norms of American life in five different decades" (Marx, Sienkiewicz, and Becker 2013, 4). Shales and Miller note that, "Television is not itself an art form, but it provides a showcase for many art forms, and the one plied and perfected by *Saturday Night Live* is the comedy sketch, a vaudeville and burlesque staple that is the theatrical equivalent of the American short story" (Shales and Miller 2002, 9). Over the years it, "has attracted and developed the best sketch-comedy writers in the business" (Shales and Miller 2002, 9).

Franken was one of the original writers of *Saturday Night Live* between 1975 and 1980. The show had its best ratings ever in 1978 with a 39 percent share, meaning that 39 percent of Americans watching TV in that time slot were watching *SNL* (Shales and Miller 2002). He returned to the show as a writer and performer between 1985 and 1995. Although *SNL*'s popularity has declined in recent years, due to competition from cable television and streaming services, the show had an average of between 10 million and 12.5 million viewers during Franken's second stint on the show (TV Ratings Guide n.d.). This is the kind of media exposure that average political candidates could only dream of.

Beyond his national fame, Franken also became a key figure for American liberals. Between 2004 and 2007 he was a radio talk show host on the Air America radio network. His goal was to create a liberal antidote to the popular right-wing radio hosts that many Americans use to get their information from. *The Al Franken Show*, originally called *The O'Franken Factor* to mock Bill O'Reilly's *The O'Reilly Factor*, used commentary along with interviews and recurring segments to argue for liberal political goals. Franken received the attention of local newspapers because the program was headquartered in Minneapolis (Rybak February 2, 2005; Rybak March 31, 2005). He was already being discussed as a potential candidate while he was in the broadcast business (Black 2005; Rybak March 31, 2005; von Sternberg 2005).

Franken made an appearance, along with Norm Coleman, on the HBO show *Real Time with Bill Maher*. Even though it was more than one year before he entered the race, the prospect of a celebrity candidate for a major political office draws in media attention that would otherwise be absent. Maher asked Coleman, "Politicians have had to run against actors before. Actors, as we all know, are witless and dumb. You're going to be running against a guy who his whole life has used humor to slice people up. Aren't you nervous a little about that?" (Covert 2005). Maher believed that Franken's gift with political satire would be difficult to defend against in a political campaign.

Franken also published several books that were geared toward the liberal activist community. *Rush Limbaugh Is a Big Fat Idiot and Other Observations* was the number one book on the *New York Times* best-selling list for twenty-three weeks in a row (Franken 2017). *Lies and the Lying Liars Who Tell Them: A Fair and Balanced Look at the Right*, "skyrocketed to the top of the bestseller list for months, selling over a million copies" after Bill O'Reilly and Fox News sued him (Franken 2017, 49). The case was dismissed on First Amendment grounds but added to Franken's liberal bona fides. The audiobook version was awarded the 2003 Grammy Award for Best Spoken Word Album (Recording Academy 2003). Franken was a well-known national personality, and he was especially prominent in liberal political circles before his run for the US Senate.

This fame translated into unusually large crowds for Franken's campaign appearances. His first campaign rally was held at his former junior high school. The attendees were described as, "a starstruck, autograph-seeking crowd of about 1,000" (Peterson 2007). A few weeks later Franken appeared on *The Late Show with David Letterman*, again giving national exposure to a state level contest (Justin 2007). During the primary battle observers noted, "The former 'Saturday Night Live' star and best-selling author has been a crowd magnet from the start. . . . Neither of his two remaining DFL rivals—Jack Nelson-Pallmeyer and Mike Ciresi—has demonstrated as much people-pulling power" (Sturdevant February 3, 2008).

RESOURCES

While hosting his radio talk show he began preparing for his senate run. Franken says,

> In my free time, I started laying the foundation for a potential campaign. That meant learning as much as I could about Minnesota issues and getting as much advice as I could from key political players. And it meant showing up everywhere I could to rally DFLers across the state for the critical 2006 midterm elections—a sort of dry run for what my own campaign might be like. I also set up a political action committee (PAC), which would allow me to meet big-shot

donors, gauge my fund-raising appeal, and build some goodwill by supporting deserving candidates in Minnesota and around the country. (Franken 2017, 58)

According to Franken, the group, called Midwest Values PAC, was remarkably successful, "mostly because I hired some people who knew what they were doing. Dinah Dale, a soft-spoken Arkansan who had overseen Paul Wellstone's fund-raising operation, was in charge of connecting me with wealthy progressives who might be interested in contributing to my PAC" (Franken 2017, 59). Franken had an easier time fundraising because of his celebrity status, and he used humor to help his cause.

> Turns out, the number one determinant of whether someone gives money in response to a mail solicitation is whether or not they open the envelope. And because I had something of a following from my books and radio show, instead of just tossing my envelopes into their trash cans—or, if they were environmentally conscious, their recycling bins—people tended to open them. Inside, they'd find a letter that didn't sound exactly like every other fund-raising letter they were getting. Mine began, "Dear Person I'm Asking for Money." Moderately amused liberals from coast to coast sent in contributions. (Franken 2017, 59)

Franken did call upon his friends in the entertainment industry to support his cause. Midwest Values PAC accepted donations from directors Gregory Berlanti, Nora Ephron, Sydney Pollack, Robert Reiner, and Jerry Zucker, from producers Norman Lear and Lorne Michaels, from actors Larry David and Larry Hagman, from talk-show host Phil Donahue, and from singer Barbra Streisand (Hotakainen September 17, 2006).

Franken is quite candid about the purpose of his PAC, "The money we raised wasn't for me. The point was to give it away to progressive candidates and causes in Minnesota and around the country. And for me to get credit for it" (Franken 2017, 59). In 2006, Midwest Values PAC and Franken as an individual, donated to several important political contests in Minnesota (Gordon 2006). The PAC raised more than a million dollars and earned Franken the admiration of many liberal activists nationally and in Minnesota (Duchschere October 20, 2008; Hotakainen 2007).

His success fundraising for the PAC translated into success in fundraising for his campaign. Franken raised $22.5 million dollars in 2008 (FEC "Al Franken"). Much of this money came from the entertainment industry. Franken received donations from Dan Aykroyd, Jason Alexander, Larry David, Ronald Bass, James L. Brooks, Bonnie Raitt, Bill Maher, Rosie O'Donnell, Kevin Bacon, and Tom Hanks (Averill 2007; Sherman July 3, 2007; Diaz and Sherman July 17, 2007). Celebrities are wealthy people with wealthy friends. This is a substantial advantage over traditional political rivals whose circle of friends may not be as well off.

In early 2007 when Franken had already collected $1.35 million, his rival for the nomination, Mike Ciresi, had raised less than $8,000 (Averill 2007). According to financial disclosure documents Ciresi was wealthier than Franken. Ciresi disclosed assets of nearly $27 million while Franken disclosed assets of $4.3 million. The Republican, Norm Coleman, had just over half a million in a retirement account (Diaz and Sherman July 4, 2007). Neither Ciresi nor Coleman could compete with Franken's star power. By July 2007, Ciresi raised $735,000, Coleman raised $1.5 million, and Franken raised $3.3 million (Sherman July 10, 2007). For the general election Coleman raised $23.7 million and Franken raised $22.5 million (Center for Responsive Politics 2008). In the primary, Franken was able to out fundraise someone who was personally wealthier than him. In the general election, he was competitive against an incumbent US Senator. This suggests that celebrities can harness their fame beyond their economic class to defeat opponents.

POLITICAL ENVIRONMENT

As a candidate, Al Franken was able to attract some of the top talent in Democratic Party politics to assist in his campaign. This included Jeff Blodgett who "had been the campaign manager for all of Paul Wellstone's Senate campaigns" (Franken 2017, 60). Although Blodgett worked for Obama in 2008, he did offer Franken sound advice and directed him to other potential staff. David Benson, who previously worked for South Dakota senator Tom Daschle, assisted with Franken's senate bid. As did James Haggar and Diane Feldman, both were former campaign staff for Wellstone. Franken's campaign manager was Stephanie Schriock who was the finance director for Howard Dean's 2004 presidential campaign and worked on Jon Tester's 2006 senate run (Franken 2017). Celebrity candidates may find it easier to attract talented staff because they have the resources to pay them and because they offer potential staff the opportunity to work with a famous person.

In Franken's case, his talented staff were of major importance. Democrat Paul Wellstone died in a plane crash and Republican Norm Coleman took his place in the US Senate. But Franken was not just facing an incumbent, he was also facing Independent candidate Dean Barkley, Jesse Ventura's campaign chairperson. Barkley had briefly served in the US Senate after Ventura appointed him to the position. Franken's staff knew that any attack on Coleman would allow Barkley to use the same successful strategy that allowed Ventura to win his statewide race. As the two major parties attack each other the third candidate can declare a pox on both their houses and call for a rejection of the status quo (Franken 2017).

Polling indicated that Barkley was drawing votes away from Franken. Voters that were upset with the status quo had two alternatives to choose from. Polling also showed that Coleman was being harmed by his close association to the Bush administration (Duchschere November 2, 2008). In a strong year for Democrats there is increased likelihood of a Republican incumbent being harmed by the presidential coattails effect. This is likely the reason for Coleman's vulnerability in that year's election. National trends increased the probability of a Republican defeat. While celebrity candidates have definite advantages, it is still the case that the political environment of the time and place of the election are of critical importance.

Political observers were comparing Franken to other celebrities that ran for office before him. Franken did not like being compared to Jesse Ventura and said he is "less like Jesse Ventura than almost anyone you'll ever meet" (Hotakainen February 27, 2006). When Republicans criticized his past work he said, "I didn't hear the Republicans complaining when Arnold Schwarzenegger was running for governor that he took steroids and ran around half-naked shooting people. That was his career. People like comedy and satire because sometimes . . . people like us tend to see the truth in a way that is helpful" (Hotakainen February 27, 2006).

Franken, however, did not rely on his celebrity to persuade Minnesota voters to support him. He laid the ground-work years before declaring his candidacy and behaved like a traditional politician by attending the numerous functions that politicians are expected to attend.

A celebrity returning to the state of his youth to run for the U.S. Senate didn't have to show up several years before the election and troop to every party picnic and legislative fundraiser he could find. He didn't have to log long hours at the State Fair, tour 10 college campuses, stomp around the Iron Range on the coldest week of the year or talk himself hoarse at a pizza place in a traditional Republican stronghold. He could have tapped his coastal friends for big contributions, said to heck with party endorsement and bought enough TV time to put himself in strong contention in the Sept. 9 primary. But that strategy would have left Franken very open to Coleman's charge that he's been too long removed from Minnesota to represent it well in the U.S. Senate. By instead running a hands-on, grass-roots campaign, and by adding a recent overlay of TV ads that reinforce his Minnesota connections, Franken gives himself a chance to blunt the inevitable Al-come-lately attack. (Sturdevant February 3, 2008)

Franken won his party's nomination with more than the 60 percent of the vote on the first ballot and was endorsed by acclamation, suggesting that his hard work paid off (Duchschere and Kaszuba 2008).

Franken's career in comedy, the very thing that gave him the fame to be successful, was also a serious potential weakness. The Democratic Party leadership was worried that too many of Franken's jokes were too offensive and would derail his senate campaign. Republicans, who were aware of the potential run of Franken, had already begun to collect a plethora of material from Franken's career in comedy that could be used against him (Black February 4, 2007). The Democrats wanted to reclaim the Minnesota seat and were worried about a candidate that had so many over the top public statements (Hotakainen and Lopez 2007). The Democratic leaders were right to be concerned. The Republicans began "aggressively circulating a compendium of Franken's rudest gibes, using them to define Franken in voters' minds as angry, divisive and potty-mouthed" (Black March 28, 2007).

Unfortunately for Franken, his jokes nearly did derail his campaign. The most prominent example was from a *Playboy* magazine article published in January 2000. Titled "Porn-O-Rama!" the article was a satire of a *Playboy* article. In the same way Franken ridiculed high school pep rallies at pep rallies, he mocked the sexually explicit *Playboy* articles with over-the-top explicit details of virtual sex acts. The story broke after Franken held a fundraiser with Christie Hefner, the daughter of *Playboy* founder Hugh Hefner. Christie Hefner was a prominent Democratic donor, was a founding member Emily's List, and served on the board of the National Women's Political Caucus (Duchschere May 21, 2008). Republicans attacked Franken for degrading women, and he started to lose support from some Minnesota Democrats as well (Duchschere June 3, 2008). Franken says, "All campaign long, I'd avoided apologizing for things I'd said or written, because it felt like doing so would mean apologizing for everything I'd done over forty years in comedy" (Franken 2017, 112). Franken apologized at the DFL convention and was able to secure the nomination by acclamation (Sturdevant June 9, 2008; Duchschere and Kaszuba 2008).

Jesse Ventura won the governor's race in Minnesota even though he had bragged about visiting a Nevada brothel. Franken survived the "Porn-O-Rama!" scandal and defeated Norm Coleman by a razor thin 312 votes (Diaz and von Sternberg 2009). Even though Franken was not seated in the Senate until the next summer due to litigation over the recount, the episode shows that celebrities can survive mistakes and scandals that would doom ordinary politicians. Franken likely benefited from celebrity slack and was given a pass for his jokes that offended many members of his constituency. This is not to say that there was no damage because of the incident, the contest was exceedingly close. But he was able to defeat a well-financed incumbent, a rarity in American politics.

CONCLUSIONS

Franken was not successful in movies like Clint Eastwood or Arnold Schwarzenegger. But he was successful on TV, like Ronald Reagan, and successful on radio, like Jesse Ventura. Franken was able to win in Minnesota because he was a talented comedian who was able to win over crowds. He was a nationally known celebrity and his run for the US Senate received national media attention. His connections with "Big Comedy" provided resources for his Midwest Values PAC and his senate bid. He became active in Minnesota politics and worked the political circuit just as any other aspiring politician would do. Franken benefited from a political environment that was favorable to Democrats. The 2008 recession and the turmoil of the Bush administration meant that the presidential coattails effect was working against Republicans that year. Lastly, Minnesota voters were willing to overlook Franken's outlandish, offensive, and obscene conduct and statements that were intended as jokes by the award-winning comedian.

Al Franken served in the US Senate until his resignation at the end of 2017. He was accused of groping and sexually harassing several women. A photograph shows Franken with his hands over the breasts of radio host Leeann Tweeden. It appears that his jokes had crossed a line that could not be tolerated by his Democratic colleagues in the Congress. However, 68 percent of Minnesota Democrats believed that he should not have resigned. Among all registered voters in the state, sixty percent believed that Franken did grope or harass multiple women, but only 41 percent believed he should have resigned because of it (Brooks and Rao 2018). Even with his resignation Franken was the beneficiary of celebrity slack. He remained popular with Minnesota voters who did not believe his conduct warranted his leaving office. He went back to his radio broadcasting career after leaving the Senate (Fang 2019).

Chapter 10

Donald Trump

Donald Trump's grandfather was an illegal German immigrant who made some money operating a hotel in a shady part of Seattle during the Gold Rush. His grandfather returned to Germany but was expelled for having dodged his required military service. Back in New York he died during a flu epidemic and his wife and sixteen-year-old son, Fred Trump, continued the family business. Fred Trump would go on to build houses on undeveloped land in Queens during a time when the population was growing tremendously. When the Great Depression forced thousands of New Yorkers into bankruptcy and foreclosure Fred Trump purchased the foreclosed homes for only a fraction of their actual value and began the family's real estate empire (Kranish and Fisher 2016).

Fred Trump's son, Donald, was a mischievous child who frequently drew the ire of his teachers. A neighbor recalls Donald assaulting another boy and Fred found a stash of switchblades in Donald's room. Fred decided that Donald needed to attend military school for the discipline he needed. After college Donald joined his father in managing a large portfolio of apartment buildings in Queens and Brooklyn. Multiple instances of racial discrimination were documented by authorities at these apartments, where whites but not blacks could rent vacant units. This had been common practice throughout the country but was prohibited after the passage of the 1968 Fair Housing Act. In *United States of America v. Fred C. Trump, Donald Trump and Trump Management, Inc.* Donald Trump adamantly denied the charges despite significant documented evidence of discriminatory actions. This would begin a lifelong pattern of denying things that were blatantly obvious to observers (Kranish and Fisher 2016).

Trump is exceptionally talented at gaining attention for himself and for developing a well-known personal brand. According to Kranish and Fisher, "Trump always took pride in knowing how to win attention for himself, knowing how to feed the media's insatiable appetite for stories about wealth, sex, and controversy—and ideally, all three blended together" (Kranish and Fisher 2016, 232). They also note what his personal brand represents, "Trumpism" consists of "boasts of wealth and influence, a highly public airing of grievances, and dramatic battles staged in gossip columns and courtrooms" (Kranish and Fisher 2016, 92). It was this Trump brand that resonated with the American public as he considered his run for office.

As early as 1987 there was speculation that Trump would run for political office, even the presidency. Some Republicans even started a draft Trump campaign to encourage him to run. They admired his business savvy and knew he connected with the everyday workingman. Richard Nixon sent Trump a letter telling him that he would succeed in politics *when* he decided to become a candidate. In 1988, on *The Oprah Winfrey Show*, Oprah asked Trump about seeking the presidency and he did not rule it out. In 1999, Trump joined the Reform Party and again publicly considered a run for the presidency. Asked by Larry King who he would he select as his running mate, Trump said Oprah. He consulted with Jesse Ventura and Ventura's advisors in Minnesota, but ultimately decided not to seek the Reform Party nomination. Interestingly, Trump won the Michigan and California Reform Party primaries because his name remained on the ballot (Kranish and Fisher 2016).

Trump views politics as a transactional endeavor and does not have a consistent ideological set of views. Trump had supported Hillary Clinton in the past. He contributed to her campaign and hosted fundraisers for her. Later, he would denounce her as "Crooked Hillary." Indeed, "Trump changed parties seven times between 1999 and 2012" (Kranish and Fisher 2016, 302). He would support whoever benefited him in the moment, Democrat or Republican. When Trump did finally decide to run, he was attacked by his Republican competitors for not being a true conservative. His lack of a stable ideological bent, however, did not prevent him from winning the Republican primaries.

There were three things in the political environment that propelled Trump to victory. The first is racism in America. Racism is not new; it is a long-standing historical fact that is part of American culture (Demby 2019). Using racial divisions to motivate voters also is not new. But, beginning in the 1970s, overtly racist appeals were deemed no longer acceptable. The idea was that one needed to win elections by appealing to the largest swath of voters possible. That meant not offending minority voters that could potentially vote for either candidate. Many whites, in particular whites with low levels of education, were not motivated to vote for these inoffensive candidates. Trump brought back overtly racist appeals to motivate poorly educated whites who remained racist because of long standing cultural traditions, but who did not have a candidate who spoke to their preferences. Trump did not do this by himself, the Republican party actively stoked racial resentment during the

Obama presidency and primed the Republican electorate for a candidate like Trump.

The second change has to do with the changing media environment. Many Americans now get their news and information from partisan sources. This means they never encounter information that may be detrimental to their party's candidates and office holders. Everything their party does is right and everything the other party does is wrong. Many Americans are now exposed to intentional misinformation and willingly believe false narratives and incorrect "facts" that support their ideological preferences. In this environment Trump's false claims were believed to be true claims by voters who preferred the false claims because they reinforced their preferred beliefs. Getting caught in a lie typically makes politicians look bad, but because celebrities are given slack when it comes to social norms Trump's falsehoods did not adversely affect him. Instead, they reinforced his support by sending his supporters a signal. His voters had been told for decades that they were not allowed to behave in certain ways and say certain things. They were tired of being politically correct. Trump broke the norms and got away with unacceptable behavior; he could do what they have been prohibited from doing for a long time. This accounts for the exceedingly high levels of enthusiasm among his supporters.

Finally, election rules played in Donald Trump's favor. He faced a primary with sixteen other candidates that allowed his plurality wins to secure his nomination without majority support among Republicans. The electoral college allowed Trump to win the presidency despite having a majority of voters prefer Hillary Clinton. Narrow victories in a few key states meant that Trump had more electoral college votes than the candidate who had more popular vote totals. Thus, the vagaries of US election procedures allowed an unpopular candidate to win.

TALENT

Donald Trump is a master in the art of branding. His name has become synonymous with victory and exaggeration. "The Trump card" is the card that defeats all the other cards, when someone has "the Trump card" they can defeat their opponents. When something is "Trumped up" it is exaggerated. A "Trumped up" charge is a charge that is overly accusatory. In this way the name Trump has entered the American lexicon as a stand in for other words. Certain ideas are represented by Trump himself.

Trump is a "winner" who doesn't like "losers." John McCain was captured by the enemy, this is losing the war, therefore McCain is a loser. Trump said of McCain, "He's not a war hero. He's a war hero because he was captured.

I like people that weren't captured, okay?" (Kranish and Fisher 2016, 325). He's a loser in Trump's view. In contrast, Trump is a winner. He tells his audiences, "We will win so much you'll get tired of winning." The amount of victory would be excessive.

Exaggeration is a crucially important part of the Trump brand. In Trump world everything is big. His bank account, his buildings, his airplane, his crowd size, his love for America, and his ego. This penchant for exaggeration is part of a deliberate media strategy. In *The Art of the Deal* Trump says,

> The final key to the way I promote is bravado. I play to people's fantasies. People may not always think big themselves, but they can still get very excited by those who do. That's why a little hyperbole never hurts. People want to believe that something is the biggest and the greatest and the most spectacular. I call it truthful hyperbole. It's an innocent form of exaggeration—and a very effective form of promotion. (Trump 2005, 58)

In 1976, "Trump had asserted to the Times that he was worth 'more than $200 million,' even though a year earlier, Penn Central negotiators had estimated the Trump family holdings at about $25 million, all of it under Fred's control" (Kranish and Fisher 2016, 89). Accusations that he was inflating the amount of his wealth came up during his campaign because Trump has a penchant for exaggerating.

Perhaps the most important part of his brand is his persona of being a successful businessman. Trump portrayed "himself as a can-do dealmaker with a showy billionaire's tastes and a populist's penchant for plain talk" (Kranish and Fisher 2016, 110). On *The Apprentice*, he proved he was a natural showman. He commanded audience attention, he came up with witty one liners, and he played to the cameras. Trump then used his TV show to secure lucrative licensing deals, "Trump himself initially saw the show as a brand extension and took advantage of his *Apprentice* success to plaster his name on ties, suits, fragrance (Success by Trump), water, lamps, and a credit card" (Kranish and Fisher 2016, 228).

> *The Apprentice* turned Trump from a blowhard Richie Rich who had just gone through his most difficult decade into an unlikely symbol of straight talk, an evangelist for the American gospel of success, a decider who insisted on standards in a country that had somehow slipped into handing out trophies for just showing up. (Kranish and Fisher 2016, 230)

Trump was an aspirational figure to millions of Americans. They viewed him as an exemplar of the American success story. They saw gumption and determination that propels people to victory.

Trump also cultivated his playboy image as a rich debonair gentleman who could woo beautiful women. Early in his real estate career, "He started attending high-voltage parties, accompanied by photogenic women whose company he obtained by calling modeling agencies and asking for help filling out his guest list" (Kranish and Fisher 2016, 172). Trump understood that physically attractive people draw attention. To gain attention Trump made sure to be at the center of a crowd of beautiful women. "In 1996, he bought a controlling share of the Miss Universe pageants, which included the Miss USA and Miss Teen USA competitions" (Kranish and Fisher 2016, 176). He used his role as owner to meet the contestants and to make sure that lots of photographs were taken of himself with them.

In at least five of Trump's resorts there hangs a framed *Time* magazine, dated March 1, 2009, with Trump on the cover. The cover is a forgery, he was not on the cover in that issue (Fahrenthold 2017). As president, the White House released digitally altered photos that fixed his hair, broadened his shoulders, reduced his gut, and elongated his fingers (Milbank 2019). This suggests that Trump is extremely concerned with projecting the right image of himself.

Trump's attempts to manage his optics do not always succeed. In June 2018, when his zero-tolerance policy was separating parents and children at the border the media was displaying images of weeping children crying for their mothers and kids behind and under security fencing that made them look like they were in cages. Trump wanted to look tough, he needed shirtless gang members covered in tattoos in hand cuffs being escorted by police. That would have made him look tough. The wailing babies made him look like a monster. He then signed an executive order maintaining zero tolerance, but that would aim to keep the family units together. His attempt to change the optics failed when *Time* magazine's cover that week featured a distraught pink coated toddler and Melania Trump decided to wear a jacket that said "I don't care" in giant letters on her visit to see the separated children (Cranley 2019). These negative optics helped Trump with a key constituency for the Republican Party.

Trump also developed a reputation for being racist, making it a part of his brand image. Marketing experts who specialize in branding would surely oppose negative associations with brands that they would like to promote. However, Trump was able to use this negative reputation to his advantage. Trump's fame began because of a housing discrimination lawsuit against his business. He stoked racial resentment among white people as a candidate. And, as president, he said white supremacists were "very fine people" (Rucker and Parker 2019).

Hughey has found that "Westernized nations with colonial histories and unequal relations between a powerful white class and a subjugated non-white class now witness a strikingly adamant discourse and movement: growing numbers of white people claim that they are racially oppressed and seek redress against policies, laws and practices that they believe discriminate against them" (Hughey 2014). The myth of white victimization is particularly important to maintain for those with a white supremacist ideology. When a dominant group harms a subjugated group it is called oppression, but victims can claim self-defense when harming their victimizer. Thus, whites need to cast themselves as victims to justify inflicting harm on minorities. This politics of white grievance is based on entitlement. Many whites, and many white men in particular, believe that they are not receiving that to which they are due. This injustice must be remedied they believe, and they support candidates that promise to rectify the unfair victimization they perceive (Kimmel 2013).

Donald Trump's belief in the theory of white victimization by minorities dates to at least the 1980s. A few months after the infamous Willie Horton ads Donald Trump took out a full-page ad in several New York City newspapers demanding the death penalty for the Central Park Five, five black and Hispanic boys who were accused of raping and nearly killing a white woman in Central Park (Kennedy 2019). Around the same time, he told Bryant Gumbel that well-educated blacks have advantages that well-educated whites do not have, suggesting that affirmative action is unfair to whites. In 1993, he told a Congressional committee that Indian casinos got unfair advantages and that the operators of the Foxwood casino "Don't look like Indians to me" (Kranish and Fisher 2016, 292). Trump is reported to have told one of his hotel managers,

> I've got black accountants at Trump Castle and at Trump Plaza—black guys counting my money! I hate it. The only kind of people I want counting my money are short guys that wear yarmulkes every day. Those are the kind of people I want counting my money. Nobody else. . . . Besides that, I've got to tell you something else. I think that the guy is lazy. And it's probably not his fault because laziness is a trait in blacks. It really is; I believe that. It's not anything they can control. (O'Donnell and Rutherford 2016, 115)

He was also accused of excluding black contestants from his beauty pageants (Kranish and Fisher 2016).

Trump also gained attention because of his attractiveness, "*Playgirl* magazine called him one of the sexiest men in America, and in March 1990, he adorned the cover of *Playboy*, brushing against a cover girl eyeing him adoringly" (Kranish and Fisher 2016, 113). It is possible the "halo effect" had some role in Trump's success. Several studies have found that both men and women prefer mates that are more physically attractive, however, women, and not men, also prefer mates that are wealthier. Evolutionary psychologists have found that women prefer these high-status men because they have the resources to provide for possible offspring (Buss 1989; Buss and Schmitt 1993; Singh 1995; Townsend and Wasserman 1998; Hitsch, Hortacsu, and Ariely 2010). Although some might scoff at the idea that Donald Trump is attractive, men and women rate attractiveness by different standards. Thus, his "sexiness" according to a magazine oriented toward women is more a function of his money than his looks. For men, Trump's displays of wealth are a signal of his status/dominance in the social hierarchy.

Trump's multi-faceted persona is a key to his success and Trump worked at maintaining the right public image. When Robert Slater was writing a biography of Trump, Trump threatened to sue if the book portrayed him negatively. Trump was given an advance copy and persuaded the publisher to remove content that he did not like. Rather than risking a lawsuit the publisher accommodated Trump. They even changed the cover to make him look slimmer (Kranish and Fisher 2016).

FAME

Trump first gained media attention because of the federal government's discrimination lawsuit against his properties. Because the Trump company had scores of buildings and thousands of units the lawsuit was a high-profile case. Trump relished the attention, denied the charges, and boasted about his wealth to reporters. In these early years Trump would pretend to be John Barron, a PR spokesperson for the Trump company, when he wanted to direct the media narrative without being directly implicated himself. Later he would use John Miller as a pseudonym. Like many entertainment industry executives, Trump understood that public perceptions of celebrities were constructed productions. Trump used the John Barron or John Miller pseudonyms to construct his public image. The reporters were aware that they were actually talking to Trump himself but went along with the ploy because it gave them a story to write about (Kranish and Fisher 2016).

Trump, who already had political and media connections, gained a boost in fame when Steven Spielberg, Michael Jackson, and Johnny Carson all purchased units in his newly constructed Trump Tower. There was even a rumor that the Prince of Wales and Princess Diana were interested in buying a unit, although the rumor was likely another one of Trump's publicity stunts aimed to lure prospective tenants (Kranish and Fisher 2016).

Trump Tower overlooked the dilapidated Wollman Skating Rink in Central Park. Trump offered to repair and renovate the rink and the city was delighted to avoid the expense. "Trump quickly turned the Wollman project into a free-media gold mine. He held half a dozen press conferences as the work unfolded, irritating city officials" (Kranish and Fisher 2016, 110). Not long after, *Trump: The Art of the Deal* was the top selling book in America. Trump's penchant for publicity helped him sell condos and books, but it also made him famous. It was a skill that would later prove useful when he ran for president.

Trump also engaged in celebrity feuds designed to keep the spotlight on him. As described in chapter 1, celebrities feud with each other to create a spectacle that directs the media attention toward them. As P.T. Barnum reportedly said, "If you want to attract a crowd, start a fight." Trump has feuded with Robert DeNiro, Rosie O'Donnell, and many others. Each side mocks, ridicules, and disparages the other, meanwhile both grab much desired media attention. These ploys are understood by both sides as beneficial to themselves and, importantly, beneficial to their opponent. It is a game where the "rivals" help each other get additional media coverage.

Even fake fighting will draw a crowd (Shafer 2019). Cyndi Lauper's feud with Lou Albano was fabricated by MTV and the WWF. Trump hosted WrestleManias 4 and 5, which began his long-lived partnership with Vince McMahon. Incidentally, this is also how Trump and Jesse Ventura first met. As president, he would appoint Linda McMahon, Vince McMahon's wife, as Administrator of the US Small Business Administration. Trump also participated in WrestleMania 23 where McMahon and Trump staged a fight with each other. The event had 1.2 million pay per view purchasers making it, at the time, the most watched pay per view wrestling event in history (Dawson 2017). The fighting, fake as it might be, compels people to watch. After that Trump made the rounds with celebrity cameos in the movies *Zoolander* and *Home Alone 2* and on sitcoms like *The Drew Carey Show*, *The Nanny*, *The Fresh Prince of Bel-Air*, *Spin City*, and *Sex and the City*. Trump was now firmly in the entertainment business.

His biggest success occurred when he was asked to host his own reality TV show, *The Apprentice*. The first show had 20 million viewers. It soared to 27 million viewers by the end of the first season. The show culminated with *Celebrity Apprentice* piling on star power on top of star power to attract the attention of the American viewer. Because of his success with *The Apprentice* he was asked to host *Saturday Night Live*, where Trump was his stereotypically boastful self. NBC would cancel the show after fourteen years because of Trump's derogatory statements about immigrants (Kranish and Fisher 2016).

By the time Donald Trump decided to seek the presidency he was already a household name with a well-established reputation, but he received nearly $6 billion worth of earned media. The free media coverage that he received dwarfed that of his primary and general election opponents. While the

Trump campaign spent $398 million, the Clinton campaign spent $768 million. Clinton, however, received less than $3 billion worth of earned media (Sultan 2017). This excess in coverage occurred, in part, because the media could not decide if Trump should get "clown coverage" or "serious coverage." The result was that Trump got the "clown" treatment and the serious treatment in equal proportions, thus overwhelming the airwaves with Trump's pontifications (Boydstun and Lawrence 2020). Earned media gives celebrities like Trump a significant advantage in electoral politics. Celebrities get more airtime than their opponents even if they raise and spend less than their competitors.

RESOURCES

Trump began to earn his money by using his political connections to get subsidized deals and tax incentives for his building projects. By 1982, Donald Trump was on *Forbes* magazine's richest 400 Americans list. He used those resources to cultivate relationships with politicians on both sides of the aisle. He provided financial assistance to both Jimmy Carter and Ronald Reagan. In New York, he sometimes donated to two rival candidates seeking the same office. His goal was to back "winners" and remain allied with whoever had the power to help his business (Kranish and Fisher 2016).

In 1990, because of overspending on a lavish lifestyle and making risky investments with borrowed money, Trump had $3.2 billion in debt and his net worth was negative $295 million. The banks put liens on his properties and repossessed his yacht and five helicopters. They sold his airline, Trump Shuttle, to another carrier. Contractors who worked on the Trump properties did not get paid and went bankrupt themselves because of Trump's actions. The bankruptcies of his casinos would tarnish Trump's reputation as a financial genius, but Trump blamed the recession for his troubles (Kranish and Fisher 2016).

Trump used sleight of hand to recover from his financial miscalculations. He created a publicly traded company to lure investors to his enterprises. He transferred ownership of his casinos to the new company, while paying himself more than what the casinos were worth. He paid himself $7 million a year as salary and transferred his debts to the new business. Investors "suddenly found themselves saddled with $1.7 billion of his debt" (Kranish and Fisher 2016, 218). When it went bankrupt, it was the people who invested in Trump that lost millions. Trump was back on the richest 400 list.

He made millions on licensing his name for Trump branded products like furniture, clothing, fragrances, eyewear, boardgames, vodka, soap, steaks, vitamins, and water. By the time he decided to run for president "Trump was receiving income from twenty-five different licensing deals" putting his name on every manner of consumer product (Kranish and Fisher 2016, 236). His most notorious Trump branded product was Trump University which would ostensibly train investors in making money in real estate. Trump University ended with two class action fraud lawsuits by his students who felt swindled by the training program. A Trump branded condominium complex in south Florida and a Trump branded mortgage lending company failed when the housing market crashed in 2008, but under the terms of the contract Trump kept his licensing fees (Kranish and Fisher 2016).

It is difficult to determine just how much money Trump actually has. When he announced that he was running for president his campaign claimed he was worth $8.7 billion. A month later his campaign claimed he was worth over $10 billion. He refused to release his tax documents, claiming that he was prohibited from doing so because he was being audited, so his boasts cannot be verified. Trump has said that exaggeration is part of what made him successful and the wild fluctuation in his statements suggests he is not giving a real assessment of his financial situation. He has also stated that his worth depends on his "feelings" about what he is worth. In 2011, a judge in one of Trump's many lawsuits found that Trump was worth between $200 and $300 million (Kranish and Fisher 2016). Clinton spent nearly double what Trump did on the presidential campaign, but Trump's fame compensated for the disparity (Sultan 2017).

POLITICAL ENVIRONMENT

The political environment was highly favorable to Donald Trump. Republicans had been priming their voters to accept a candidate like Trump with racially divisive appeals that effectively nationalized Nixon's southern strategy. The changing media environment allowed for information bubbles where disinformation could be harnessed for political advantage. These bubbles also downplayed Trump's offensive comments or characterized them in a more favorable light for conservatives. Most important were the election rules. Trump won the Republican primaries with plurality, not majority, support. The electoral college system allowed Trump to lose the popular vote but still carry enough states to secure the presidency.

To understand today's political environment, it is important to begin with some historical perspective. America's most prominent founders were themselves slaveowners. "The Deep South was for at least the three centuries from 1670 to 1970 a caste society. . . . The system's fundamental rationale was that blacks were inherently inferior, a lower form of organism incapable of higher thought and emotion and savage in behavior" (Woodard 2011, 94).

Later, after the Civil War ended the practice of slavery, the authority of the state was used to oppress blacks through Black Codes, Jim Crow, segregation, and discrimination. Vigilante groups of white men, mostly but not exclusively from the south, terrorized and lynched blacks. Racist attitudes also led to the Chinese Exclusion Act as a mechanism to protect white workers. The civil rights movement of the 1950s and 1960s ended state enforced discrimination, but it produced a white backlash that reverberates to this day.

The rise of Donald Trump to the presidency was possible because of the rise of the Dixiecans in the Republican Party. The Dixiecrats were segregationist Democrats whose base of support was in the states of the old confederacy. When LBJ signed the 1964 Civil Rights Act the Dixiecrats began abandoning the Democratic Party. Strom Thurmond, leader of the Dixiecrats, switched from the Democratic Party to the Republican Party and actively opposed the 1964 Civil Rights Act. LBJ also created the Great Society welfare programs designed to alleviate poverty. Because poverty is concentrated among minority groups due to active discrimination, the welfare programs are linked to race. Over the next fifty years Republicans would continue to use racial animus to woo these former Democrats toward the Republican Party (Hughey and Parks 2014; Strickland 2017). They succeeded, and the Dixiecans can now be considered a significant force in Republican Party politics. Yes, they lost the Civil War, but they believed that Trump would give them a victory.

"From the outset, Deep Southern culture was based on radical disparities in wealth and power, with a tiny elite commanding total obedience and enforcing it with state-sponsored terror" (Woodard 2011, 88). These cultural traditions persist, but their loss in the Civil War meant that their preferred society could not be advocated for directly. Southern whites learned to use pretense to accomplish their aims. They claimed that the Civil War was not about defending slavery, it was about protecting state's rights. They argued that segregation was not harmful to blacks; it was used to help blacks be with their own kind in a caring paternalistic manner. They stated that the southern states were not trying to stop blacks from voting, they were merely promoting literacy. Lynchings, they said, occurred because whites had to defend themselves from violent attackers, it was necessary for their own self-preservation. They oppose affirmative action not because they oppose equality for minorities, but because they do not want minorities to be embarrassed by their lack of ability by being put into situations they are cognitively unprepared for. Pretense was used to cast an evil system of racial oppression into a virtuous endeavor that had nothing to do with racial hostility.

Today's undergraduate students understand pretense. If a date invites you to their residence to "watch Netflix and chill," there may be some hanky-panky on this date. Codewords are used to give the appearance of propriety when anything but is the desired outcome. Words like "state's rights" and "welfare" were used as codewords to promote anti-black policies. These "dog whistles," in the parlance of political operatives, surreptitiously motivated southern whites to support Republican candidates. Northern whites did not quite hear the dog whistle. As the section of the country that was home to both Federalists and Unionists the North was not predisposed to state's rights as a political aim. Welfare meant aid to the poor, not a bad idea if you were a working-class person who could, with the loss of a job, easily find themselves in a financial bind. No, pretense did not work for northern working-class whites.

This is where Donald Trump's not so innovative idea comes in. No pretense. Just come out and say it and say it loud! Mexicans are rapists and murders! We need to ban all Muslims from this country! Poorly educated northern whites said, "That's our man!" White nationalists like David Duke and Richard Spencer hailed Trump's victory because they believed their racist ideology was now mainstream and accepted (Strickland 2017). Trump's success did not emerge in a vacuum. The electorate had been primed by many years of GOP efforts to stoke racial resentment among white voters. The election of America's first African American president spurred the Dixiecans to step up their efforts and a surge of white enthusiasm against Barack Obama specifically, and minorities generally, caused the Republican Party to embrace openly racist rhetoric. The Tea Party movement, whose acronym stands for Taxed Enough Already, was superficially about lower taxes and limited government. However, because all Republicans want lower taxes that is not the distinguishing feature of Tea Party supporters. The item that sets Tea Party Republicans apart from Establishment Republicans was racial animus (Hughey and Parks 2014; Gervais and Morris 2018).

The seeds of the Tea Party predate Obama's election. Sarah Palin said that Obama was, "palling around with terrorists" (Alberta 2019, 55). During the final weeks of the 2008 campaign,

> Shouts of "terrorist!" echoed at Republican events nationwide. Conservative websites exploded with last-minute allegations that Obama had been born overseas; that he was a Muslim; that he was a Manchurian candidate. Rock bottom was reached at an October 10 rally in Minnesota, where McCain was repeatedly booed for telling his town hall audience that they should not be scared of Obama. . . . Obama brought out the worst in the Republican base. The seeds of anger and resentment, of nativism and victimization, were sown by forces outside his control long before his ascent. (Alberta 2019, 56)

Ann Coulter specified just how right wingers planned to beat Obama. They would tell people, "You're electing a black guy and he only cares about African Americans" and that "He has a middle name that sounds like a 'terrorist' therefore he's 'soft' on terror and national defense" (Palermo 2008). Indeed, "The right-wing tactic of drawing audience attention to Obama's full name as evidence of his quintessential otherness has been continually deployed to the effect of it becoming a slur" (Hughey and Parks 2014, 75). Emphasizing the *Hussein* in Barack *Hussein* Obama was meant to elicit fear among American voters.

This racial animus was propagated by Republican elected officials. They used race baiting to motivate white voters on the premise that their place in American society was being subverted and that they were in danger of losing their way of life because minorities and immigrants were "taking over" and actively seeking to harm whites. Because the law has been used to oppress blacks and other minorities for most of America's history, it is not a far-fetched or fantastical idea to believe that once in power these minorities would use the law to favor themselves and oppress whites. The theory of white oppression fits in with a world view that views the state as the enforcer of dominant group privileges against those of a subjugated class.

Whites are by no means oppressed, but for many whites, white identity is framed within a set of cultural norms and beliefs in which they are rightfully the heirs of an American system of government where they were to rule and possess a privileged position. The election of Barack Obama and the ongoing demographic changes that will in a matter of time see whites as a numerical minority themselves, causes fear and anxiety among many white Americans. It is an easily understood fear. What if whites get treated the way whites treated minorities? They are smart enough to know that minority groups, and blacks in particular, were not treated well for a long part of America's history.

This fear of retribution was actively used by Republican elected officials and right-wing commentators to motivate white voters to oppose Barack Obama. Glenn Beck and Rush Limbaugh were prominent figures in promoting this campaign. "The narrative of Obama as a racial revenge seeker was repeatedly used to paint Obama as an 'angry' affirmative action president ready to act out 'retribution' against whites and protect other blacks who held antiwhite ideologies. Fox News repeated this trope throughout the spring and summer of 2012, as the GOP geared up for the November election" (Hughey and Parks 2014, 60). Levels of prejudice against blacks as measured in public opinion polls increased from 2008 to 2012, even as a shift occurred from anti-black to anti-immigrant, and specifically anti-Hispanic, rhetoric in the Republicans' "racially divisive appeals" to white voters (Pasek, Stark, Krosnick, Tompson, and Payne 2014; Brown 2016). This suggests that Republican efforts were effective at increasing racist sentiments among white Americans.

In 2011, Rick Perry was booed at a Republican presidential debate for supporting in-state tuition for undocumented immigrants (Marlantes 2011).

Perry is from Texas, a state with a large and growing Hispanic population. An overwhelming 87 percent of Hispanics believe that illegal immigrants who graduate from high school in their state should be eligible for in-state tuition at a public college (Pew Hispanic Center 2011). Rick Perry's views, however, would not win him support with Republican voters. At the other extreme, 86 percent of self-identified Republicans believe that the children of illegal immigrants (who themselves may have been born in the United States) should not qualify for in-state tuition rates (CBS News 2011). In 2015, Perry said "Let no one be mistaken—Donald Trump's candidacy is a cancer on conservatism, and it must be clearly diagnosed, excised and discarded . . . He offers a barking carnival act that can be best described as 'Trumpism': a toxic mix of demagoguery, mean-spiritedness and nonsense that will lead the Republican Party to perdition if pursued" (DelReal 2015).

Even before Trump sought the Republican nomination, discussion of a border wall was occurring. When asked if the United States should build a fence along the border with Mexico, 67 percent of Republicans said we should and 52 percent of Democrats said we should not (CNN/ORC International 2011). When asked, "What should be the main focus of the US government in dealing with the issue of illegal immigration—developing a plan that would allow illegal immigrants who have jobs to become legal US residents, or developing a plan for stopping the flow of illegal immigrants into the US and for deporting those already here?" Seventy-one percent of Republicans supported deportation, while 56 percent of Democrats supported legalization (CNN/ORC International 2011). Additionally, when asked if immigration levels should be increased, decreased, or stay the same a plurality of Republicans said decrease while a plurality of Democrats said stay the same (Gallup Poll 2012).

> Nearly two-thirds (64%) of Americans say that the U.S. becoming a majority-nonwhite nation by 2045 will be a mostly positive change. While about eight in ten Hispanic (80%) and black (79%) Americans say that the impact of the U.S. becoming a majority-nonwhite country will be mostly positive, significantly fewer (55%) white Americans hold this view. Eight in ten (80%) Democrats and two-thirds (67%) of independents, compared to only 36% of Republicans, say that the growth of the nonwhite population will be a positive change. More than six in ten (61%) Republicans believe that the shift to being a majority-nonwhite country will be a mostly negative development. (Vandermaas-Peeler, Cox, Najle, Fisch-Friedman, Griffin, and Jones 2018)

These differences between the parties contribute to why so few Latinos believe that the Republican Party serves their interests and why many believe the Republican Party is hostile toward them. It also gives entrepreneurial candidates issues to support and emphasize if they want the support of Republican voters.

Republicans relied on racist stereotypes to demean and ridicule President Obama. Hughey and Parks studied how "political movements both rely upon and reproduce racist imagery, representations, and symbols (such as apes, witch doctors, fried chicken, watermelons, etc.) under the pretense that their cause is racially neutral or even color-blind" (Hughey and Parks 2014, 11). All these images were used in attacks on Obama. These racist images and symbols were not being propagated by overzealous misguided GOP supporters; they were being used by Republican elected officials to reinforce negative stereotypes about blacks that have a long history in American culture. Soon after Obama's election, "Republicans like Senator Richard Shelby (AL), Senator Roy Blunt (MO), and newly elected governor of Georgia, Nathan Deal, all publicly questioned the legitimacy of Obama's presidency, while several Republican members of Congress signed on to a bill requiring presidential candidates to provide their birth certificates" (Hughey and Parks 2014, 44).

Trump entered the political fray by echoing and amplifying the Tea Party's attacks on Obama. He used his celebrity to garner attention toward the plight of white America in this new dystopian world where blacks can not only vote and win local elections, but also get elected president. "In the spring of 2011, Donald Trump cast himself as a Birther—questioning the legitimacy of Obama's national origin—and also questioned whether he was a mere affirmative action beneficiary and not intellectually equipped to compete at Columbia University and Harvard Law School, Obama's two alma maters" (Hughey and Parks 2014, 12). In one fell swoop Trump employed two racist attacks on President Obama, Trump said,

Now, we have to look at it [the "long form"]. We have to see. Is it real? Is it proper? What's on it? . . . I'm going to look at it and many other people are going to look at it. You're going to have many people looking at it. And obviously, they're going to have to make a decision. Because, it is rather amazing that all of a sudden it materializes. But, I hope it's the right deal. I'm sure, I hope it's the right deal. We have to look at it. A lot of people have to look at it. Experts will look at it. . . . The word is, according to what I've read, that he was a terrible student when he went to Occidental. He then gets to Columbia. He then gets to Harvard. . . . How do you get into Harvard if you're not a good student? Now, maybe that's right, or maybe it's wrong. But I don't know why he doesn't release his records. Why doesn't he release his Occidental records? (Hughey and Parks 2014, 46)

The first attack was that Obama was not a "real American." By promoting the idea that Obama was born in Kenya he was explicitly stating that Obama was not an American. Many Republicans believed that they were being governed by a foreigner, something expressly forbidden by the Constitution. Indeed, 42 percent of Republicans and 75 percent of southern whites believed that Obama was not born in the United States (Hughey and Parks 2014). These "birther sentiments were predominant among conservatives/Republicans and individuals holding anti-Black attitudes" (Pasek, Stark, Krosnick, and Tompson 2015, 482).

The second attack was that Obama was unintelligent. The white supremacist ideology supports the idea that whites are intellectually superior to other races, that other races are inherently less intelligent than themselves. When a minority is successful this is viewed as a violation of the natural order. It only occurs when something nefarious happens. "The tactic of deriding black accomplishment as due to white handouts works to both negate black meritocratic actions and paint the white majority as a group from which resources are being stolen" (Hughey and Parks 2014, 76). Somewhere there was a highly intelligent white who was not admitted to Harvard and Columbia because Obama, a less intelligent black, took something that was theirs through an unfair policy. This reverses the narrative to claim that whites are the victims of racism. An overbearing federal government is harming whites with its affirmative action policies and welfare programs. The limited government ideal is appealing to Republicans because they believe that minorities are guilty of abusing government services and harming white taxpayers. Then, the pretense that smaller government is not about race attempts to reframe the narrative in more appealing terms.

In 2012, Trump "demanded that the president's transcripts be released in order to disprove Trump's claims of Obama's academic mediocrity and to dispel the supposed mysteries surrounding his educational background" (Hughey and Parks 2014, 13). This demand for proof also has racist origins. Prior to the Civil War free blacks had to possess manumission papers to prove they were free. Whites could demand that these papers be presented when encountering any black person and these documents were often deemed to be forgeries even when they were legitimate, thus making the papers nearly useless as a means to prevent capture by entrepreneurial slave traders.

Per the Black Codes, without written documentation, nonwhites were forced to pay poll taxes and/or pass literacy tests in order to vote. Even with documentation or successful passage of tests, many blacks faced charges that documents were forgeries, they were told that more documentation was required, or vigilante groups like the Ku Klux Klan simply intimidated them away from civic and political participation. (Hughey and Parks 2014, 41)

Trump's demand that Obama prove he is a citizen and prove that he had good grades was reminiscent of centuries worth of white demands that blacks prove their worthiness. When proof was provided, the proof was deemed a forgery, and this was taken as evidence that blacks were a deceitful and dishonest group. Dixiecans understood that Trump was on their side even before he announced his run for the presidency.

Once he announced his intentions to seek the presidency, he merely increased his race-baiting. His opening salvo as he announced his candidacy was, "When Mexico sends its people, they're not sending their best. . . . They're sending people that have lots of problems. . . . They're bringing drugs. They're bringing crime. They're rapists. And some, I assume, are good people" (Kranish and Fisher 2016, 323). It was reminiscent of his claims against the alleged Central Park rapists. It was the next day that Dylann Roof murdered nine African American churchgoers in South Carolina. Just a few months later a terrorist attack in San Bernardino California killed 14 people. In response, Trump called for a "total and complete" ban on Muslims entering the country (Kranish and Fisher 2016, 331). Later, he called for a wall to span the entire length of the southern border to stop drugs and illegal immigration. Afterall, the Mexicans are dangerous, he claimed. A majority of Republican voters supported the travel ban and the border wall (Shepard 2017; Sheffield 2019).

The judge assigned to preside over the Trump University fraud case was a Mexican American who had been born in Indiana. Trump said Judge Curiel could not be trusted to treat his case impartially because, "We are building a wall. He's a Mexican. We're building a wall between here and Mexico. . . . This judge is giving us unfair rulings. Now, I say why? Well, I'm building a wall, OK? And it's a wall between Mexico. Not another country" When the interviewer, Jake Tapper, said, "But he's not from Mexico. He's from Indiana." Trump retorted, "He's of Mexican heritage and he's very proud of it" (Wolf 2018). This exchange highlights Trump's acceptance of white grievance politics. He believes he is a white victim of minority unfairness. Even other Republican recoiled at his remarks. Paul Ryan said the comments were, "absolutely unacceptable" and "the textbook definition of a racist comment" but continued to support the Trump campaign (Kranish and Fisher 2016, 342). This begs question, why do they support unacceptable racism? Because the Dixiecans are a core constituency. This group of Americans has been around since before the nation itself was free from British rule (Woodard 2011). We could argue that, as Americans, they deserve political representation, but we must also acknowledge that their goal is to enforce a tyrannical caste system based on race.

Trump's use of "racially divisive appeals" continued as president. He said that Representatives Alexandria Ocasio-Cortez (D-NY), Ilhan Omar

(D-MN), Rashida Tlaib (D-MI) and Ayanna Pressley (D-MA) should "go back and help fix the totally broken and crime infested places from which they came" (Dwyer and Limbong 2019). These anti-immigrant sentiments aimed at people of color are part of a deeply rooted sentiment among many white Americans who, ironically, are themselves descended from immigrants.

> On January 11, 2018, during an Oval Office talk with several U.S. senators about protecting immigrants from Haiti, El Salvador, and African countries in a new immigration package, President Donald Trump unleashed a word that Americans aren't accustomed to hearing from their president. "Why are we having all these people from shithole countries come here?" Trump reportedly asked. (He later denied having said this.) Months earlier, Trump had reportedly complained that Nigerian immigrants would never "go back to their huts" and Haitians "all have aids." He doubled down at the Oval Office meeting. "Why do we need more Haitians?" Trump said. "Take them out." In their stead, Trump spoke of taking in immigrants from great European countries like Norway, and also from Asian countries, since they could help America economically. . . . White House staffers immediately predicted that the leaked conversation would resonate with his base. Perhaps it did. Perhaps it still does. Perhaps racist Americans see the browning of America as the shitholing of America. (Kendi 2019)

After the killing of George Floyd under the knee of a white police officer Trump and other GOP elected officials continued to stoke racial tensions.

> For a glimpse of what the total absence of faith and character looks like, see the Republican Party of Texas. In the aftermath of Floyd's death, a dozen elected leaders of the GOP wrote or retweeted racist memes and conspiracy theories. Comal County Republican Party Chair Sue Gafford Piner propagated the idea that philanthropist George Soros is funding a race war. Bexar County GOP Chair Cynthia Brehm suggested that Floyd's death was staged to hurt President Trump's reelection chances. Texas Agriculture Commissioner Sid Miller wrote that the civil rights protesters are "domestic terrorists who were organized and paid for by George Soros." (Gerson 2020)

What has become abundantly clear is that Donald Trump's views about minorities is not an aberration in American politics. Views like his have a long history and are supported by millions of European-Americans and their elected representatives.

The other important element in Trump's victory has to do with the changing media environment. Partisans acquire their information from biased sources. These sources include websites, radio, and television. It often begins with someone inventing a horrible act committed by a politician. Then the rumors are spread on social media. Websites and blogs that are created and maintained by crackpots and trolls then report on the rumor. Soon after, radio and television hosts get wind of the allegation and report what is being said. People without a capacity for critical thinking may believe that the reports are true. This is how the belief that "Hillary Clinton and her top aides were . . . running a child-trafficking ring out of a Washington pizza parlor" came to pass (Aisch, Huang, and King 2016). The partisan bias is clear, "Faced with alternative realities, Americans are increasingly inclined to choose the one associated with their party, even if a moment's reflection would indicate that it's less plausible" (Patterson 2019, 22). Republicans were more likely to believe Hillary Clinton was a child sex trafficker and Democrats were more likely to believe that George W. Bush was complicit in the 9/11 terrorist attacks (Patterson 2019).

Often, it is politicians themselves who are responsible for spreading the rumor. When Barack Obama was working to pass his health care proposal Republicans like Sarah Palin, John Boehner, and Chuck Grassley spread the "Death Panels" rumor. This was the idea that the health care plan included provisions to euthanize seniors to reduce health care costs. The false statements are designed to scare the public to support their own position, in this case opposition to the plan. Two-thirds of Republicans believed the claim was true and nearly every American had heard about the "Death Panels" (Patterson 2019).

Things become dangerous when Americans take make believe as reality, "Rationality goes out the window when citizens lose touch with reality. The problem of the misinformed is not their logic. Their decisions make perfect sense given what they believe. The problem is that they are living in an alternative world" (Patterson 2019, 17). When it comes to the ACA, "for those who believe there are no benefits and lots of costs, opposition to the law and support for repeal is rational" (Longoria 2018, 99). If one believes the government has a plan to actively take steps to kill seniors, then opposition to the plan would be the right choice and fear of the people trying to kill grandma would make sense. American voters now use delusions as a basis for their political preferences. More philosophically, subjectivist reality seems to be the new norm in American politics, "For some, your empirical evidence is a lie and their make believe is 'reality.' For a subjectivist, their reality is as real to them as your reality is real to you" (Longoria 2018, 99).

Thomas Patterson pins some of the blame on journalists, "Rather than take responsibility for the facts, journalists strive for 'balance'—giving each side a chance to make its case. It's a sensible approach in many situations and protects the journalist from accusations of bias. Yet the approach breaks down when one side is making things up" (Patterson 2019, 26). Climate scientists agree that climate change is a man-made phenomenon and that it is causing severe harm to our planet. Donald Trump said that "The concept of global

warming was created by and for the Chinese in order to make U.S. manufacturing non-competitive" and "Global warming is an expensive hoax!"
(Dodgson 2016). Now it becomes a choice of who to believe. Two perspectives were presented in the media and the person who was given the different
views is left alone to indicate their preference. Giving equal weight to made
up fabrications gives it more credence than it deserves and perpetuates the
false narratives. Trump's claim was even more ingenious because it perpetuated a racist stereotype, that the Chinese are devious people. So, in addition
to the liberals lying about climate change, it is also non-white foreigners that
are dishonest and malicious in their intent.

Donald Trump used partisan biases and alternative realities to his advantage. His false claims were reported as truthful statements by media outlets
that favored his candidacy. When the media reported that his claims were
false, Trump claimed the media was biased against him. Their accusations,
calling him a liar, was proof of their bias. We live in an extremely dangerous
political environment where facts do not matter because facts and fabrications have equal footing. Echoing Glynn's "alternative popular knowledges"
(Glynn 2000, 231), Trump's campaign manager, Kellyanne Conway, infa-
mously stated that their campaign had "alternative facts" than those being
reported by the mainstream media (Gajanan 2017). After his defeat in the
2020 presidential election Trump began to falsely claim the election was
stolen and that there had been massive voter fraud. Mitt Romney compared
this lie to professional wrestling, "Here in the U.S., there's a growing recognition that this is a bit like WWF, that it's entertaining, but it's not real"
(Vakil 2021). In other words, Republicans know it's a fabrication, but they
like it anyway.

Lying is not a new strategy for politicians and savvy politicians have been
long aware of how voter biases can be utilized for their own advantage. Adlai
Stevenson said, "You will find that the truth is often unpopular and the contest between agreeable fancy and disagreeable fact is unequal" (Stevenson
1958, 386). The false narratives that have been constructed by conservative
commentators and amplified by conservative news outlets perpetuated long
standing racist beliefs.

Fox News and associates constantly constructed the average white viewer as a
hard-working American who is, at base, frightened by the unfair and racialized
agenda of Obama. Characterizing the white viewer as an American under the
assault of a dark and dangerous "other" implies a racial bystander in the racial
drama directed by the Obama administration. For example, in July of 2008
Glenn Beck engaged in a pithy race-based fear-mongering remark on his Fox
News show. He stated that Obama "has a deep-seated hatred for white people

or the white culture" and that Obama "is, I believe, a racist." (Hughey and Parks 2014, 68)

The view that black people are on a mission to harm white people creates fear among white people and it justifies actions to be taken in "self-defense" to protect white interests. Sadly, some whites act to "defend themselves" by walking into churches and Wal-marts to kill blacks and Hispanics as Dylann Roof and Patrick Crusius did.

Trump's brand of white victimization had been stewing in the American perception of him for decades. Blacks were out to hurt a white man's business with the discrimination charges. Blacks and minorities hurt the white taxpayers when they were awarded a settlement for their wrongful convictions, they should have been executed according to Trump. The Indian casinos had unfair advantages over his white owned casinos. The injustices that Trump claimed to endure resonated with whites who were now being told through all manner of media that they were the victims of minority oppression. At the Republican nominating convention only 18 of the 2,472 delegates were black (Kranish and Fisher 2016). Republicans are almost exclusively the party of white people.

The 2016 election results demonstrate a highly racialized vote. A majority of white voters, 58 percent, supported Trump. This included 53 percent of white women and 63 percent of white men. Further analysis found that "Among white voters, racial resentment and anti-immigration views, along with a negative outlook on the national economy, all boosted support for Trump (along with a number of demographic factors, including education)" (Gervais and Morris 2018, 224). Meanwhile, 88 percent of African Americans, 65 percent of Hispanics, and 65 percent of Asians supported Clinton (Tyson and Maniam 2016). Keep in mind that many of these minorities live in an information universe where whites are, every day, discriminating against them and often murdering them in cold blood just because of their ethnicity.

More than any other candidate Donald Trump likely benefited from celebrity slack. He unleashed a barrage of outrageous statements any one of which probably would have doomed ordinary politicians. Leaving aside the racist comments already discussed, Trump made demeaning comments about women. When debate moderator Megyn Kelly asked Trump to explain his degrading comments toward women he tried to deflect by saying he only made those comments about Rosie O'Donnell. By stoking another celebrity feud he could keep himself the center of attention. Just before the election a recording from Access Hollywood caught Trump discussing his interactions with women,

Chapter 10

I moved on her, and I failed. I'll admit it. . . . I did try and fuck her. She was married. . . . I've got to use some Tic Tacs, just in case I start kissing her. You know, I'm automatically attracted to beautiful—I just start kissing them. It's like a magnet. Just kiss. I don't even wait. . . . And when you're a star, they let you do it. You can do anything. . . . Grab them by the pussy. . . . You can do anything. (Kranish and Fisher 2016, 367)

Trump understands that he benefits from celebrity slack. Indeed, the damning video seemed not to adversely impact his electoral prospects. He knew he could get away with it and he did.

Multiple accusations of sexual assault were leveled against Trump. His ex-wife Ivana claimed to have been assaulted during their divorce proceedings, but later recanted. Contestants from the beauty pageants he owned said Trump made unwanted sexual advances and that they endured "inspections" where he would rate the women's bodies. He was accused of unwanted kissing and groping. In all, twenty-five women accused Trump of similar behavior. Trump bragged about his actions on the *Access Hollywood* video and on the *Howard Stern Show*, but he would later call the women liars and claim that some of the women were too ugly for him to be interested in to begin with (Kranish and Fisher 2016; Relman 2019).

He would often advocate violence against protestors at his campaign rallies. Trump's violent rhetoric gave license to those with personal hatreds to act on them. ABC News "identified at least 36 criminal cases where Trump was invoked in direct connection with violent acts, threats of violence or allegations of assault. . . . The perpetrators and suspects identified in the 36 cases are mostly white men . . . while the victims largely represent an array of minority groups—African-Americans, Latinos, Muslims and gay men" (Levin 2019). One man, Cesar Sayoc, whose van was covered with pro-Trump stickers, sent mail bombs to Democratic critics of Trump and to members of the media (Levin 2019).

Trump was not harmed politically for any of his uncouth behavior. Trump succeeded because he likely benefited from celebrity slack and because his personal brand fit the moment.

Trump won because he intuited that his celebrity would protect him from the far stricter standards to which politicians are normally held—one bad gaffe and you're finished. He won because he understood that his outrageous behavior and intemperate comments only cemented his reputation as a decisive truth-teller who gets things done. And he won because he had spent almost forty years cultivating an image as a guy who was so rich, so audacious, and so unpredictable that he would be beholden to no one. (Kranish and Fisher 2016, 363)

He disparaged P.O.W.s. He mocked disabled people. He made racist comments. He bragged about assaulting women. Trump's supporters were not turned off by his behavior, many of them cheered it.

Like some of the other celebrities that won elected office, Trump benefited from idiosyncratic election rules. He faced 16 other candidates in a crowded GOP primary. This allowed him to secure the Republican nomination without winning a majority of the votes among Republican primary voters. The electoral college, a system where states are given electors to vote in presidential elections, allowed Trump to lose the popular vote and get elected president. "The margin of the GOP victory was found in three states—Pennsylvania, Michigan, and Wisconsin—which Trump won by a total of 77,744 votes" (Alberta 2019, 538). Overall, Clinton received 3 million more votes than Trump did (Pilkington 2020). Unsatisfied, Trump claimed millions of illegal votes were cast for Clinton and that he had won the popular vote of qualified voters. There was not any actual evidence to support his assertions (Struyk and Pearle 2017). Trump was merely attempting to reinforce his "winner" brand by making the claims and his "victim" brand by blaming undocumented immigrants for vote totals.

The general election was peculiar because both Trump and Clinton were unpopular. For both, a majority of American voters had a negative opinion of them. Although Trump's unfavorable ratings were worse than Clinton's (Cillizza 2016). Thus, many voters had to choose between two candidates they did not like. It is possible, if not likely, that had Trump faced a candidate that had approval ratings above 50 percent he would have lost the contest.

CONCLUSIONS

Trump is what Lasswell would call a "dramatizing character." The central feature "is the demand for immediate affective response in others. The dramatizing character may resort to traces of exhibitionism, flirtatiousness, provocativeness, indignation; but in any case all devices are pivoted around the task of 'getting a rise out of' the other person" (Lasswell 1976, 62). Trump has many of the characteristics of dramatizing characters, including erratic judgements, disinterest in details, a penchant for being a "publicity hound," a belief that others are stupid, breaches of decorum, use of language "studded with 'color' adverbs and adjectives," displays favoritism toward the young and physically attractive, is repelled by and overreacts to "hysteria among women," is mercurial in the treatment of others, and is impressed with "nationalistic and totalitarian regimes" (Lasswell 1976, 78–81).

Dramatizing characters are "persons who consciously seek power in spite of unconscious tendencies that handicap them" (Lasswell 1976, 94). Lasswell writes, "In addition to arrogance, power holders often undermine themselves by provoking revenge against the terror and degradation which they impose upon others" (99). Donald Trump got himself impeached as president because he enraged his opponents. He also willingly provided the evidence of his own wrongdoings. He would publicly ask foreign governments for help in his re-election efforts and then cry foul when Democrats accused him of seeking foreign assistance for his re-election efforts. When he selected a new person for a high-level executive branch position, he would lavish praise upon their character and accomplishments. When he would fire these same people, he would ridicule them for their ineptitude and stupidity. Many of them would retaliate by publicly exposing the president's own ineptitude and character flaws. In short, Trump actively creates dramatic contests between himself and his allies and adversaries.

Donald Trump was highly skilled at gaining attention for himself and developing a personal brand that resonated with many Americans. He was well known as a prominent real estate developer whose ostentatious lifestyle drew attention. He actively sought out tabloid headlines that exposed his private life to the general public. He metamorphosed from a businessman to an entertainer with his hit show *The Apprentice*. Although he is likely exaggerating his wealth, he is probably worth several hundred millions of dollars. Like other celebrity politicians, his wealth, and his connections with other wealthy people, while helpful in election efforts, are less important than the tremendous amount of free media coverage they receive from the press. He also benefited from celebrity slack, his outrageous statements would cause a stir, upset many people, and would promptly be dismissed as par for the course. Trump, like other celebrities, was able to break social norms and conventions, without lasting repercussions. The most important reason for his victory, however, was an electoral system that allows someone to win without majority support from the voters.

Chapter 11

Reverse Migration and Celebrity Losers

This chapter will explore politicians that went on to become celebrities and celebrities that lost elections. Many authors have argued that celebrification allows for entertainers and politicians to be interchangeable (Street 2003; West and Orman 2003; Van Krieken 2012; Wheeler 2013). Industry professionals can move back and forth between industries. This chapter adds further evidence of this by looking at politicians who became entertainers. While the power trifecta of talent, fame, and resources are an advantage in electoral politics it is not enough to secure victory for most celebrity candidates. This chapter explores the election losses of several high-profile celebrities. It is, ultimately, the political environment that seems to be the decisive factor in whether a celebrity can successfully win an election.

Fred Thompson, Sarah Palin, and Jerry Springer were politicians before they became celebrities. Their career trajectories are evidence that the skills that are necessary for success in politics are useful in the entertainment industry. Other former politicians also transitioned to a career in the entertainment industry. Former Arkansas governor Mike Huckabee became a political talk show host on Fox News, Al Gore worked on the Oscar winning film *An Inconvenient Truth*, and Barack Obama produced and won an Oscar for *American Factory*. Pete Buttigieg guest hosted *Jimmy Kimmel Live!* and seemed poised to make a similar move before being picked for Secretary of Transportation by the Biden administration. The linkages and similarities between the two industries is remarkable.

Of course, not every celebrity is successful in their bid for elected office. Shirley Temple ran for California's 11th congressional district in 1967 but was defeated in the primary. Gary Coleman ran for governor of California and lost to Schwarzenegger during the recall election. Linda McMahon ran for the US Senate in 2010 and 2012, in both cases she won the Republican primary but lost the general election to the Democratic candidate. Roseanne Barr ran for president under the Green Party label but lost the nomination to Jill Stein in 2012. Cynthia Nixon ran for governor of New York in 2018 but lost the primary to incumbent Andrew Cuomo. Stacey Dash ran for California's 44th congressional district in 2018 but withdrew a month later.

When celebrities lose, they lose for conventional reasons. Despite having high name recognition and a tremendous amount of free media coverage they often lose because they are running in an unfavorable district or state for their party. They also lose if they have public personas that do not match the politics of the time. Their fame can work against them when they advocate for unpopular ideas or are typecast in an unfavorable way. At other times, their candidacies are viewed as publicity stunts, and they are not taken seriously. Celebrities are by no means guaranteed a victory if they decide to run for public office.

FRED THOMPSON

Fred Thompson grew up in rural Lawrence County, Tennessee in a family that was active in local politics. The area was a Democratic stronghold dating back to the Civil War and remained so through the Great Depression as FDR's Tennessee Valley Authority promised jobs to unemployed locals. His dad unsuccessfully ran for sheriff of Lawrence County, a position that had become highly corrupt due to the influence of bootleggers during Prohibition. Thompson indicates that he supports the ideas of checks and balances and limited government because, "Mistakes, miscalculations, and corruption have too often accompanied the ambitions of individuals as well as governments" (Thompson 2010, 66). That, he argues, "is the essence of conservatism" (Thompson 2010, 66). These sentiments are what drove Fred Thompson to support Republican Party politics.

In 1968, Thompson was John T. Williams's campaign manager in Williams's losing race for Tennessee's 7th congressional district—against Ray Blanton. Thompson was able to meet Ronald Reagan when Reagan appeared at some campaign rallies for Tennessee Republican candidates that year. Because Nixon won the presidency that year Republicans were looking for district attorneys and assistant district attorneys to be appointed by the president. Thompson secured one of the ADA jobs prosecuting federal criminal cases. In 1972, Thompson was Senator Howard Baker's campaign manager for Baker's successful re-election to the US Senate—against Ray Blanton. In 1973, Thompson gained national fame when he was minority council during the Watergate impeachment proceedings. It was Thompson's questioning of Alexander Butterfield that led to the public revelation of a secret White House audio recording system. Thompson proved that he could be cool under pressure and be effective in front of television cameras (Gill 2007; Thompson 2010).

Because of this fame he was called upon to take a case against Tennessee governor Ray Blanton. The case involved the wrongful termination of a parole board appointee and accusations of executive interference in parole board decisions. The governor's office had been taking bribes in exchange for releasing convicted criminals and the FBI was investigating when Thompson filed his civil case against the governor. Dramatically, one of the witnesses against the governor was murdered a few days before the trial began. Thompson won his case and criminal charges against the governor soon followed. The governor and his associates were convicted of bribery and removed from office (Gill 2007; Thompson 2010).

Thompson helped his client secure a book deal to tell the story and the book was turned into the biographical film *Marie* in which Thompson played himself as the lead attorney. Thompson landed the role because the producers of the film went to Tennessee to interview the actual participants of the story to gain context and details that may be useful for the film. When it was time to cast the film, the producers invited Thompson to audition. His performance was superior to that of the other aspirants for the role of "Fred." One should hope that one could play oneself pretty well. He was offered the role and was asked if he had an agent to contact about the contract. Thompson did not have an agent, but since he was a lawyer, he felt he could negotiate the contract himself. He accepted what he believed was a fair payment and did not take the enterprise with any great deal of seriousness. Being a movie star was not one of Thompson's goals in life. Later, he found out from real Hollywood agents that he should have gotten paid a lot more for the role. The other actors in the film included Sissy Spacek, Jeff Daniels, and Morgan Freeman. Thompson's first acting lesson was done by observing the actors in the film he was already in. Thompson said, "I didn't mean to be an actor or be in the movies. It just kind of happened with no planning on my part" (Thompson 2010, 80).

He went on to appear in twenty-four movies and four television shows between 1985 and 1994. The movies included *The Hunt for Red October*, *Days of Thunder*, *Die Hard 2*, *Cape Fear*, and *In the Line of Fire* (IMDb "Fred Thompson"). By the time he decided to run for the US Senate in 1994, he had mastered the skills necessary for on screen performances. Thompson, "tends to play characters like himself, bigger-than-life political guys who speak in a withering Dixie cadence and don't blink much. In one movie, 'Born Yesterday,' he even played a U.S. senator" (Powers 1994). Because Al Gore was now Vice President Tennessee had a special election to fill Gore's seat. Even before becoming a big-time actor, Thompson was already well known in Tennessee for his role in ousting the former governor and for his role in the Watergate hearings. On the campaign trail Thompson signed auto-graphs from movie fans and recreated scenes from the movies he was in. The fans/voters would cheer as he recreated scenes from their favorite movies live in front of them (Powers 1994).

Thompson knew the importance of image management and leased a pick-up truck for his campaign. The truck symbolized the life of hardwork-ing rural Americans, though Thompson himself drove a Lincoln Continental. The rented truck became a campaign issue. Thompson's opponent said that Thompson was, "a lobbyist and actor who talks about lower taxes, talks about change, while he drives a rented stage prop and plays the role of sena-tor" (Powers 1994). At least one voter was skeptical of Thompson because of his past as an actor. The Tennessee resident said, "I'm concerned that Mr. Thompson used a lot of his acting abilities and props and sets to persuade Tennessee voters to vote for him" (*Pittsburgh Post-Gazette* November 15, 1994). Ultimately his past as an actor was not a barrier to his success.

A *Washington Post* reporter noted that "the truck, which is all about being true to one's country origins, is closer to the heart of what this race is about than any policy differences between the two men. It is the antithesis of Washington, and the embodiment of all things good and honest and unpre-tentious and hardworking about the true America. After all, in 'The Hunt for Red October,' one of the defecting Russian officers wants nothing more than to live in Montana and own a pickup truck" (Powers 1994). Reporters cover-ing celebrity politicians often weave in elements from the celebrity's films in their political reporting of the campaign. This serves to reinforce the imagery the polebrity is utilizing to gain votes.

He made use of his acting skills in his run for the US Senate. Reformulating a line made famous by George Burns, Thompson said, "In politics they say that sincerity is very important. Once you are able to fake that the rest of it is easy" (Thompson 2010, 107). He developed a brand as an authority figure. He looked like someone who should be a high-ranking government official and so he often portrayed military commanders, cabinet officials, district attorneys, and senators (Gill 2007; *Pittsburgh Post-Gazette* November 15, 1994). It was not that much of leap in the public imagination to see Thompson as an actual high-ranking government official, he had been pretending to be one for nearly a decade.

He handily defeated his Democratic opponent with more than 60 percent of the vote (*Washington Post* November 10, 1994). Like other polebrities Thompson benefited from earned media and won despite raising less money. Thompson raised $3,887,713 and his opponent Jim Cooper raised 4,016,192 (FEC "Fred Dalton Thompson"; FEC "Jim Cooper"). Thompson served eight years in the US Senate, completing a partial term, and being reelected to one full term. Thompson retired from politics to return to acting. Recalling his decision Thompson said, "I had resumed my acting career. (Having been in law and politics, some might say, I'd never left it.)" (Thompson 2010, 193). The quip is suggestive. Thompson, more than others, knew the remarkable similarities in the two professions. The skills of image management and stagecraft are vitally important in both.

Thompson then spent the next five years on one of America's longest running shows, *Law and Order*, where he portrayed a district attorney. The blurring of the lines between entertainment and politics is especially true in Thompson's career path. He pretended to be a US senator before becoming an actual US senator. He was an actual district attorney who later pretended to be a district attorney on TV (IMDb "Fred Thompson"). In 1993, just before his bid for the US Senate, he was in *In The Line of Fire* with Clint Eastwood who had returned to the movies after his stint as mayor. It is likely the two Republicans talked about politics, and Fred Thompson may have been inspired by Eastwood's back and forth transitions from acting to public service.

In 2007, Thompson decided to make a bid for the White House. In true Hollywood fashion he made his announcement on *The Tonight Show with Jay Leno* (O'Donnell 2007). He entered the race late, only a few months before the Iowa caucuses. After poor showings in the early states Thompson dropped out on January 19, 2008 (Thompson 2010). He lost despite having remarkably high name recognition. He had developed a brand as an authority figure. He portrayed and had come to symbolize the Establishment. This was exactly the wrong thing to be in 2008. Barack Obama would become the first African American president and his opponent, John McCain, was himself a maverick who bucked Republican orthodoxy on several occasions. The public was in a very anti-establishment mood, so Thompson's persona worked against him. He did, however, continue to act in television and movies utilizing the skills he had first learned in politics.

SARAH PALIN

Sarah Palin's family moved to Wasilla when she was 8 years old. She married Todd Palin in 1988 and had five children with him. She earned a journalism degree and after college she covered sports for a local television station and was the sports anchor during weekend broadcasts. This is where she learned to be comfortable in front of television cameras (Palin 2009). Having been extremely religious since childhood Sarah's first foray into politics was an attempt to change the Wasilla school board to promote creationism and remove Darwinian evolution from science classes. The public hospital in the area was overseen by a governing board. In 1992, Palin was actively involved in local church efforts to elect a pro-life majority to the board and ban abortions. They succeeded and the new board declared that abortions would no longer be performed at the hospital. In that same year Palin ran for city council by canvassing the less than 8,000 residents of Wasilla. With support from the evangelical community Palin won her first election. With a court injunction preventing the hospital from stopping abortion procedures, the evangelical community urged Palin to run for mayor. The Alaska Supreme Court eventually made the injunction permanent (McGinniss 2011).

Palin had supported the creation of Wasilla's first ever police force in 1992. The city was experiencing a crime wave due to pain killer addiction in the community. There were also problems with drunk driving and domestic abuse. Bars in Wasilla were open until 5 a.m. but were closed at 2 a.m. in Anchorage. The mayor had proposed a 2 a.m. closing for bars in Wasilla because drunks from Anchorage would drive to Wasilla to keep drinking until 5. In addition, domestic violence calls peaked in Wasilla just after 5 a.m. when drunk husbands and boyfriends returned home. But backlash from the over 200 DUI arrests in the first year of the police force was gaining momentum in the community (McGinniss 2011).

Palin sided with the bar owners who viewed the mandated 2 a.m. closing as a violation of their freedoms. Palin had also secured political support from Lyda Green, the local state senator. Green asked her staff to help Palin in the mayor's race. Tuckerman Babcock was a Republican political strategist and Laura Chase would be Palin's campaign manager. As a result, "Big jars into which Palin campaign donations could be placed appeared on all Wasilla bars and were filled to the brim nightly. In the same saloons, pictures of incumbent mayor Stein were placed inside the urinals" (McGinniss 2011, 68). With a coalition of evangelicals, drunks, and bar owners Palin was elected mayor of Wasilla in 1996 by a vote of 661 to 440 (McGinniss 2011).

The Palin campaign spread a series of lies about the incumbent mayor. Even though he was a member of the NRA, the Palin campaign claimed he was anti-gun. Even though he was a Lutheran, they claimed he was Jewish. Both charges were deal breakers for the pro-gun evangelicals that dominated local elections. They played up the "hockey mom" persona and called attention to Palin's part in the Wasilla High School women's basketball team that won the state championship in 1982. The community still had a great deal of pride in the team Sarah was a part of more than a decade prior. By capitalizing on local political issues and her long-standing relationships with community members Sarah Palin began her ascent in Alaska politics (McGinniss 2011).

An acquaintance that knew Sarah very well during her time as mayor recalled Palin's strategy for city council meetings, "I remember she'd say, 'I have to go to a fuckin' meeting tonight.' And she'd be like, 'I got on my biggest push-up bra. I'm gonna get what I want tonight.' Like she had some motion before the city council and she was gonna use her titties to get their votes" (McGinniss 2011, 125). Palin likely has not read the academic litera-ture around the "halo effect," but as a physically attractive person she learned to use her physical attractiveness to get what she wanted. She knew from experience that when she looked good, she could persuade people and get what she wanted from them.

In *Going Rogue* Palin acknowledges how her physical attractiveness has helped her become successful.

> Then I shocked my friends and family, put on a sequined Warrior-red gown, danced the opening numbers, gave the interview, and uncomfortably let my butt be compared to the cheerleaders' butts. I played my flute, and I won. In fact, I won every segment of the competition, even Miss Congeniality. The Miss Wasilla Scholarship paid my college tuition that fall. The following summer, I progressed to the next round and was crowned second runner-up and Miss Congeniality in the Miss Alaska Scholarship Pageant. I had to admit it was good tuition money, as well as a good testing ground for public speaking and issue advocacy, and I was happy to be even more involved in the community via this nontraditional adventure that took me out of my comfort zone. I went on to pay for two more years of college the same way. (Palin 2009, 60)

Palin was awarded scholarship money because of her looks. She learned to speak in front of an audience and to perform for them. Reagan, Eastwood, and Schwarzenegger became celebrities because of their good looks and then became politicians. Palin became a politician and then a celebrity television host. The "halo effect" has a real impact on individual outcomes and it is powerful in both the entertainment and political industries.

In 2002, she ran for lieutenant governor but lost in the primary to Loren Leman. Because of her strong performance she was appointed to the Oil and Gas Conservation Commission by the new governor. Randy Ruedrich was another member of the commission. He was also chairman of the Alaska GOP and an RNC member. According to Palin, "Ruedrich was the key fund-raiser for the GOP and naturally solicited party dollars from the oil and gas industry players we were to be regulating, something that should have immediately been pegged as a conflict of interest" (Palin 2009, 112). While serving on the commission Palin played a key role in uncovering Ruedrich's corruption and gained a reputation as someone who would stand up against her own party leaders to protect the interests of Alaskans.

Then, in 2006, she ran for governor amid another major public corruption scandal in Alaska. Eleven Republicans were indicted and convicted on charges of public corruption, including US Senator Ted Stevens. Tony Knowles was the Democratic candidate for governor; however, he had previously served as governor from 1994 to 2002 and ran a strong campaign for the US Senate two years earlier, narrowly losing to Lisa Murkowski. He was certainly viewed as part of the old guard in Alaskan politics. Palin was an anti-establishment fresh face and won the gubernatorial election (McGinniss 2011).

Palin won despite having extremist religious views,

> For at least ten years, since first learning about it at Mary Glazier's prayer group and at the Assembly of God, Sarah had subscribed to an evangelical Christian ideology frequently referred to as dominionism. The goal of dominionists is to put Christian extremists into positions of political power in order to end America's constitutionally mandated separation of church and state. Dominionists believe that America was founded as a specifically Christian republic and that Christians should control all levels of government. (McGinniss 2011, 71)

During her campaign for governor, she said that public schools should teach creationism, a view she had held since her days in Wasilla politics. Her campaign staff convinced her to back pedal on the remarks, but these were her actual beliefs. She believed she was called on by God to lead Alaska and the United States (McGinniss 2011).

Palin had a genuine talent for dealing with people, "She could be charming in superficial social situations. She had the knack of making people feel they knew her, even if all they ever glimpsed was the façade. This was no small talent" (McGinniss 2011, 127). During the debate with her rival, "the candidates engaged in an exchange of 'there you go again' remarks that would've made Ronald Reagan proud. It was classic schoolyard one-upmanship: 'There you go again,' Palin said in the sing-songy voice she uses when trying to score a zinger" (Bragg 2006, B1). A reporter noted, "It was her most impressive sparring of the campaign, and she won the round by sounding knowledgeable but not nasty" (Bragg 2006, B1).

Palin was an extremely popular governor early on. In May 2007, she earned a 93 percent job approval rating in the state, making her the most popular governor in America (Cauchon 2007). Bumper stickers began to appear all over the state, they read, "ALASKA—THE COLDEST STATE WITH THE HOTTEST GOVERNOR" (McGinniss 2011, 218). However, Palin used the office to satisfy her personal biases. The previous governor had hired more than twenty members of minority communities to work in his administration. Palin fired all non-white personnel that reported to the governor's office because she was not comfortable with them. She also sought to fire Alaska State Trooper Michael Wooten. Wooten was Palin's sister's ex-husband and the chief of the Alaska State Troopers, Walt Monegan, refused to comply because there were not any legitimate grounds for the termination. Palin retaliated by firing Monegan for refusing to fire Wooten. The legislature investigated and found that Palin had violated state ethics laws and abused her power by attempting to have Wooten fired (McGinniss 2011).

The controversies over the firings were overshadowed by Palin's being selected by John McCain as his vice presidential running mate. Initially, it seemed as though McCain had selected a "working mom extraordinaire" that could cut into the Democrats advantage with women voters (Alexander 2010, 212). Unfortunately, she performed poorly in media interviews including the infamous interview with Katie Couric in which she could not name any newspapers she read. She also claimed that Alaska's proximity to Russia gave her foreign policy credentials and experience (Alexander 2010). It was clear that she was not prepared for the situation she found herself in. Her folksy ineptitude was parodied on *Saturday Night Live*. Tina Fey's "I can see Russia from my house" and winking "Ya Betchas" became comedic gold. *SNL*'s audience increased to 14 million viewers and many millions more than that in on-line viewing after the original air dates. Many Americans could not differentiate between the real Sarah Palin and Tina Fey's impersonation of her,

> The conjoining of the real and fictional political personas can also occur because the sketches may not venture too far from the ridiculousness of political reality itself, using the raw material of the actual words and events that arise each week. A particularly powerful example occurred in 2008 when the show's writers used many of Sarah Palin's words verbatim from a news interview, with occasional satiric additions and comedic inflections to drive the point home. (Marx, Sienkiewicz, and Becker 2013, 84)

The satire was effective because it highlighted real personality attributes. It also propelled Palin to "media and pop culture stardom" (Marx, Sienkiewicz, and Becker 2013, 81).

Despite the ridicule, she became the *de facto* leader of what would become known as the TEA Party Movement (Payne 2014). Her discomfort with minorities and her accusations that Obama was "palling around with terrorists" resonated with a growing group of Republican voters (Alberta 2019, 55). She resigned as governor in July 2009 claiming that she could no longer perform her job effectively because of the media attention and ethics complaints being filed against her (Balz 2009). McGinniss writes, "Quitting her job as Alaska's governor enabled Sarah to make the jump from politician to full-time celebrity" (McGinniss 2011, 305). She became a pop culture phenomenon,

> It would be cruel and wrong to dub Mrs. Palin the "Paris Hilton of politics," but her career did exploit a similar dynamic. As in Hilton's case, the media was simultaneously fascinated and repelled by Palin—appalled by her errors of judgment but never quite able to turn off the camera. Palin was elevated to fame not on the basis of experience but of personality. (Stanley 2014, 250)

She began touring the country to participate in TEA Party events and claimed that "death panels" were part of the Affordable Care Act.

In November 2010 *Sarah Palin's Alaska* on The Learning Channel premiered to an audience of more than 5 million viewers (Hibbard 2010). In 2014 and 2015, Palin starred in another program, *Amazing America with Sarah Palin*, on The Sportsman Channel (Wemple 2014). Besides herself, the show featured professional wrestler James Storm (Silver 2014). As with Ventura and Trump, professional wrestling seems to have infected Palin's professional life. She even created The Sarah Palin Channel, a "site full of news, videos, chats and exclusive insights into the life of the mamma grizzly" (Payne 2014). In 2020, she rapped "Baby Got Back" on television's *The Masked Singer* (Brammer 2021). Palin metamorphosed from politician to television star by using her charm, good looks, and well-crafted persona to captivate audiences.

JERRY SPRINGER

Jerry Springer was born in London in 1944 during the German bombing campaign. His parents were German Jews who fled from Berlin in 1939. His grandparents were killed in concentration camps. In 1949, his family moved to America to start a new life. He grew up in New York City and admits to having a family that was extremely interested in politics. Unbeknownst to his mother, his dad skipped work and he and his sister skipped school to watch the election returns from the Kennedy-Nixon race in 1960. Eventually, he attended Tulane University in New Orleans and was politically active in the civil rights movement. As a college student he went to Mississippi to register black voters. He also participated in protests, sit-ins, and other acts of civil disobedience (Springer and Morton 1998; Markham-Smith and Hodgson 1999).

His first experience mixing entertainment and politics came in college when he was a DJ for the college radio station. He was on air when Kennedy was assassinated. After reading the teletype and confirming the news, he made the announcement to his radio listeners. After college he attended Northwestern Law School because he thought being a lawyer would be a good stepping-stone for a career in politics. The self-described "pinko lefty, a total liberal" got a job at Frost and Jacobs, the premier corporate law firm in Cincinnati (Springer and Morton 1998, 47). Within a few weeks of arriving in Cincinnati he went to work in a campaign to lower the voting age to nineteen. He was appointed the Hamilton County chair for Vote 19, the group seeking to lower the voting age. Although the measure lost statewide, he was proud that he was successful locally. It was during this campaign that he gained the attention of Democratic leaders. He had given rousing and well received speeches at fundraisers and was courted by top Democrats in the state to set his goals higher. It was clear that Springer had a natural talent to perform in front of audiences (Springer and Morton 1998; Markham-Smith and Hodgson 1999).

In 1969, he decided to run for Congress as an anti-Vietnam War candidate. Having already gotten the attention of top Democratic party leaders he was invited by Senator Birch Bayh to testify before the Senate Judiciary Committee on the proposed amendment to lower the voting age. While in Washington he was introduced to other Democratic party leaders. He managed to gain the support of Sargent Shriver, Arnold Schwarzenegger's future father-in-law, who would travel to Ohio and campaign for the up-and-coming Jerry Springer. Springer quit the law firm after having been there for less than a year to pursue his political career full time. He ran against the 10-year incumbent Don Clancy and performed surprisingly well in the conservative leaning district. Springer earned 46 percent of the vote in the 1970 election (Markham-Smith and Hodgson 1999).

Because he nearly defeated an incumbent congressman, the new governor, Jack Gilligan, appointed Springer to serve on his cabinet. Soon after, party leaders wanted him to return to Cincinnati to run for city council. Even in those days Springer was an entertainer. While campaigning for city council he attended the fundraiser of a judicial candidate. He jumped on stage and gave a stellar rendition of "Blowing in the Wind" to the amazement of the local political crowd (Markham-Smith and Hodgson 1999). In 1971, Springer was elected to the Cincinnati city council by appealing to a particular demographic group. Springer's campaign manager, and life-long friend, Mike Ford, notes, "the less educated were always part of Jerry's audience. That coalition has certainly transferred into his viewing audience today" (Springer and Morton 1998, 63). As a council member he worked on increasing transit service, health programs, and public housing (Markham-Smith and Hodgson 1999).

Springer quickly became a showboat with various schemes to gain publicity for himself. He persuaded local authorities to allow him to spend the night in jail incognito. He wanted to learn first-hand what conditions were like at the local jail, but his plan to be anonymous failed when the radio reported that Councilman Springer was there that morning. His cellmates quickly deduced Springer was a fraud, but Springer used the opportunity to create a town hall with the inmates. He asked them what they thought about the conditions and what improvements they would like to see. He took their concerns to the city council and proposed a full-time doctor in the facility and the building of a new jail with better rehabilitation programs (Markham-Smith and Hodgson 1999).

He also made an appearance on the *50–50 Club*, a television talk show where he sang several songs with the band. Thereafter, he recorded several songs written by Cincinnati residents. These songs were played on local radio stations and Springer gained a reputation as a young and hip politician. Within a year, the city council selected Springer to serve as vice-mayor. He took an old RV and created Vice-Mayor Springer's Mobile City Hall. He would take the van into the various neighborhoods and talk with the residents about the issues facing the city. Springer says, "it was my first talk show" (Springer and Morton 1998, 66). He would make sure that every resident that had a question would receive an official reply from the city within two weeks. These actions increased his popularity as the residents believed that Springer was actively trying to solve their problems (Markham-Smith and Hodgson 1999).

Jerry Springer lost is virginity to a Bourbon Street prostitute paid for by his Tulane fraternity brothers his first year in college. This is important because in 1974, after being re-elected to the city council, a massage parlor was raided as part of a prostitution sting and Springer was found out to be a client. Springer was humiliated and resigned from the city council. In exchange for not being prosecuted he agreed to become a witness for the prosecution (Markham-Smith and Hodgson 1999).

During the ordeal Springer was asked not to resign by some his fellow council members and from voters in the community. Afterward, and at the behest of his supporters, he ran for city council again in 1975 and won. The voters did not seem to mind his involvement with the prostitutes. He championed issues that impacted the most impoverished residents of the city and in 1977 he was the top vote getter in the at-large city election. Because of his resounding victory his fellow council members appointed Springer to be the mayor of Cincinnati (Springer and Morton 1998; Markham-Smith and Hodgson 1999).

While serving as mayor he secured a gig recording two-minute commentaries for WEBN, a local radio station, that aired four times a week. The commentaries were not just his take on local politics, he also talked about culture and current events. Springer used his position as mayor to meet celebrities. Whenever a celebrity came to town for a performance, he would offer them a key to the city. He met Billy Joel, Dolly Parton, Joni Mitchell, Bruce Springsteen, Bob Dylan, and the Beach Boys. He got a campaign contribution from Glen Frey, the lead singer for The Eagles, for his work fighting against nuclear energy. When the Russian circus came to town, he volunteered to wrestle a bear on live television. Springer knew what it took to create a spectacle (Springer and Morton 1998; Markham-Smith and Hodgson 1999).

At thirty-three years old he was the youngest mayor in Cincinnati history and party leaders anticipated that he would continue to rise in the ranks. He ran for governor but lost in the primary to Richard Celeste. Springer was a formidable opponent and raised more than $2 million dollars which he used for television advertisements and traditional canvassing and phone banking operations. His opponents, however, used attack ads to criticize Springer's involvement with the prostitutes (Markham-Smith and Hodgson 1999).

Because of his highly rated radio commentaries he quickly secured a job as a news anchor for WLWT and would interview Celeste the night Celeste was elected governor. Springer would go on to work for ten years as a TV news anchor. In that time, he would earn ten local Emmy awards for his broadcasting. The company that owned WLWT also produced several television talk-shows. These included *Braun & Company*, the *Phil Donahue Show*, *Sally Jesse Raphael*, and *Rush Limbaugh*. With Phil Donahue nearing retirement the company set out to find a replacement (Springer and Morton 1998; Markham-Smith and Hodgson 1999).

The Jerry Springer Show first aired in 1991 and was designed as a carbon copy of the *Phil Donahue Show*. Springer says, "The original idea was to do important and serious topical interviews with politicians, celebrities, and other prominent people" (Springer and Morton 1998, 85). In the second season it was decided that the show would be taped in Chicago and that the format would change. Richard Dominick, the new executive producer, decided to push the boundaries of televised entertainment. Dominick says, "My idea was to turn the show into a spectacle, so if you clicked it on at any moment, you'll stop and watch the show" (Markham-Smith and Hodgson 1999, 8). The show would be outrageous, silly, and often uncivilized. When a fight breaks out between the guests, the audience chants, "Jer-ry! Jer-ry! Jer-ry!" (Springer and Morton 1998; Markham-Smith and Hodgson 1999).

Why have a show about incest, when you could have a show about twins who have sex with other? Why have a show about adultery, when you could have a show about a woman who cheats on her husband with his brother? Every show includes a pitch to his viewers, "Do you or does somebody you know live a bizarre or unusual lifestyle? Do you have a secret? Are you having an affair? Do you need a paternity test?" (Springer and Morton 1998, 107). The popular paternity test shows feature a woman accusing a man of being the father of her child. Sometimes he is and sometimes he isn't! The confrontations make for exciting and entertaining television drama.

A sampling of the show titles provides a sense of just how outrageous the show is. The titles include: "Hey, I've Slept With Your Husband," "I Caught My Husband Having An Affair With My Aunt," "Sorry Honey, I'm Gay," "I Am Pregnant by a Transsexual," "Granny Works In A Brothel," "My Sister Slept With My Three Husbands," "I'm Pregnant and Have to Strip," "I Slept With 251 Men in Ten Hours," "My Girlfriend Is A Man," "My Teenager Worships Satan," "I'm Raising My Daughter To Hate Men," "Honey, Please Don't Join The Klan," "I Want Your Man," "I Stole My

12-Year-Old's Boyfriend," and "Paternity Test: I Slept With Two Brothers" (Markham-Smith and Hodgson 1999). While his critics say that Springer is "the most loathesome [*sic*] man on TV who has successfully lowered the standards of talk shows to their most base and debauched," Springer believes the show "is nothing more than entertainment and should not be taken seriously" (Markham-Smith and Hodgson 1999, xii).

Springer makes it a point to book racists on his show. Because of his family's experience in Nazi Germany, he invites neo-Nazis and Ku Klux Klan members on the program. Springer says,

> Our show is about outrageousness—those things that are either abnormal or outside the bounds of cultural acceptability. Surely racism fits that description. But I also think it's important to expose this cancer in our society every time we spot it so people will see how evil and crazy and downright stupid it is. (Springer and Morton 1998, 16)

Springer suggests that the civil rights movement was successful in the 1950s and 1960s because, for the first time, the South's brutality against African Americans was visually witnessed on television. Television has the power to uncover important truths about our society. Thus, despite the often outlandish nature his show, he does try to convey a meaningful message to his viewers about justice and kindness (Springer and Morton 1998).

Springer talks about the similarity between his career as a politician and his career as an entertainer. Springer notes, "my audience hasn't changed a bit over the years. From politics, to news, to talk show host, my constituency has always been the same" (Springer and Morton 1998, 105). He says, "When I'm not taping the six shows a week that we do, I'm usually off promoting the heck out of '*The Jerry Springer Show*.' In politics, we called that campaigning" (Springer and Morton 1998, 106). In the first instance he was trying to convince people to vote for him, in the second, he was trying to convince people to watch his show. He relies on the same skill set for both functions. He must harness his inner salesman to promote his latest endeavor. Entertainers that became politicians, like Arnold Schwarzenegger, make similar observations.

The show got exceedingly high ratings. In 1995, his show had more viewers than David Letterman and Jay Leno (Springer and Morton 1998). It airs in over fifty countries and has annual revenues of over $400 million. In 1998, after seven years on the air, his ratings were higher than Oprah's (Markham-Smith and Hodgson 1999; Glynn 2000). Springer had a penchant for creating a spectacle that cut across his multiple careers.

As a politician Jerry Springer wrestled circus bears on live television. Even then, he understood "the value of a good gimmick or publicity stunt"

(Markham-Smith and Hodgson 1999, 163–64). He appealed to less educated constituents and practiced his interview skills in his mobile city hall. He was comfortable in front of cameras and would be a news anchor before hosting his own talk show. *The Jerry Springer Show* offers a kind of low brow entertainment that his devoted fans love. Springer himself draws parallels between his career as a politician and his career as an entertainer.

OTHERS

In addition to Thompson, Palin, and Springer there are a few other politicians who transitioned into the entertainment industry or have taken steps in that direction. Mike Huckabee was the governor of Arkansas and a presidential candidate. A few months after dropping out of the 2008 presidential election he was hired by Fox News to host his own political commentary show (DeMillo 2008). Al Gore was a US Senator representing Tennessee and later the Vice President of the United States. After his own unsuccessful bid for the White House, he participated in the production of *An Inconvenient Truth*, a documentary about climate change. The film won two Oscars and led to *An Inconvenient Sequel: Truth to Power*, a follow up film seeking to capitalize on the success of the first (Murray 2007; Collin 2017).

When President Obama left office, he started Higher Ground Productions. The production company's first film was *American Factory*, a documentary about a Chinese company re-opening a shuttered factory in Ohio. The film won an Oscar for best documentary and Higher Ground has now added several films including a new series on national parks narrated by the former president (Rao 2020; Weprin 2022). Mayor Pete Buttigieg, after his unsuccessful presidential run, guest hosted the late-night show *Jimmy Kimmel Live!* where he gave an opening monologue, interviewed and played a Star Trek trivia game with Patrick Stewart, and showed off his own musical talents with the band (CNN 2020). Buttigieg's telegenic charm and enthusiastic supporters could launch him into the entertainment business when his political career ends, though he is currently the Secretary of Transportation. Stacey Abrams, a candidate for governor in Georgia, made a guest appearance on *Star Trek: Discovery* demonstrating that her skill in front of cameras advocating for voting rights can be used for other purposes (Mark 2022). Just as entertainers harness their talents to become politicians, politicians sometimes use their talents join the entertainment industry.

CELEBRITY LOSERS

Shirley Temple

Ronald Reagan became a Hollywood star in the 1930s and won elected office in the mid-1960s. But not every celebrity who tries their hand at electoral politics is successful. Shirley Temple was a child star in the 1930s but failed when she ran for Congress in the mid-1960s. The differing outcomes for Reagan and Temple are illustrative. Temple was unsuccessful because her persona was not suited for the politics of the time. The political environment was not suitable for her to find success.

Shirley Temple's claim to fame was that of a cute boisterous little girl who could sing and dance. Her career in film began at the age of three and her most iconic films were released before she reached the age of ten. It was at the age of ten when she got her first taste of politics. She was accused by the House Committee on Un-American Activities of unwittingly serving the purposes of the Communist Party. The American Communist Party took offence and declared that Temple was not a communist (Temple Black 1988). Her films as a child star were enormously successful and Temple became rich from merchandising her image and endorsing various products, most popularly dolls and dresses. Unfortunately for her, substantial amounts were misappropriated by the adults in charge of her earnings. She began to lose her audience appeal as a teenager and retired from film at the age of twenty-two (Edwards 1988). Near the end of her film career, she co-starred in *That Hagen Girl* with Ronald Reagan. She and Reagan discussed HUAC, and Reagan declared that he took the communist threat seriously (Temple Black 1988).

She married Charles Alden Black in 1950 and would be known as Shirley Temple Black from then on. In the late 1950s she narrated a television series called *Shirley Temple's Storybook* featuring fairy tale adaptations. After that she made guest appearances on the occasional television show in the early 1960s. She also began making appearances at campaign rallies and fund-raisers for Republican candidates. In 1966, she worked to support Ronald Reagan's campaign for governor and was appointed to a state advisory board upon his victory. She says in her autobiography, "To me Washington political and business celebrities seemed no different from celebrities anywhere. Products and ideas need to be peddled, things need doing, politics need be pursued, and sometimes self-delusion and pretension need be served" (Temple Black 1988, 496). By 1967, she was ready to step off the sidelines and into the arena herself (Edwards 1988).

That was the year Shirley Temple Black would run for Congress in a special election for California's eleventh district. In 1967, however, there were only twelve women serving in Congress, representing about 2 percent of the total membership. Women were not typically viewed as fit for leadership positions. It did not help that Shirley Temple's public persona was inextricably linked with the curly haired little girl of her early days in Hollywood. As it happened that was the same year *Curley McDimple*, a musical spoof of Shirley Temple's early career, opened off Broadway. It was not long before the moniker was used against the first-time candidate. Temple's best-known adult accomplishment was narrating children's fairy tales. The Cold War and Vietnam were serious issues and public perceptions could not conceive of Shirley Temple Black as anything other than kids' entertainment. Despite her fame Temple finished second in the primary with 22 percent of the vote. She advocated for escalation in Vietnam while her opponent Paul McClosky supported withdrawal (Daily News-Post 1967). Despite getting a campaign contribution from Bing Crosby Shirley Temple came in third in fundraising totals. Paul McClosky raised $121,678, William Draper raised $65,200, and Shirley Temple raised $33,251 (*San Francisco Examiner* 1967). The political environment was not favorable to women candidates and the persona that made her a Hollywood icon worked against her. She remained active in Republican party politics and would be appointed US ambassador to Ghana in 1974 (Edwards 1988).

Ben Jones

Ben Jones is famous for his role as "Cooter Davenport" in *The Dukes of Hazzard* which aired on American television from 1979 to 1985. In the 1980–81 season it was the second most popular show in America with a 27.3 rating, meaning that more than 27 percent of television viewers in that time slot were viewing *The Dukes of Hazzard* (Brooks and Marsh 2007). A year after the show ended, in 1986, Jones ran for Congress in Georgia's 4th district, but his TV persona worked against him. He portrayed an unsophisticated bumbling hayseed and commentators argued that this image harmed him during the election ("Industry Impact" 1986).

He ran again in 1988 and defeated incumbent Pat Swindall by a large margin (61 percent to 39 percent). In that race, Jones admitted that his past alcoholism contributed to his three divorces. Fortunately for Jones, Swindall was indicted just three weeks before the election on charges of perjury and money laundering. This caused the electorate to swing in Jones's favor (Wallace and Ducanin 1988; Hall 1988; Schwartz 1988). He was re-elected in 1990 but lost in the 1992 Democratic primary. Because of redistricting Jones was forced to run in a new district (Cooper 1992). Jones also bounced seven checks and was caught up in the House banking scandal of that year. The scandal was effectively used against him by state Senator Don Johnson who was an established figure in Georgia politics (McCarthy 1992). Jones quickly got to work proposing a political situation comedy to TV networks based on his congressional career (Cooper 1992). He sought to return to TV but instead became a radio talk show host (Yandel 1992).

In 1994, Jones tried again. He ran against Newt Gingrich in the election that saw Newt Gingrich become the Speaker of the House and Republicans taking control of the lower chamber for the first time in nearly forty years. Redistricting and realignment were making it increasingly difficult for Democrats to win in the South (Smith 1994). As a southern Democrat running in a year that favored Republicans, the political environment was not in Jones's favor. He would return to acting in the movie *Primary Colors* and the television series *Sliders* (IMDb "Ben Jones"). He would lose a fourth election in 2002 when he ran against Eric Cantor in Virginia's 7th district (Bell, Meyer, and Gaddie 2016). Jones was a Democrat running in a Republican dominated district and had little chance of winning despite his celebrity.

Gary Coleman

Gary Coleman was a child star made famous by his role in the TV situation comedy *Diff'rent Strokes* which aired from 1978 to 1986 (Brooks and Marsh 2007). His tagline "Watchoo talkin' 'bout, Willis" would be requested of him for the rest of his life. He earned more than $18 million but the money was "chewed away by family feuds, bad decisions, lawsuits, agents and greedy managers" leaving him broke and working ordinary working-class jobs as an adult (Stuever 2003). An independent newspaper, the *East Bay Express*, paid for Coleman's filing fee and collected the necessary signatures to get him on the ballot in the California gubernatorial recall election in 2003. The newspaper did this to mock the California election system and "Coleman has walked a line of believing in his own legitimacy and mocking it" (Stuever 2003). Observers noted "that Coleman's sole purpose as a candidate is to be on hand to watchoo, etc., his diminutive heart out, to pop some one-liners about the mess the state is in, and to pose for pictures with all manner of quasi-celebrities, voters, the buxom, the marginalized, the masses" (Stuever 2003). His job was to participate in the spectacle of the 2003 California recall election. Coleman said, "I am probably the most unqualified person to run for governor, but I'm willing to do it as a goof" (Van Susteren and Housley 2003). He continued, "of course I'd vote for myself. And, you know, I'm a big Arnold Schwarzenegger fan, if you will, and I also believe that because of the abilities and the connections that he has to politics, he's going to make a great governor. So I'd vote for him, too" (Van Susteren and Housley 2003). Coleman lost to Schwarzenegger but earned 12,683 votes and came in eighth place (*Weekly Standard* October 20, 2003).

Linda McMahon

Linda McMahon, along with her husband Vince McMahon, were the CEOs of World Wrestling Entertainment. They employed Jesse "The Body" Ventura and made him a famous professional wrestler. They worked with Donald Trump to secure venues for their wrestling events and even featured him in their phenomenally successful WrestleManias. Linda McMahon ran unsuccessfully as a Republican candidate in 2010 and 2012 US Senate races in Connecticut.

Her political career began when Governor M. Jodi Rell appointed her to the Connecticut Board of Education in 2009. She survived approval from the Connecticut House and Senate even though some legislators thought that her appointment would send the wrong message to children because of the violence and overt sexuality at WWE events (Associated Press February 26, 2009). McMahon was an influential Republican donor and state Republican leaders were excited about her bid for the US Senate (National Journal August 17, 2009). She faced US Representative Rob Simmons, state Senator Sam Caligiuri, and former US Ambassador Tom Foley for the Republican nomination (Miga 2009).

Simmons attacked McMahon for the poor safety record of the WWE and for "selling graphic sex and violence to children of all ages" (Haigh May 20, 2010). Others noted the WWE's tasteless content, "including a developmentally disabled character being beaten and a performer simulating sex with a woman's corpse in a casket" (Haigh May 20, 2010). McMahon was nominated at the Republican Party convention, but Simmons secured enough votes to force a primary contest (Haigh and Eaton-Robb 2010). Much was made of "the footage of McMahon herself in the ring, being called a bitch and slapped to the ground by her daughter, kicking one man between the legs and then having her head inserted between the legs of another man as he pile-drove her down to the mat" (Horowitz 2010). But in a year in which the Tea Party would come to dominate the political scene the "fans who respond to the anti-elite, nationalist jingoistic sentiment stoked by WWE scripts" would come out in force to support McMahon (Horowitz 2010). McMahon, who spent $22 million of her own money in the primary, defeated Simmons by more than 20 points (Haigh August 11, 2010; Haberman and Toeplitz 2010).

Incumbent Senator Chris Dodd was consistently behind Rob Simmons in early polls and decided not to seek re-election (Sidoti 2010). When the highly popular Richard Blumenthal announced his candidacy for the Democratic side early polls showed that he had a 40-point lead over all his Republican rivals (Associated Press January 14, 2010). The race narrowed but Blumenthal defeated McMahon 55 percent to 43 percent despite McMahon's enormous spending of her own funds (Associated Press November 11, 2010; Farnam

2010). McMahon spent more than $50 million while Blumenthal spent less than $9 million (FEC "Richard Blumenthal"). Most of the criticism leveled at McMahon had to do with the content of WWE programming, which she considered to be unfair (Haigh November 12, 2010). Jesse Ventura survived the crudeness of WWE programming because he was in a three-way race and did not need a majority to win. In a one-on-one contest, McMahon's association with the lowbrow entertainment was too much to overcome.

She ran again in 2012 and spent another $50 million (FEC "Linda McMahon"). This time she lost to Representative Chris Murphy in another open seat race after Senator Joseph Lieberman retired. Because Connecticut is a state that favors Democrats, McMahon released an advertisement with voters who planned to vote for Obama and herself—splitting their ticket. The move upset Republican Party leaders and did not help her convince Democrats to vote for her (Stoller 2012; Weiner 2012). Forty percent of voters said that McMahon's wrestling background played a role in their decision, and they broke 9 to 1 in favor of Representative Murphy (Applebome and Maker 2012). Her tremendous financial resources could not overcome Democratic dominance in the state and her association with crude and vulgar entertainment. She remained active in Republican politics, donating $7 million to Trump's campaign, and Trump appointed her administrator of the Small Business Administration after his presidential victory in 2016 (*New York Times* Editorial Board 2017).

Roseanne Barr

Roseanne Barr was a comedian best known for her self-titled sitcom *Roseanne*. The show aired from 1988 to 1997. It was tied for the number one rated show in television in the 1989–1990 season. It was the second rated show in the 1988–1989 and 1990 to 1993 seasons, beaten only by *The Cosby Show*, *Cheers*, and *60 Minutes* (Brooks and Marsh 2007). The show was nominated for an Emmy twenty-seven times and won the prestigious award on four occasions (Television Academy "Roseanne"). She sought the Green Party nomination for president in 2012 making her announcement on *The Tonight Show with Jay Leno*. She said she would create a new party called the "green tea party" because she was "not for either party because they both suck, and they're both a bunch of criminals" (Global Broadcast Database 2011). She continued by saying, "There will be no taxes," "I forgive all student loans," and "I'm getting rid of money. . . . There will be no more money" (Global Broadcast Database 2011). Leno was skeptical about her seriousness but congratulated her making the announcement.

The following month she attended an Occupy Wall Street protest and said, "I first would allow the guilty bankers to pay—you know, the ability to pay back anything over $100 million of personal wealth because I believe in a maximum wage of $100 million, and if they're unable to live on that amount then they should, you know, go to the reeducation camps and if that doesn't help, then be beheaded" (Hannity 2011). Later she got into a Twitter feud with Beyoncé and said, "Beyoncé's fans are really ignorant-she should not be proud of entertaining drooling mutants!" and "just finished telling all of Beyoncé's cheesy stupid a— fans who slammed me to go and f--- themselves! It was fun!" (AOL Music 2012).

It was not at all clear whether Barr was running a serious campaign or just engaging in a publicity stunt. Jill Stein trounced Roseanne Barr and won 193.5 delegates, while Barr only secured 72 at the Green Party nominating convention (Witte 2012). After her defeat Barr continued her campaign and won the nomination of the Peace and Freedom Party (Yoon 2012). She appeared on the ballot in several states and was a write in candidate in others (Associated Press October 3, 2012; October 25, 2012; International Business Times November 6, 2012). Barr said, "I'm here to tell the voters: if you want to tell the government and the two domineering parties that you're sick and tired of all their evil, register in the Peace and Freedom Party and vote for me and Cindy" (Yoon 2012). Barr did manage to earn 67,326 protest votes nationally (FEC "Federal Elections 2012 Results").

Cynthia Nixon

Cynthia Nixon is an actress best known for her work on the HBO series *Sex and the City*. She won an Emmy Award for her work on the show and a second Emmy Award for her work on *Law and Order: Special Victims Unit* (Television Academy "Cynthia Nixon"). *Sex and the City* aired from 1998 to 2004 and focused on the sexual exploits of four friends who were all "catty, self-absorbed, and constantly gossiping about their latest conquests" (Brooks and Marsh 2007, 1221). She challenged incumbent governor of New York Andrew Cuomo in the Democratic primary of 2018 and lost.

The Working Families Party is a minor third party in the United States that recruits liberal candidates to run in Democratic Party primaries (Working Families Party). Because of her work as a liberal activist, Nixon, who supported a single-payer health system, secured the nomination of the Working Families Party of New York in April 2018. Major labor unions then abandoned the Working Families Party because they feared a 3-candidate field in November would allow a Republican to win the general election (McKinley 2018). In May, Andrew Cuomo secured the nomination of the Democratic Party of New York. Nixon then organized a petition to force a primary election (Goldmacher May 22, 2018). She lost the primary in September 2018 by a large margin, receiving just 34 percent of the vote. Observers noted that Cuomo's fundraising advantage and strong support from labor unions were important factors in his victory (Goldmacher September 14, 2018). The Working Families Party quickly proceeded to remove Nixon from their line on the ballot and to endorse Andrew Cuomo (McKinley and Goldmacher 2018).

Nixon made marijuana legalization the top issue of her campaign. Cuomo had ended prosecution of small amounts of marijuana and legalized marijuana for medical use, but Nixon wanted full legalization for recreational use and release from prison and compensation for those previously arrested on marijuana charges. Nixon faced an uphill battle to begin with. Early polls had Nixon far behind Cuomo. In 2014, the moderate Andrew Cuomo defeated the progressive Zephyr Teachout by a two to one margin in the Democratic primary (Wang 2018). This suggests that Democratic primary voters in New York have a strong preference for more moderate Democrats. Nixon was simply too far to the left for the electorate. Nixon's fame did give her increased publicity, but the media publicized positions that made her less popular with the public.

Stacey Dash

Stacey Dash is an actress best known for her roles in *Clueless* and *Mo' Money*. She is also known for her stunning good looks and posed for *Playboy* in 2006 (Bradwell 2014). Dash was a former Democrat who supported Obama in 2008, but she switched parties and supported Romney in 2012 (Hare 2012; Morgan 2012). In 2018, she decided to run for Congress in California's 44th district. The district is predominantly Hispanic and represents south Los Angeles, Compton, and Long Beach (Heil 2018). After the 2010 redistricting the district became a Democratic stronghold with Hillary Clinton getting 83 percent of the vote in 2016 (Modesti 2018).

In 2014 Dash was hired as a contributor on Fox News (Bradwell 2014). Over the next several years she made several incendiary comments. In 2015 she said that Obama "didn't give a sh—" about terrorism (Stelter 2015). In 2016 she was dismissive of the protests over the lack of African American Oscar nominees. She said, "We have to make up our minds. Either we want to have segregation or integration, and if we don't want segregation, then we have to get rid of channels like BET and the BET Awards and the Image Awards, where you're only awarded if you're black. If it were the other way around, we would be up in arms. It's a double standard" (Pallotta 2016). She went on to say, "There shouldn't be a Black History Month. We're Americans, period. That's it" (Pallotta 2016). Minority groups were especially galled by the comments because Dash is herself of African American and Mexican American ancestry (Carroll 2018). When her contract expired in 2017 Fox News decided not to renew it. *The Hollywood Reporter* noted that Dash had an "abrasive persona on social media" and was an early supporter of Trump's presidential bid (Rahman 2017).

In February 2018 Dash announced she would run as a Republican for California's 44th congressional district (Heil 2018). She was critical of the Republican Party, Education Secretary Betsy DeVos, and Donald Trump. She said, "We have a billionaire sec. of education who is against public school we even have a president whose children did not go to public school and there are cries from the federal government to fix this shooting problem?" (Downs 2018). Political reporters said, "It is a quixotic bid. Dash is a political outcast in liberal Hollywood, scorned for saying Black History Month should be abolished and that transgender people should pee in the bushes and waxing lyrical about the Mad Men era when 'men were men'" (Carroll 2018). She criticized inner city voters for supporting Democrats saying, "I want to free people from the shackles of a plantation mentality" (Carroll 2018). She supported Trump's border wall proposal, dismissed his "grab them by the pussy" comments, and defended Trump's moral equivalency between neo-Nazis and the counter-protestors in Charlottesville. Dash said, "The anti-fascists were just as violent" (Carroll 2018).

After just five weeks of campaigning Dash dropped out of the race. She said,

At this point, I believe that the overall bitterness surrounding our political process, participating in the rigors of campaigning, and holding elected office would be detrimental to the health and wellbeing of my family. I would never want to betray the personal and spiritual principles I believe in most: that my God and my family come first. (Hamedy 2018)

She continued to scold minority voters saying, "Because I'm Black I'm supposed to therefore be a Democrat, which is absurd. They're supposed to be the party of tolerance. I don't see any tolerance. I've made a choice to stand up for what I believe in and don't think I should be condemned" (*Guardian* 2018). As an outspoken, and abrasive, conservative she had little chance in a heavily Democratic district.

Others

A few other celebrities are worth briefly mentioning. Ralph Waite was most famous for his role as "John Walton Sr." on *The Waltons*. In 1990, he ran in the Republican dominated 37th congressional district of California. The four-term Republican Al McCandless got support from Mayor Sonny Bono and former President Ronald Reagan. Waite, a Democrat, lost the heavily Republican district despite outspending the incumbent nearly 2 to 1 (Willis 1990). When Sonny Bono died in 1998 Waite ran in the special election to replace him and lost to Mary Bono. He tried again in the regularly scheduled general election but lost a second time to Mary Bono. Bono's congressional district was also a Republican stronghold, making Waite's bid to succeed him unlikely (Claiborne 1998; Connolly 1998).

Nancy Kulp was known for her role in *The Beverly Hillbillies*. In 1984, with Ronald Reagan serving as president, she ran for Pennsylvania's 9th congressional district. She ran as a Democrat in a Republican dominated district against six-term incumbent Bud Shuster. Shuster held the seat from 1973 to 2001 and Democrats had virtually no chance in the uncompetitive district (Barker 1984; Comegys 1984).

Kanye West is a hip-hop musician who is one of the top selling artists in the United States and has won twenty-two Grammy Awards (Recording Academy "Kanye West"). He spent $12.5 million of his own money for his 2020 presidential run. He received help from Republican consultants to gain ballot access and his name appeared on the ballot in twelve states. He received 70,296 votes nationally (FEC "Official 2020 Election Results"). His wife filed for divorce and asked the public for compassion because of West's bipolar disorder. It wasn't clear why he was running for office because he had previously stated his support for Donald Trump (Neumann 2021).

Caitlyn Jenner, a former Olympic athlete and reality TV star, announced she would run for California governor in 2021 (Marinucci and Shepard 2021). She was most recently famous for her role in *Keeping Up with the Kardashians* but appeared in many television shows since the 1970s including *CHiPs*, *Silver Spoons*, *The Fall Guy*, *Murder, She Wrote*, *The Weakest Link*, *The Apprentice*, *Transparent*, *The Masked Singer*, and others (IMDb "Caitlyn Jenner"). Beginning in 2015 she became a prominent transgender activist. Despite getting more media attention than many of the other forty-six candidates in California's recall election Jenner received approximately 73,000 (1 percent) votes (Roos 2021). Ultimately, Republicans were unable to oust Democratic governor Gavin Newsom in the heavily Democratic state.

CONCLUSIONS

Politicians and entertainers rely on the same skill set to be successful. They need to be good in front of cameras, they need to be good in front of audiences, it helps if they are telegenic, they should be able to remember a script, and they need to be skilled at gaining attention for themselves. Many entertainers have used these skills to succeed in politics. But it is also true that some politicians can use those same skills to become entertainers. Thompson, Palin, and Springer are examples of reverse migration. They moved between industries in the opposite direction from the likes of Reagan, Schwarzenegger, and Ventura.

Not every celebrity, however, is able to succeed in electoral politics. Sometimes they lose because their persona is not compatible with the politics of the time. Shirley Temple was known as a sweet little girl at a time when tough men needed to solve serious problems. Thompson represented the Establishment by portraying authority figures in TV and movies. This was detrimental to him in an anti-establishment year. At other times the campaigns are correctly perceived as publicity stunts and not taken seriously; this was the case for the Coleman and West campaigns.

Celebrities can also lose for more mundane reasons. At times, the partisan political environment is not favorable to celebrity candidates. McMahon and Dash were Republicans in Democratic districts. Waite and Jones were Democrats in Republican districts. In New York, Democratic primary voters have a history of supporting more moderate candidates and rejected the too liberal Nixon. Fame and fortune are not able to overcome unfavorable electorates. Celebrities have many advantages over other candidates, but if they advocate unpopular ideas their fame brings added attention to policies voters prefer to reject.

Chapter 12

The Perils and Promises
of Celebrity Politics

The previous chapters have provided case studies of celebrities that have sought elected office. This chapter will summarize the conclusions that can be drawn from these case studies. It will also explore the costs and benefits of celebrity involvement in American politics. What, if anything, does it mean for American democracy if celebrities become our elected leaders?

Hollywood elites have been active in American politics for a long time. Louis Mayer and Jack Warner used their movie studios to influence Americans' political views. The techniques of the entertainment industry were used for political ends. Celebrities used their ability to draw attention to advocate for favored policies. Many celebrities have gone beyond advocacy and ran for office themselves. Some celebrities were able harness the power of their celebrity to achieve success in electoral politics. They had *the power trifecta*, the talent, fame, and resources to be successful in the political arena.

Their talents are well suited to a career in politics. They are good in front of audiences. Al Franken's ability to read a crowd and pivot was possible because of his career as a stand-up comedian. They are good in front of cameras. From movies to television the celebrities in this book were experienced with on screen presentations of themselves. Reagan noted that the presidency required these skills, and he could not image that the job could be done without skill in front of the cameras. They can memorize scripts and deliver a performance. Schwarzenegger and Ventura understood that they had to put on a show for the audience. They had to become characters on a show called the Evening News. Celebrities are excellent at drawing attention to themselves. Ventura and Bono used crazy outfits make a spectacle of themselves. Once they garnered attention, they started talking about politics. Some benefited from the "halo effect" of their good looks. Reagan, Schwarzenegger, and Eastwood were successful because of their physical appearance. The social psychology literature shows that being physically attractive provides social benefits that are effective in politics as well.

Most importantly, they were superb at creating a personal brand that resonated with audiences and voters. The voters already knew the celebrity candidates because they had developed a "para-social" relationship with them. Their fans provided a base of support among the voting public, at the start of their campaigns favorable approval ratings are based on their careers as entertainers. Reporters noted that many of the attendees at their campaign rallies were autograph seekers who were drawn to the event by the prospect of seeing a famous person up close. They had tremendous name recognition and earned media attention that their opponents could not replicate. This was especially devastating for the opponents of Eastwood, Bono, and Ventura in their mayoral races. In all cases, the overwhelming media attention benefited the celebrity candidates. The media often conflates the actors with the roles they have played, suggesting that voters are influenced by the imagery of the candidacy. Schwarzenegger's Terminator became the Governator. Eastwood had bumper stickers that said, "Go ahead, make me mayor" as if Dirty Harry was running for office. On screen personas were part of the public's imagination when evaluating these candidates.

Celebrities are wealthy people with wealthy friends who can help them finance a political campaign. Reagan's campaign contributors included many Hollywood elites. Franken was not ashamed to say he was supported by "Big Comedy," by his friends and co-workers in the entertainment industry. Schwarzenegger noted that wealthy donors were more likely to take his calls because of his celebrity status and more likely to contribute since they viewed him as an equal. Eastwood self-financed his campaign and overwhelmed his opponent financially. The money was superfluous, however, because the free media attention meant they did not need to spend on advertising to get their message out. Trump received twice as much free media coverage than Clinton. Ventura used public financing but was the biggest political story of the year.

Yet the long list of celebrities that have lost elections suggests that the power trifecta is not enough, the political environment was the difference between winning and losing for celebrities who seek elected office. The unique circumstances of their city, district, or state are important. Items like the partisan composition of the district, the election laws of the state, or the characteristics of their opponent can propel a celebrity candidate to victory or a resounding defeat. As many celebrities have lost elections as won elections. Much depends on who counts as a celebrity and which elections are considered.

Wright's list of celebrity politicians suggests that 58 percent of celebrities win their first race (Wright 2019). This list is questionable. She includes

Jerry Springer as a winner, but he was freshly out of law school and not yet a famous personality at the time of his city council victory. Star power had nothing to do with his win. She lists Ben Jones as a winner in 1988, but Jones lost his first race in 1986. He won re-election and then lost three races after that. Fred Thompson won his first race in 1994, but lost his presidential bid in 2008. Dropping out should be considered a loss since it demonstrates a pitifully poor level of support. Sonny Bono was elected as a mayor and congressman but lost his Senate bid. Congressman Fred Grandy lost a primary contest for governor. If one were to count the losses of these winners, the results could well be more losses than wins in total. Facing a new constituency should count as a new first race. For these last four in particular their previous electoral success and celebrity fame was still insufficient to win. This casts some doubt on the claim that celebrities are inherently serious political contenders. They have advantages for sure, but they are not totally immune from the normal laws of politics (Longoria 2022).

The ability to create a personal brand is advantageous, unless that brand is viewed negatively in a particular environment. Shirley Temple's cute little girl persona was used against her when the serious issues of Vietnam and nuclear proliferation called for tough hard-nosed solutions. Fred Thompson's Mr. Establishment persona was exactly the wrong thing to be in an anti-establishment year when the economic collapse called for new and innovative thinking. Fame is not enough when a campaign is viewed as a publicity stunt. Roseanne Barr, Gary Coleman, and Kanye West were not taken seriously even though they received media coverage and were well known by the public. Resources are not enough when the political environment favors the other party. Linda McMahon, a Republican, lost two self-financed races

Table 12.1. Winning Celebrity Candidates

Winning Candidate	Type of Seat	Vote Percentage	Fundraising Winner
Ronald Reagan (Gov)	Incumbent	57%	Yes
Ronald Reagan (Pres)	Incumbent	51%	Yes
Clint Eastwood	Incumbent	72%	Yes
Fred Grandy (House)	Open	51%	Yes
Sonny Bono (Mayor)	Open	44%	Yes
Sonny Bono (House)	Open	56%	Yes
Ben Jones (1988)	Incumbent	61%	No
Jesse Ventura (Mayor)	Incumbent	n/a	n/a
Jesse Ventura (Gov)	Open	37%	No
Fred Thompson (Senate)	Open	60%	No
Arnold Schwarzenegger	Recall	49%	Yes
Al Franken	Incumbent	42%	No
Donald Trump	Open	46%	No

Source: Author's analysis.

costing $50 million each to Democrats who spent far less than she did, but were in a Democratic state.

Incumbents are difficult to beat, even for celebrity candidates. Celebrities defeated an incumbent in six of the thirty races they ran in, they won an open seat race in six of the thirty races and won one recall election. Reagan (in the gubernatorial and presidential races), Eastwood, Ventura (in the race for mayor), Franken, and Jones defeated an incumbent office holder. Franken won by a few hundred votes in a statewide race and Jones was facing an incumbent who was criminally indicted on federal charges. Grandy, Bono (in the races for mayor and the US House), Thompson, Ventura (in the race for governor), and Trump were running in open seat contests where there is a greater chance for victory, even without their celebrity advantages. Schwarzenegger ran in a recall election in which there is no primary contest and is not a direct one on one against the incumbent.

Not counting re-election campaigns celebrities won thirteen of the thirty races they ran in. This is better than the average political upstart but is not overwhelming evidence for the power trifecta of celebrity politics. On seven occasions the celebrity candidate won with a majority, they got less than half of the total vote on twenty-three occasions. Again, Jones's majority was the result of the incumbent being indicted a few weeks before the election. Of those that won, five won with less than a majority of the vote suggesting their victories were accidents of a plurality rule or electoral college system where a popular majority is not necessary for victory. Bono (44 percent in the race for mayor), Ventura (37 percent in the race for governor), Schwarzenegger (49 percent), Franken (42 percent), and Trump (46 percent) all had plurality victories, not overwhelming support. This diminishes the idea that celebrities are super popular figures that use their fan base to propel them to victory. Celebrities do win, and they do have many advantages, but we can't say the results are overwhelming. Eastwood's 72 percent happened in a town with 4,000 voters (Longoria 2022).

Wealthy celebrities can use their own funds to run for office and are very good at getting their wealthy friends to donate to their campaigns. But they won the fundraising battle in only nine of the thirty races presented here. In seven of the thirteen victories celebrities raised more money than their opponent. In the other victories they won despite being outspent by capitalizing on their earned media. In fifteen of the seventeen losses celebrities raised less than their opponent. They sometimes lose even when they have the financial advantage. Overall, they seem to follow the normal laws of politics. They tend to win when they raise more and lose when they raise less. The underwhelming victories along with the long list of losing celebrities, suggests that winning, while easier for the celebrity candidate, is still a very difficult thing to achieve.

Table 12.2. Losing Celebrity Candidates

Losing Candidate	Type of Seat	Vote Percentage	Fundraising Winner
Sonny Bono (Senate)	Open	17%	No
Ben Jones (1986)	Incumbent	47%	No
Ben Jones (1992)	Open	30%	No
Ben Jones (1994)	Incumbent	36%	No
Ben Jones (2002)	Incumbent	30%	No
Fred Thompson (Pres)	Open	Dropped Out	No
Shirley Temple	Open	22%	No
Gary Coleman	Recall	0.2%	No
Linda McMahon (2010)	Open	43%	Yes
Fred Grandy (Gov)	Incumbent	48%	No
Roseanne Barr	Incumbent	0.05%	No
Cynthia Nixon	Incumbent	34%	No
Stacey Dash	Incumbent	Dropped Out	No
Ralph Waite	Incumbent	45%	Yes
Nancy Kulp	Incumbent	34%	No
Kanye West	Incumbent	0.04%	No
Caitlyn Jenner	Recall	1%	No

Source: Author's analysis.

Celebrities can benefit from their outsider status. They can present themselves as a challenge to the status quo and can benefit from an anti-incumbent mood when it exists. Because "they are not a politician" the public may be willing to dismiss their mistakes. The book argued for the idea of *celebrity slack*. As celebrities they do not face the usual repercussions of socially unacceptable behavior. They can get away with statements and actions that would doom non-celebrities. Some limitations to the concept of celebrity slack should be acknowledged. Except for Reagan, all of the winning celebrity candidates were accused of sexual misconduct of lesser or greater seriousness. In the case of Grandy, the accusation of making offensive statements did not occur until after his victory. With the others their alleged misconduct was an issue during the campaign, or widely known prior to their seeking office.

It could just be that American society is permissive of these deviant or offensive sexual predilections. Afterall, Bill Clinton survived a sex scandal. But many others have not. Eliot Spitzer, John Edwards, and Roy Moore did not survive sex scandals. Because each individual case is unique and because different people have different moral standards it is difficult to compare the cases to each other and definitively state that a particular scandal was survivable or not. We can only compare and attempt to make reasonable inferences. Eliot Spitzer, the governor of New York, did not survive politically after being caught with prostitutes. Jesse Ventura bragged about his adventures with prostitutes and was elected governor of Minnesota. But a plurality win for Ventura creates doubts. Maybe he was harmed politically, just not enough to lose in a three-way race. Springer resigned after getting caught with prostitutes but was re-elected after the scandal. Then he lost a race for governor where the prostitution scandal was used against him by his opponents. Roy Moore lost a Senate race in Alabama after being accused of sexual misconduct by a person who was a minor at the time of the incident. It was well known that Sonny and Cher's romance began when Cher was a minor, yet Sonny went on to win mayoral and congressional races. It remains an interesting observation that the winning celebrities survived scandals that may have been career ending for non-celebrity candidates even though some qualification is necessary.

One of the most glaring observations is that all the celebrity winners were white males. Leaving aside Ben Jones, Fred Gandy, Sonny Bono, and Fred Thompson, who both won and lost elections, 9 of the 10 celebrity losers, those who never won, were not white males. There is a large academic literature on systemic racism (Feagin 2013; Elias and Feagin 2016; Feagin and Ducey 2017; Tourse, Hamilton-Mason, and Wewiorski 2018) and systemic sexism (Ng 1993; Stoll 2013; Ochoa 2019; Gilbert 2021). There is also evidence that racist and sexist attitudes influence vote choice in US elections (Sanbonmatsu 2002; Buyuker 2020). Given the observations the effects of racial and gender prejudice seem apparent.

One must always be careful when attempting to draw broad conclusions from a small sample. Except for Shirley Temple, where sexism was clearly an issue, and Donald Trump, where racist attitudes helped him secure votes, these candidates won or lost for more conventional reasons. Stacy Dash, a black female, lost (or more accurately dropped out) because she was a Republican in a strongly Democratic district—her partisan affiliation was the dominant reason for the outcome. Taken individually, reasons other than race or gender seemed to play a more prominent role in the defeat of minority celebrity candidates. Taken together, the effects of race and gender seem evident.

These are complex issues with multiple factors that influence who wins and who loses elections. Because this is a small-N case study approach the unique circumstances of each election were considered. The similarities and dissimilarities point to several possible explanations as to why some candidates win while others lose. Race and gender no doubt influence vote choice and have an impact on US elections, however, in the cases presented here there seemed to be other factors that were generally found to be more influential. Is celebrity slack merely a white male "halo effect"? Possibly. Black celebrities do have the power to focus public attention to issues of racial inequality, but they often face a backlash in which they are demonized for their public pronouncements (Jackson 2014). This suggests that celebrities are subject to the same social prejudices as everyone else and that some people may be given more slack than others. More research in the area of celebrity politics will be necessary to expand upon the evidence presented here.

Another area for further study would be the international character of the American phenomena described in this book. Volodymyr Zelensky, the president of Ukraine, pretended to be the president of Ukraine in a television show before seeking the actual office. *Servant of the People*, the name of his show, became the moniker for is newly established political party. After the Russian invasion of Ukraine Zelensky was praised for his handling of the situation suggesting that actor comedians can be excellent political leaders (Parker 2022). In the Philippines former boxer Manny Pacquiao was elected to the House of Representatives and later the Senate. He has recently announced his intention to seek the presidency. The merging of entertainment and politics is a global trend worthy of additional study.

Because entertainers and politicians rely on the same skill set to succeed, entertainers can become politicians and politicians can become entertainers. But not every celebrity has been able to achieve electoral success. Celebrities in unfavorable districts for their party cannot overcome their partisan disadvantage. Sometimes the carefully crafted persona that led to their professional success in Hollywood was a detriment when they sought public office. And sometimes their office seeking is viewed as just another publicity stunt designed to keep them in the headlines.

Another reason that there is a back and forth between entertainers and politicians is because the two enterprises attract the same kind of people. According to Blumenthal, "the presidential campaign and the entertainment industry share more than the cash nexus. Its players are in the same business—the business of popularity. They both seek to captivate the masses: Viewers are voters. The themes that work in politics also work on the screen, especially an antiestablishment populism against corrupt and venal authority" (Blumenthal 1988). It is no wonder that entertainers would be good at politics.

Where does this leave us as a nation? Many authors have begun to consider the perils and promises of our celebrity politics.

PERILS

There are three main critiques of celebrity politics. The first is that celebrities are not good at governing. The second is that the public's attention is distracted away from serious matters and toward trivial controversies. The third is that it is fundamentally elitist and undemocratic. Taken together we should be alarmed by celebrities' electoral victories.

The first critique is that celebrities lack the skills to make them good at governance. Traditional problem-solving skills are replaced with spectacle creating skills. West and Orman believe that "Most entertainment figures do not have the training, background, or experience to offer much other than opinions about important national and international events" (West and Orman 2003, 116). Archer et al.. state that "One important feature of celebrity epistemic power is that it frequently extends beyond the celebrity's legitimate area of expertise. That is, celebrities are routinely perceived as credible on subjects *outside* their relevant expertise" (Archer et al. 2020, 35). Tsaliki et al. note that "Raising and setting global issues and problems on the agenda is not the same thing as solving them" (Tsaliki et al. 2011, 303). Anyone can have an opinion, but solving the problems requires different skills.

Stanley also agrees, "there is a worrying fusion between entertainment and politics going on. Worrying because it elevates celebrities beyond their skill set, bestowing upon them an authority that they do not deserve" (Stanley 2014, 16). The Republican cowboy archetype solves problems with violence. But there are few problems where violence is a workable solution, it is simply not a model for good governance (Stanley 2014). The lack of governing skills seems to define the presidencies of Reagan and Trump.

The Iran-Contra Affair is an example of Reagan's penchant for delegating authority coming back to haunt him. In that case, Oliver North devised a plan that was approved by National Security Advisor John Poindexter to divert money from weapon sales to Iran to aid the Contra rebels in Nicaragua. Although there were differing accounts, the ultimate White House statement on the matter was that Reagan did not know about the scheme. The Tower Report that investigated the matter found that Reagan was derelict in his duty to supervise his top-level staff who orchestrated the arrangement that violated American laws (Brands 2015). Reagan was an actor; the writers and directors were making the decisions.

More recently, Donald Trump's handling of the Coronavirus pandemic has caused consternation among many. Trump's contradictory messages have left states and citizens to their own devices regarding the best approach to handle the deadly disease (Newmyer and Griffiths 2020). The White House issued guidelines on social distancing measures and Trump praised protestors flouting those same measures (McCord 2020). Trump said states should re-open their economies and when Georgia decided to do just that the President admonished the reckless action (Olorunnipa and Dawsey 2020). Trump claimed that a vaccine would be ready by the end of the year, while his scientific advisors claimed that goal was not realistic (Johnson et al. 2020). Trump said schools could safely re-open in the fall while Anthony Fauci, the top public health official, said it would not be safe (Strauss 2020). Donald Trump appeared bewildered in the face of a pandemic that public health officials had developed robust plans for. At one point, Trump said that people should inject themselves with disinfectant because he heard that disinfectant kills the virus. This caused the makers of Lysol and other cleaning products to issue a statement on the danger of ingesting their products. Poison control centers recorded a large uptick in poisonings (Masterson 2020). Skill at gaining attention is not skill at coordinating a multi-leveled federal bureaucracy. Celebrities have many advantages that help them win elections, but the skills that win elections are not the same skills that effectively manage a government (Wright 2019).

Hyde agrees with these assessments. She argues that "Entertainers have vastly exceeded their mandate" (Hyde 2009, 2). She says, "we live in a celebocracy, which means that a celebrity's voice is worth approximately 10,000 times what yours is" (Hyde 2009, 94). They are not the right people for the job.

> Celebrities tend to react emotionally to problems. There is nothing wrong with this tendency—in fact, it's likely to make them much better actors or musicians. But these are absolutely not qualities you'd look for in a public intellectual. Complex problems like the humanitarian fallout from counter-insurgencies need to be approached analytically, not emotionally. (Hyde 2009, 115)

Hyde acknowledges that celebrities can bring attention to a problem, but they also, "degrade the suffering they are attempting to highlight" (Hyde 2009, 115). She is critical of the UN's goodwill ambassadors saying they, "have been created as a way to say 'sorry about the bombing/famine/pestilence—we've sent you a celebrity as a goodwill gesture'" (Hyde 2009, 97). Hyde believes that entertainers should stick with providing entertainment and that policy experts and diplomats should be solving our political problems.

The second criticism revolves around the new media environment and its ill-effect on the public. It causes a dumbing down of political discourse that makes problem solving difficult. West and Orman argue that the media's focus on celebrity opinion pushes out expert analysis of the issues (West and Orman 2003). Instead of covering serious issues seriously, political issues become trivialized and personal scandals dominate the headlines. In an ideal democracy the media would report, and the public would be interested in, expert analysis about public policy issues, not celebrity opinion.

Turner seems to accept the critique presented by West and Orman. Celebrity is criticized "as the epitome of all that is trivial, superficial, meretricious and deplorable about contemporary popular culture" (Turner 2014, 26). He believes the "celebritised persona of the politician" overwhelms the public debate on issues of genuine importance (Turner 2017, 154). Furthermore, "the work of the political spin doctor is primarily intended to interrupt public access to information" (Turner 2014, 155). Again, the concern is about diminishing what should be serious discourse. The public gets distracted by trivialities and does not acquire important information.

Many Americans get their political news from talk shows and late-night comedians. Others rely on social media. The traditional news outlets are not as powerful as they once were in shaping public opinion and perceptions. West and Orman are particularly worried about the destructive effect of comedians on our public figures' credibility, "These stand-up comedians with their nightly forum can engage in a comedic feeding frenzy and destroy a politician with the cumulative weight of their pointed jokes" (West and Orman 2003, 95). Tina Fey's impersonation of Sarah Palin effectively ended Palin's political career. Palin would resign as governor six months after she and McCain lost the election.

West and Orman argue that "As the line between news and entertainment breaks down, it becomes harder for readers and viewers to distinguish fact from fiction in news reporting and to respect the new norms that govern press behavior in terms of information gathering" (West and Orman 2003, 103–4). In short, the media environment puts fact and fiction on equal footing and causes millions of Americans to dismiss information from established and credible news outlets. They start to conflate the fantasy world with the real world. Worse yet, they make decisions using fantastical and false information (Anderson 2017).

They believe voters should reject celebrity politics,

> If we don't take back the celebrity political system, citizens might well face a political contest between a basketball player versus a football player, or a comedian versus a rock star, or a movie star versus a television situation comedy star. Elections are the key vehicle by which representative democracy takes place. Unless citizens receive proper information and candidates provide meaningful choices, it short-circuits the democratic procedures that all Americans value. We all deserve better choices than that currently provided in our regime based on celebrity politics. (West and Orman 2003, 119)

The top-level disfunction of the Trump administration would seem to suggest that West and Orman were correct in their assessment of celebrity politicians.

The third critique is that celebrity politics is elitist. The ability of celebrities to increase awareness of issues through their agenda setting powers effectively limits the voices of less privileged actors in a democracy who can't set the agenda or draw attention to issues (Archer et al. 2020). The new era of celebritized politics, "serves to retrieve and concentrate power in the hands of an elite that controls certain aspects of mass media access and content in order to protect their own interests" (Turner 2014, 155). When a celebrity endorses a politician both the celebrity and the politician make the headlines.

This should help both their careers as they stay in the limelight, but "associating with celebrities also can do a politician more harm than good, making them appear elite, out of touch, even dangerously radical" (Stanley 2014, 103). If celebrities are part of the power elite, we lose sight of the powerless.

It may also create a public desire for an all-powerful president. Growing up watching fantastical tales of heroic men saving the planet, the public might very well expect too much from its leaders. Conflating the real world with the fantasy worlds of Hollywood entertainment creates expectations that cannot be attained democratically. Democracy is messy. In America, the federal government, and the state governments each have their own powers and responsibilities. The same is true of the three branches of government, each have their own powers and responsibilities. Conflicts arise, partisan battles erupt. But when Donald Trump claimed he had "total authority" over the states, things are made simple (Kim, Dawsey, and Dennis 2020). Who would not want total authority? But that is not how democracy works because total authority in the hands of one man is dangerous. That is why we have federalism and checks and balances.

Taken together these three critiques suggest that something is dangerously wrong when entertainers become the political leaders of a society. Stanley admonishes, "Modern American democracy has become like a movie in which people play two-dimensional characters rather than real-life statesmen, all rehearsing lines that are meant to appease their audience rather than tackle the real problems of the world with genuine insight and honesty" (Stanley 2014, 271). In mixing entertainment with politics, we have also mixed reality with make believe.

PROMISES

Not everyone interested in the subject is so pessimistic about the consequences of celebrity politics. There are three potential advantages. Celebrities can draw attention to important issues, they can engage people that were previously bystanders in the political process, and they can provide democratic representation.

Bringing attention to important issues is the first advantage of celebrity political activism. Wheeler suggests that "Celebrities engaging in partisan or casual affairs can bring a guile and persuasiveness in using the media, which may reinvigorate politics with new ideas" (Wheeler 2013, 33). Perhaps celebrities can bring needed change to a stagnant political landscape. Cooper agrees, "The best celebrity diplomats have figured out far more successfully than their professional counterparts how a sophisticated form of public diplomacy can be operated. Direct appeals to a massive public audience are at the core of this approach" (Cooper 2008, 127). Celebrities can create a global public will to pressure governments to take the necessary actions.

Many celebrities engage in activism to bring attention to a large variety of causes. Angelina Jolie has brought attention to the global refugee crisis. Richard Gere wants us to pay attention human rights abuses in Tibet. Bono from U2 supports debt relief for developing nations. Leonardo DiCaprio wants people to protect the environment. George Clooney has been attempting to solve the genocide and refugee crisis in Darfur (Street 2002; West and Orman 2003; Huddart 2005; Cooper 2008; Tsaliki et al. 2011; van Krieken 2012; Wheeler 2013). In March 2022 as Russian missiles pounded Ukraine Arnold Schwarzenegger recorded a video message to the Russian people asking them to oppose the war and to provide them with information they were not getting on Russian state television (Hesse 2022). As global citizens celebrities can use their soft power to act as an agent of change in situations where the hard power of nation-states would be ineffective or counterproductive (Tsaliki et al. 2011).

Celebrities can use their power to direct the public's attention to issues of political importance (Archer et al. 2020). By increasing their relative importance, they hope to move the issue up on the list of agenda items for world leaders and to popularize possible solutions. Harvey has found that celebrities are often viewed as credible agents in the public sphere on issues of political importance. He also found that they can successfully persuade their audiences on those issues. Lastly, they "are potentially as capable as politicians at using the media for agenda setting purposes" (Harvey 2017, 158). Celebrities can have a real impact in the policy arena.

Celebrities are often recruited to fundraise for humanitarian causes. This comes in the form of benefit concerts and branded merchandising (Brownstein 1990). With the RED campaign U2's Bono, Oprah Winfrey, Scarlett Johansson, Penélope Cruz, and other celebrities teamed up with American Express, Apple, Converse, Dell, Gap, Emporio Armani, Hallmark, Microsoft, Motorola, and Starbucks to sell RED branded products. The sales raised $160 million for AIDS relief in Africa. While both the celebrity and the corporation use such philanthropy to build their brand image, there may be some good that comes from such efforts (Richey and Ponte 2011). Paul Newman's charitable work has donated more than $460 million to sick children through the sale of Newman's Own branded products (Raphael 2017). The goal is to get people to contribute money that they may not have if it were not for the attention that the celebrity brought to the cause.

The second advantage celebrities have over traditional politicians is that they can engage people that were previously disengaged from politics. They can draw in new voters and persuade the public by using their media savvy to convey meaningful messages. Wheeler believes that celebrity politics provides "a realistic means through which to promote political engagement" and that "The dialogue between celebrity politicians and the public has allowed for new opportunities for political participation" (Wheeler 2013, 114). Drake and Higgins argue that "Celebrities perform a public service in bringing politics to an audience that traditionally feels excluded from political discourse" (Drake and Higgins 2006, 99).

In the case of Jesse Ventura in Minnesota citizens who were not previously registered to vote registered and voted because they felt that Ventura's campaign spoke to their concerns. His hostility toward the status quo was their hostility toward the status quo. Innovative advertising, a campaign ad made to resemble an ad for children's toys, and the selling of action figures to raise political funds were new methods aimed at increasing political engagement. Celebrities can be innovative in exactly the ways that Wheeler suggests.

Van Zoonen argues that citizens are analogous to fans and that we now have a "fan democracy."

> There are, however, more fundamental and helpful similarities between the active fans of participatory multimedia entertainment and the committed citizen the political parties and politicians look for. Both fans and citizens emerge as a result of performance, of pop-cultural and political actors respectively; both fans and citizens seek information about their objects, talk and discuss, try to convince others of their preferences, and propose alternatives; both fans and citizens have a necessary emotional investment in their objects that keeps their commitment going. Thus, the way fans are positioned, the activities they undertake, and the relation they have with their objects is not fundamentally different from what is expected from good citizens in modernist discourse of politics. (van Zoonen 2005, 145)

When a politician walks onto a stage at a political rally the audience reaction is not all that different from a sports team taking the field or a rock star taking the stage. Fans and voters cheer victories and mourn losses (Hersh 2020). Street's analysis of Donald Trump suggests that van Zoonen is on the right track, "It does appear that Trump elicits a form of adoration that closely resembles the behaviour of fans" (Street 2019, 11). Van Zoonen further believes that engaging with citizens through the forms of communication they are familiar with, i.e., entertainment modalities, that politicians can reach out to groups previously left out of political discussions and thereby enhance democratic participation.

That is why Bill Clinton famously played the saxophone on late night television. He was reaching a demographic group whose support he wished to acquire by appealing to them in terms they found entertaining and pleasing. Van Zoonen is correct that voters and fans are interchangeable. What this means, however, is that celebrities with a fan base can transfer their fans to form their political base of support. When entertainment and politics converge celebrities become candidates and fans become voters. We could lament the passage of bygone days when entertainment and politics were distinct realms and attempt to clamor for serious policy discussions and an informed citizenry. Or we can recognize the world we live in and make the best of it.

Third, celebrities can represent groups of people (Marshall 1997). This is true even when the media seems to be preoccupied with aesthetics over substance. Pels acknowledges that the new media environment tends to focus on political style. It gives "equal attention upon allegedly trivial details (such as sartorial appearance, competitional motives, sexual exploits or other 'private' matters) as upon those elements that the traditional image of political representation focuses as the heart of the matter (the policy issues themselves)" (Pels 2003, 48). But he tends to believe that this is helpful toward democratic aims, "The style concept appeals to the capacity for discernment of citizens without placing excessive weight upon their political competence and their propensity for political action" (Pels 2003, 56). Ultimately, he argues "that the media show that is called 'politics' similarly promotes forms of emotional realism, which enable ordinary citizens, in spite of their political 'passivity' and even 'indifference,' to react adequately to whatever their political representatives are putting on" (Pels 2003, 60).

Street has a very particular definition of celebrity politics that leads to his defense of it. He argues, "Celebrity politics is a code for the performance of representations through the gestures and media available to those who wish to claim 'representativeness'" (Street 2004, 445). Sonny Bono was cognizant of the fact that he represented hippies who were turned off by the Establishment and were ostracized from mainstream culture. In his attire and behaviors Bono embodied a group of people, he publicly represented their lifestyle. Corner argues, "There is a symbolic excess at work in the figure of the politician, a relationship between person and political system, and often between person and nation" (Corner 2003, 80). The persona of the politician gives citizens the ability to connect with their leaders in more effective ways.

Street believes that the "Adoption of the trappings of popular celebrity is not a trivial gesture toward fashion or a minor detail of political communication, but instead lies at the heart of the notion of political representation itself" (Street 2004, 447). Politicians behave like celebrities to communicate their political message to audiences and celebrities become activists to communicate their political messages as well. Both are representing a constituency, and this is what representative democracy is all about. Street is clear,

> The capacity to claim to speak politically as a celebrity is determined by a
> number of conditions and structures, as well as by the affective bond which is

created by the relationship between the celebrity and their admirers. In certain contexts and under particular conditions, performers can lay claim to represent those who admire them. They give political voice to those who follow them, both by virtue of the political conditions and by means of their art. (Street 2004, 449)

Marshall agrees with Street. He argues that "celebrities are human agents in the public sphere who act as proxies" (Marshall 1997, 249). Through their carefully crafted public persona they come to "embody the collective in the individual" (Marshall 1997, 241). In the end, "the celebrity figure is con- structed by these apparatuses to contain the public—in effect, to represent the public" (Marshall 1997, 242). Celebrities can, and do, represent people who want representation in government. They come to symbolically embody a character with qualities that voters desire. Far from being undemocratic, it fosters democracy by giving voice to those who want to be heard.

CONCLUSIONS

Turner is correct when he says, "Celebrity has the potential to operate in ways that one might deplore or applaud, but neither potential is intrinsic" (Turner 2014, 157). It is not inherently good or bad that celebrities have an advan- tage in electoral politics. Advocacy groups have long sought-after celebrities to serve as their spokespersons. Bringing attention to the plight of starving children, abused animals, or environmental degradation can serve to solve our collective problems. Conversely, the power of celebrity could distract us from those problems when they start fighting about who has the bigger hands, as Trump did in 2016. Or consider Al Franken in the Senate. He shunned the national media and only spoke with Minnesota reporters. He became a "work-horse" instead of a "show-horse" precisely because he did not want his celebrity to distract us from the serious issues. Celebrities who have a genuine interest in serving the common good could very well transform soci- ety for the better by making us pay attention to our serious problems. Those without that interest could make our society worse by distracting us from the serious issues.

Biases against actors' involvement in politics due to their fabricated sincer- ity forgets that anyone is capable of the same deception.

Granted, actors can rely on tricks of the theatrical trade in evoking support from the voters. Yet so can former trial lawyers, a breed of communicator that is even more common in politics than thespians. And, thanks to show biz-inspired campaign consultants, even politicians who come from academe or business can

find themselves in a starring role on television—in a 30-second spot. Whether
they are sincere or not requires careful study of their records, not their rushes.
(*Pittsburgh Post-Gazette* November 15, 1994)

Entertainers are not the only professionals whose skills at fakery are used to
persuade and convince audiences. There is no reason to expect more deception from actors than from any other professional turned politician.

Despite lamentations to the contrary, there is nothing wrong with politics
being entertaining. Indeed, the more entertaining it is the more people will
participate in it. Rather than fantasizing about an ideal democracy with sub-
stantive civic engagement elites could harness the power of celebrity for the
common good. Celebrities have the attention capital to garner media and
public focus. Consultants, pollsters, speech writers, and other political insiders have the tools to craft winning messages. Policy experts have solutions
to our most pressing problems. Working together they can be an integral part
of the political system and make real change that is supported by the mass
public. The line between celebrity spokesperson and celebrity politician is
only a matter of content, the skill is the same; to sell the public on an idea.

Realists understand the media environment is not going to change overnight. As such they can harness the power of celebrity to effect positive
change, they can use the system as it is to create the world they would prefer.
Public policy experts still offer in-depth analysis, and they still create plans
that would solve many of our most pressing social and political concerns.
Their next job is to find a good spokesperson and to convince the public that
their solution is a good one. If the media gravitates toward covering celebrities, recruit a celebrity to advocate for your cause or run for office with your
preferred policy agenda. The world of celebritized politics does not neces-
sarily mean the demise of good policy solutions. It simply means that good
policies need to be sold to the public using the existing mechanisms of power.

Political activists and political consultants understand that fundraising to
advertise is a difficult endeavor. The public understands it creates bias that
favors wealthy interests. But the celebrity's ability to use earned media makes
fundraising less important. With celebrity fame working for them policy
advocates can use someone else's fame for political ends. Persuading an influential person, like a celebrity, to take up one's cause allows more people to
be persuaded through the power of free media attention. Companies harness
the power of celebrity to sell products with celebrity endorsements. Political
activists could harness the power of celebrity to sell ideas and win elections.

The power trifecta of talent, fame, and resources that celebrities have can
be harnessed by party leaders to win elections. They key for party leaders is
to find celebrity candidates who understand their role. The celebrity candidate
is likely to succeed if they remember they are spokespersons for the party

and allied interests. If they stick to the script created by political consultants, strategists, and speechwriters they will say what they need to say to win. Campaign managers hate it when their candidate "goes rogue" and veers off script. They open the campaign to unplanned occurrences and the designed image falters. Image management requires sticking to the script, in political parlance—staying "on message." The celebrity candidate will best succeed when they understand they are not the decision maker, they are the spokesperson, they are the actor portraying a politician as the screenwriters intended it. Interviews and press conferences require improvisation, but it must be "on message" improvisation. When candidates start to believe they know better than the consultants and handlers, they lose elections. This is not only bad for them; it is bad for everyone who works for the campaign and everyone who supports the campaign.

With all these advantages why don't more celebrities seek elected office? The most obvious answer is opportunity cost. High profile actors can earn millions of dollars for a single movie role. A celebrity's income would decline dramatically if they pursued a career in public service. There is also the risk of the celebrity damaging their brand image. Celebrities can remain apolitical and maintain goodwill among their fans. Celebrities who speak out on controversial issues run the risk of alienating or angering fans who have different political views. Today's "cancel culture" seeks to punish individuals who have offended the sensibilities of political activists. Celebrities who get involved in politics face the very real possibility of a backlash that results in financial losses and a damaged reputation.

Wright, like others before her, argues that celebrities lack the skills for effective governance. But we need to make a distinction between what is good governance and what is good representation. Are celebrities, once elected, effective at solving problems? There is evidence to suggest they are not. Do celebrities come to embody the hopes, dreams, wishes, and desires of their fans? Do they represent a group of people? There is evidence to suggest they do. Democrats would argue that Trump completely mishandled the Coronavirus pandemic due to his lack of governing skills. Republicans would argue that Trump represented the interests of millions of Americans who were concerned with government overreach and above all else wanted their freedoms protected. Bureaucrats and policy experts can design and implement effective government. The role of the elected politicians is to represent the people and that is something that celebrities can surely do.

More research will need to be done to answer this question. What makes someone a good leader? Passing bills and solving problems or representing the interests of the constituencies that elected them? Many celebrities, once elected, were re-elected suggesting that their constituents thought they were doing a good job in office. Others were not re-elected. One should note that even established politicians with decades of experience have difficulty getting their agenda passed, especially in this era of hyper-partisanship. Traditional legislative experience is no guarantee of success.

Ultimately, this book presents some contradictory evidence. On the one hand celebrities have many advantages when they seek office—the power trifecta and celebrity slack. But they are not immune from the normal laws of politics. If they belong to the minority party in a one party dominated district or state, they get crushed no matter how famous they are. If they lose the fundraising battle, they tend to lose the election. Sometimes earned media can allow them to squeak out a just barely plurality win - sometimes. And sometimes a wood tick or federal indictment turns a likely loser into a winner. It doesn't look like the celebrity advantage is as strong as some suggest.

There is an air of elitism in West and Orman's critique. If Americans want the movie star, or TV star, or rock star, to be their leader they should go ahead and select that person. If that person turns out to be completely ignorant and produces social upheaval and discord along with policies that harm millions of people, then the public has every right to suffer the consequences of their decisions. If Americans want boring technocrats to solve our collective problems, then they should select them. But if they want fabulous heroes with great smiles and charming personalities, then they have every right to select them as well. Democracy is about giving the people what they want, even when the people will hurt themselves in the process. That said, James Madison understood that an elected body of discerning representatives should be in place to put a check on the unrestrained passions of a populist mob.

Because celebrities have the talent, fame, and resources to run an effective campaign on their own, they are less beholden to the political establishment. Rather than needing to rely on party leaders and a small number of mega-donors to organize and finance their campaign, they can operate independently and challenge the existing system. This could be a good thing when the system is failing to serve the interests of ordinary Americans. But it could also pose a danger. Celebrity slack may allow celebrities to break social norms with impunity. If the celebrity politician breaks political norms that are fundamental to a functioning democratic republic, it could irreparably alter the political landscape. Because celebrities are trend setters, they can set in motion a political trend that disrupts the peaceful transfer of power, the rule of law, and other cherished ideals.

In the end, there is nothing inherently wrong, or inherently right, with celebrities taking an active interest in our politics. As citizens they have just as much right to participate in politics as anyone else. Their preeminence in the entertainment industry makes them well suited to appeal to mass audiences and a mass electorate. They can use their platform to inform citizens, or at least to persuade them to vote for one party over another. If done carefully, and with regard to the possible dangers, we can harness the power of celebrity to further democratic aims. When celebrities talk about political issues or take a stand for or against certain policies people listen.

Bibliography

60 Minutes. 2011. "Lady Gaga on 'Mastering the Art of Fame.'" February 10. Accessed May 20, 2020. https://www.cbsnews.com/news/lady-gaga-on-mastering -the-art-of-fame/.

Advertiser. 1987. "Former Pop Singer to Run for Mayor." February 9.

Associated Press. 1986. "Clint Eastwood Runs for Mayor in California Town." January 31.

Associated Press. 1987. "Sonny Runs for Palm Springs Mayor." February 6.

Associated Press. 1988. "Sonny Bono's Mayoral Campaign Put on Hold After Wife Hospitalized." March 31.

Associated Press. 1988. "People in the News." April 3.

Associated Press. 1988. "Sonny Bono Headlines Elections in California, Texas." April 12.

Associated Press. 1988. "Sonny Bono Elected Mayor of Palm Springs." April 13.

Associated Press. 2009. "Wrestling exec wins bid for Conn. school board." February 26.

Associated Press. 2010. "Poll: Blumenthal ahead in Conn. Senate race." January 14.

Associated Press. 2012. "Roseanne Barr, Ex-Va. Congressman on W.Va. Ballot." October 3.

ABC News Transcripts. April 8, 1987.

ABC News Transcripts. April 10, 1988.

Adams, John. 1805. *Discourses on Davila: A Series of Papers on Political History*. Boston, MA: Russell & Cutler.

Adler, Jerry, Ron La Brecque, Jon Lowell, and Martin Kasindorf. 1981. "Frankie and Ronnie." *Newsweek*, January 19.

Aisch, Gregor, Jon Huang, and Cecilia King. 2016. "Dissecting the #PizzaGate Conspiracy Theories." *New York Times*, December 10. Accessed May 27, 2020. https://www.nytimes.com/interactive/2016/12/10/business/media/pizzagate .html?searchResultPosition=1.

Alberta, Tim. 2019. *American Carnage: On the Front Lines of the Republican Civil War and The Rise of President Trump*. New York: HarperCollins.

Alexander, Jeffrey C. 2010. *The Performance of Politics: Obama's Victory and the Democratic Study for Power*. Oxford: Oxford University Press.

Alter, Jonathan. 1986. "Taking CBS News to Task." *Newsweek*, 15 September 1986.

Anderson, Kurt. 2017. *Fantasyland: How America Went Haywire a 500 Year History*. New York: Random House.

Andrews, Nigel. 2003. *True Myths: The Life and Times of Arnold Schwarzenegger*. New York: Bloomsbury.

AOL Music. 2012. "Roseanne Barr: Beyonce, Jay-Z 'Arrogant,' Fans Are 'Stupid.'" January 24.

Applebome, Peter, and Elizabeth Maker. 2012. "Murphy Defeats McMahon After Bitter U.S. Senate Race in Connecticut." *New York Times*, November 7.

Archer, Alfred, Amanda Cawston, Benjamin Matheson, and Machteld Geuskens. 2020. "Celebrity, Democracy, and Epistemic Power." *Perspectives on Politics* 18 (1): 27–42. https://doi.org/10.1017/S1537592719002615.

Averill, Brady. 2007. "Celebrities, Small Donors Make Up Franken Fundraising List; His Campaign Said the Donors in the Entertainment Industry Are Friends and People He's Worked With." *Star Tribune* (Minneapolis, MN), April 14.

Baden, Patricia Lopez. 1996. "Redford, Now Batting for Wellstone." *Star Tribune* (Minneapolis, MN), October 27.

Baden, Patricia Lopez. 1998. "This Candidate Knew How to Market Himself; Never Camera-Shy, He Knew Creativity Wasn't a Risk at All." *Star Tribune* (Minneapolis, MN), November 5.

Balz, Dan. 2009. "With Act II Unwritten, Palin Can Define Her Role." *Washington Post*, July 27. Accessed May 28, 2020. https://www.washingtonpost.com/wp-dyn/content/article/2009/07/26/AR2009072602580.html.

Barker, Jeff. 1984. "Jed Clampett and Miss Hathaway Rejoin 1960s Battle in House Campaign." Associated Press, November 2.

Barreiro, Dan. 1990. "War? The Body Coos Like a Dove." *Star Tribune* (Minneapolis, MN), December 9.

Barthes, Ronald. 2005. "The World of Wrestling." In *Steel Chair to the Head: The Pleasure and Pain of Professional Wrestling*, edited by Nicholas Sammond, 23–32. Durham, NC: Duke University Press.

Beekman, Scott M. 2006. *Ringside: A History of Professional Wrestling in America*. Westport, CT: Praeger.

Beeman, Perry. 1986. "Love Boat's Fred Grandy in Close Congress Race." *Lansing State Journal*, October 26.

Bell, Lauren, David Meyer, and Ronald Gaddie. 2016. *Slingshot: The Defeat of Eric Cantor*. Washington, DC: CQ Press.

Bentley, Rosalind, and Susan Hogan/Albach. "Ventura Gets Votes from All Walks of Life." *Star Tribune* (Minneapolis, MN), November 5.

Bergholz, Richard. 1966. "Lynch Is Only Democrat to Win Statewide Post; Reagan Names Key Aide." *Los Angeles Times*, November 10.

Bergholz, Richard. 1966. "Reagan Calls Brown His Main Asset for Victory in Election." *Los Angeles Times*, September 30.

Bernstein, Carl. 1992. "The Idiot Culture." *New Republic* 206 (23), June 8: 22–28.

Black, Eric. 2005. "Filling Dayton's Seat; In, Out and In-Between." *Star Tribune* (Minneapolis, MN), February 11.

Black, Eric. 2007. "The Big Question; A Franken Candidacy." *Star Tribune* (Minneapolis, MN), February 4.

Black, Eric. 2007. "Still a 'Standup' Guy?; Has Al Franken's Acid Tongue Singed His Candidacy? Franken Says the Race Isn't a Vote on His Sense of Humor. But Some Minnesota Republicans Think They Might Get the Last Laugh." *Star Tribune* (Minneapolis, MN), March 28.

Blumenthal, Sidney. 1988. "Hollywood's Search for a Political Leading Man." *Washington Post*, January 22.

Bono, Sonny. 1991. *And the Beat Goes On*. New York: Pocket Books.

Boorstin, Daniel J. 1992. *The Image: A Guide to Pseudo-Events in America*. New York: Vintage Books.

Box Office Mojo. 2019. "Clint Eastwood." Accessed May 15, 2019. https://www .boxofficemojo.com/people/chart/?view=Actor&id=clinteastwood.htm.

Boydstun, Amber E., and Regina G. Lawrence. 2020. "When Celebrity and Political Journalism Collide: Reporting Standards, Entertainment, and the Conundrum of Covering Donald Trump's 2016 Campaign." *Perspectives on Politics* 18 (1): 128–43. https://doi.org/10.1017/S153759271900238X.

Bradwell, Matt. 2014. "'Clueless' Star Stacey Dash Joins Fox News." United Press International, May 28.

Bragg, Beth. 2006. "Palin-Knowles Radio Debate Didn't . . . Did Too . . . Didn't . . . Did Too." *Anchorage Daily News* (AK), November 3.

Brammer, John Paul. 2021. "Nero Fiddled as Rome Burned. Sarah Palin Rapped as America Did." *Washington Post*, March 11. Accessed May 3, 2022. https://www .washingtonpost.com/opinions/2021/03/11/covid-anniversary-sarah-palin-masked -singer-tom-hanks-nba/.

Brands, H.W. 2015. *Reagan: The Life*. New York: Doubleday.

Braun, Gerry. 1987. "Entertainer Bono Runs for Mayor; Sonny Seeking Share of Power in Palm Springs." *The San Diego Union-Tribune*, 7 December 1987.

Braun, Gerry. 1992. "Campbell Done in by His Own Negative TV Ads, Bono Candidacy." *San Diego Union-Tribune*, June 14.

Brooks, Jennifer and Maya Rao. 2018. "Most Believe Franken's Accusers." *Star Tribune* (Minneapolis, MN), January 16.

Brooks, Tim, and Earle Marsh. 2007. *The Complete Directory to Prime Time Network and Cable TV Shows 1946–Present*. 9th ed. New York: Ballantine Books.

Brown, Jessica A. 2016. "The New 'Southern Strategy': Immigration, Race, and 'Welfare Dependency' in Contemporary US Republican Political Discourse." *Geopolitics, History, and International Relations* 8 (2): 22–41.

Brownstein, Ronald. 1990. *The Power and the Glitter: The Hollywood–Washington Connection*. New York: Vintage Press.

Budesheim, Thomas L., and Stephen J. DePaola. 1994. "Beauty or the Beast? The Effects of Appearance, Personality, and Issue Information on Evaluations of Political Candidates." *Personality and Social Psychology Bulletin* 20 (4): 339–48.

Bumiller, Elisabeth. 1980. "The Elephant's Ecstasy & Washington in Wait; Get Ready for The Country Club Presidency—Now!" *Washington Post*, November 6.

Burke, Shane. 1994. "Congressman Bono Has the Last Laugh." *Advertiser*, November 11.

Buss, David M. 1989. "Sex Differences in Human Mate Preferences: Evolutionary Hypotheses Tested in 37 Cultures." *Behavioral and Brain Sciences* 12 (1): 1–14. https://doi.org/10.1017/S0140525X00023992.

Buss, David M., and D.P. Schmitt. 1993. "Sexual Strategies Theory: An Evolutionary Perspective on Human Mating." *Psychological Review* 100 (2): 204–32. http://dx.doi.org/10.1037/0033-295X.100.2.204.

Buyuker, Beyza, Amanda Jadidi D'Urso, Alexandra Filindra, and Noah J. Kaplan. 2020. "Race Politics Research and the American Presidency: Thinking About White Attitudes, Identities and Vote Choice in the Trump Era and Beyond." *Journal of Race, Ethnicity, and Politics* 6 (3): 1–42. https://doi.org/10.1017/rep.2020.33.

California Journal's Election Weekly. June 8, 1992.

California Journal's Election Weekly. August 31, 1992.

Campaign Finance Institute. n.d. "Major Presidential Candidates' Pre-Nomination Receipts, Individual Contributions and Matching Funds, 1976–2004." Accessed June 25, 2018. http://www.cfinst.org/pdf/federal/2016Report/pdf/CFI_Federal-CF_16_Table1-01.pdf.

Cannon, Lou. "Clinton Secures Party Nomination; Perot Factor Grows, Exit Poll Show; Women Triumph in California Senate Contests." *Washington Post*, June 3.

Cannon, Lou. 2000. *President Reagan: The Role of a Lifetime*. New York: Public Affairs.

Carroll, Rory. 2018. "Stacey Dash on Being a Conservative in Hollywood: 'I've Been Blacklisted'; The Clueless Actor Hopes for Trump's Endorsement as She Runs for Congress: 'He's Representing the People That I Want to Represent.'" *Guardian* (London), March 11.

Cashmore, Ellis. 2014. *Celebrity Culture*. 2nd ed. New York: Routledge.

Cauchon, Dennis. 2007. "The New Bipartisans: At State Level, GOP, Dems Learn to Get Along." *USA Today*, June 21. Accessed May 28, 2020. https://usatoday30.usatoday.com/news/politics/2007-06-21-state-bipartisanship_N.htm.

CBS News Poll. September 2011. Retrieved January 10, 2013 from the iPOLL Databank, The Roper Center for Public Opinion Research, University of Connecticut. http://www.ropercenter.uconn.edu/data_access/ipoll/ipoll.html.

Center for Responsive Politics. 2008. "Minnesota Congressional Races 2008." Accessed May 10, 2019. https://www.opensecrets.org/races/election?cycle=2008&id=MN.

Cillizza, Chris. 2016. "Get Ready for Nastiest Presidential Race You've Seen; Each Candidate May Just Try to Make the Other Look Bad." *Dayton Daily News* (Ohio), May 5.

Claiborne, William. 1998. "Mary Bono Wins House Seat; Widow Takes 65% in California Race." *The Washington Post*, April 8.

CNN. 2020. "Pete Buttigieg Fills In for Jimmy Kimmel." March 13. Accessed May 2, 2020. https://www.cnn.com/videos/media/2020/03/13/pete-buttigieg-guest-host-jimmy-kimmel-orig.cnn.

CNN/ORC International Poll. November 2011. Retrieved January 17, 2013 from the iPOLL Databank, The Roper Center for Public Opinion Research, University of Connecticut. http://www.ropercenter.uconn.edu/data_access/ipoll/ipoll.html.

Collin, Robbie. 2017. "An Inconvenient Sequel: Truth to Power Review: In the Age of Trump, Al Gore's Follow-Up Already Feels Dated." *Telegraph* (UK), August 17.

Comegys, Lee. 1984. "Kulp Gulp." United Press International, November 8.

Conklin, Ellis E. 1985. "The Town Where Time Stopped; UPI News Feature; Carmel-by-the-Sea: Coping with No-Growth." United Press International, December 22.

Connolly, Ceci. 1998. "Politics." *Washington Post*, September 1.

Cooper, Andrew F. 2008. *Celebrity Diplomacy*. Boulder: Paradigm Publishers.

Cooper, Kenneth J. 1992. "A Sitcom About Congress? 'Cooter' Says Stay Tuned." *Washington Post*, November 18.

Corner, John. 2000. "Mediated Persona and Political Culture: Dimensions of Structure and Process." *European Journal of Cultural Studies* 3 (3): 386–402.

Corner, John. 2003. "Mediated Persona and Popular Culture." In *Media and the Restyling of Politics: Consumerism, Celebrity, and Cynicism*, edited by John Corner and Dick Pels, 67–84. London: Sage.

Corner, John, and Dick Pels, eds. 2003. *Media and the Restyling of Politics: Consumerism, Celebrity, and Cynicism*. London: Sage.

Covert, Colin. 2005. "For Maher, No Shortage of Outrage." *Star Tribune* (Minneapolis, MN), June 24.

Cranley, Ellen. 2019. "Melania Trump Expert Says 'I Really Don't Care, Do U?' Jacket Was a Jab at Ivanka." *Business Insider*, December 3. Accessed May 27, 2020. https://www.businessinsider.com/melania-trump-i-really-dont-care-do-u-jab -ivanka-2019-12.

Crosby, Jackie. 2005. "2005 Election; St. Paul Mayor's Race; All Politics is Local? Think Again; In St. Paul on Monday, U.S. Sen. John Kerry Stumped for Chris Coleman, and Former New York City Mayor Ed Koch Headlined a Fundraiser for Randy Kelly." *Star Tribune* (Minneapolis, MN), October 11.

Cullen, Jenny. 1987. "Do Drop In to The City of Hype." *Sunday Mail* (QLD), December 13.

Dahl, Robert A. 1961. *Who Governs?: Democracy and Power in an American City*. New Haven, CT: Yale University Press.

Dahlgren, Peter. 2009. *Media and Political Engagement: Citizens, Communication, and Democracy*. Cambridge: Cambridge University Press.

Daily News-Post. 1967. "Today's a Big Day for Shirley Temple." November 14.

Dallek, Matthew. 2000. *The Right Moment: Ronald Reagan's First Victory and the Decisive Turning Point in American Politics*. New York: Free Press.

DeMillo, Andrew. 2008. "Huckabee Joining Fox as Commentator." Associated Press International, June 13.

Des Moines Register. 1986. "Primary Races at a Glance." June 4.

Des Moines Register. 1986. "Choices for Congress." October 19

Des Moines Register. 1986. "Grandy, Nagle Stress their Iowa Roots." November 6.

Des Moines Register. 1986. "Winners, Losers and Never—Rans . . . " November 9.

Des Moines Register. 1986. "It's a Stupid, Stupid New Culture and It's Getting More Stupid." November 26.

Des Moines Register. 1986. "Can You Imagine? . . . " November 30.

Des Moines Register. 1986. "Appointment Flight Becomes More Than Legislative Politics as Usual." December 8.

Des Moines Register. 1986. "Official Results of State's Nov. 4 Election." December 12.

Des Moines Register. 1987. "On Your Mark." February 1.

Davis, Ivor. 1980. "Queen May Be Hobnobbing with Clint, Bob and Frank." *Globe and Mail* (Canada), November 29.

Dawson, Alan. 2017. "The 51 Best-Selling Pay-Per-View Fight Nights in History." *Business Insider*, August 25. Accessed August 23, 2018. https://www.businessinsider.com/the-50-best-selling-pay-per-view-events-boxing-ufc-wrestling-tv-history-2017-8.

De Fiebre, Conrad. 1998. "The Campaign Money Rolls In; Candidates, Parties Raised $4.8 Million in Past 2 Months." *Minneapolis Star Tribune*, October 27.

De Fiebre, Conrad. 1998. "Ventura's Big Contributors Don't Quite Fit the Big-Money Mold." *Minneapolis Star Tribune*, December 7.

De Garis, Laurence. 2005. "The 'Logic' of Professional Wrestling." In *Steel Chair to the Head: The Pleasure and Pain of Professional Wrestling*, edited by Nicholas Sammond, 192–212. Durham, NC: Duke University Press.

DelReal, Jose A. 2015. "Perry: Trump's Campaign 'A Barking Carnival Act' and 'A Cancer on Conservatism.'" *Washington Post*, July 22.

Demby, Gene. 2019. "White Supremacy Has Never Been Fringe." *NPR Code Switch*, August 10. Accessed May 27, 2020. https://www.npr.org/sections/codeswitch/2019/08/10/749202273/white-supremacy-isnt-emerging-from-the-fringes-its-part-of-americas-core.

Diaz, Kevin and Jake Sherman. 2007. "Ciresi's Personal Wealth Dwarfs That of Potential Senate Opponent; The Lawyer's Fortune—Assets of $26 Million—Vastly Exceeds Democratic Candidate Al Franken's Holdings." *Star Tribune* (Minneapolis, MN), July 4.

Diaz, Kevin and Jake Sherman. 2007. "FEC Report; Minnesota Senate Campaign; Franken Raises More Money, Spends More; Donor Reports Confirm Stereotypes: Celebrities for Franken, Lawyers for Ciresi and Business Interests for Coleman." *Star Tribune* (Minneapolis, MN), July 17.

Diaz, Kevin, and Bob von Sternberg. 2009. "$12 Million Later and Still No Senator From Minnesota; Spending by Franken and Coleman Since Election Day Amounts to About One-Fourth of the Overall Cost of the Senate Race." *Star Tribune* (Minneapolis, MN), April 16.

Dickenson, James R. 1986. "Clint Eastwood's Race for Mayor." *Washington Post*, February 2.

Dodgson, Lindsay. 2016. "The Biggest Threat to Earth Has Been Dismissed by Trump as a Chinese Hoax." *Business Insider*, November 11. Accessed May 27, 2020. https://www.businessinsider.com/donald-trump-climate-change-chinese-hoax-2016-11.

Downs, Ray. 2018. "Actress Stacey Dash to Run for Congress in California." United Press International, February 26.

Drake, Philip, and Michael Higgins. 2006. "'I'm a Celebrity, Get Me Into Politics': The Political Celebrity and the Celebrity Politician." In *Framing Celebrity: New Directions in Celebrity Culture*, edited by Su Holmes and Sean Redmond, 87–100. New York: Routledge.

Duchschere, Kevin. 2008. "Playboy, Junta Tied to Senate Hopefuls; Supporters of DFLer Al Franken and Republican Sen. Norm Coleman Swapped Barbs Over the Sources of Campaign Donations." *Star Tribune* (Minneapolis, MN), May 21.

Duchschere, Kevin. 2008. "Campaign 2008: The U.S. Senate Race; GOP Legislators Say Franken Has History of Sexist Jokes That Aren't Funny; The Two Lawmakers Say the Candidate's Controversial Playboy Article Wasn't His Only Piece of Humor That Demeans Women. His Campaign Again Points to His Work as Satire." *Star Tribune* (Minneapolis, MN), June 3.

Duchschere, Kevin. 2008. "Race for the Senate: Al Franken's Record; Career Success, Just Not in Politics; Al Franken Has Had to Play Catch-Up as He Has Moved Away from Comedy." *Star Tribune* (Minneapolis, MN), October 20.

Duchschere, Kevin. 2008. "The Minnesota Poll: The Senate Race; Franken, Coleman Are Neck and Neck." *Star Tribune* (Minneapolis, MN), November 2.

Duchschere, Kevin, and Mike Kaszuba. 2008. "DFL State Convention: Moving Forward; Good Losers Help DFL to End on a Good Note; The Party Left Rochester on Sunday Feeling United over Obama and Franken." *Star Tribune* (Minneapolis, MN), June 9.

Durkheim, Emile. 1996. *The Division of Labor in Society*. New York: Free Press.

Duscha, Julius. 1967. "Reagan Gives a Surprising Performance: Not Great, Not Brilliant, But a Good Show." *New York Times*, December 10.

Dwyer, Colin, and Andrew Limbong. 2019. "'Go Back Where You Came From': The Long Rhetorical Roots of Trump's Racist Tweets." NPR Morning Edition, July 15. Accessed May 27, 2020. https://www.npr.org/2019/07/15/741827580/go-back-where-you-came-from-the-long-rhetorical-roots-of-trump-s-racist-tweets.

Easly, Cameron. 2017. "Mitch McConnell—Still America's Least Popular Senator (April 2017)." *Morning Consult*, April 11. Accessed February 24, 2019. https://morningconsult.com/senate-rankings-april-2017/.

Edwards, Anne. 1988. *Shirley Temple: American Princess*. Guilford, CT: Lyons Paperback.

Efrain, Michael G. and E.W.J. Patterson. 1974. "Voters Vote Beautiful: The Effect of Physical Appearance on a National Election." *Canadian Journal of Behavioural Science* 6 (4): 352–56. http://dx.doi.org/10.1037/h0081881.

Elias, Sean, and Joe R. Feagin. 2016. *Racial Theories in Social Science: A Systemic Racism Critique*. New York: Routledge.

Eliot, Marc. 2009. *American Rebel: The Life of Clint Eastwood*. New York: Three Rivers Press.

Fahrenthold, David A. 2017. "A Time Magazine with Trump on the Cover Hangs in His Golf Clubs. It's Fake." *Washington Post*, June 27. Accessed May 27, 2020. https://www.washingtonpost.com/politics/a-time-magazine-with-trump-on

-the-cover-hangs-in-his-golf-clubs-its-fake/2017/06/27/0adf96de-5850-11e7-ba90
-f5875b7d1876_story.html.

Fang, Marina. 2019. "Looks Like Al Franken's Career Comeback Is Complete: The Former Minnesota Senator has a New Public Platform, Continuing the Pattern of Accused Serial Sexual Predators Getting Career Comebacks." *Huffington Post*, September 25. Accessed May 26, 2020. https://www.huffpost.com/entry/al-franken -career-comeback-sexual-misconduct-allegations_n_5d8b7ac7e4b0c6d0cef4e9ee.

Farah, Judy. 1988. "Sonny Bono Says He's Taken Seriously in Candidacy for Mayor of Palm Springs." *Associated Press*, April 9.

Farnam, T.W. 2010. "At $97 Per Vote, Top Spenders Lost." *Washington Post*, November 9.

Feagin, Joe. 2013. *Systemic Racism: A Theory of Oppression*. New York: Routledge.

Feagin, Joe R., and Kimberley Ducey. 2017. *Elite White Men Ruling: Who, What, When, Where, and How*. New York: Taylor & Francis.

Federal Election Commission (FEC). n.d. "Al Franken." Accessed May 27, 2022. https://www.fec.gov/data/candidate/S8MN00438/?cycle=2008&election _full=true.

Federal Election Commission (FEC). n.d. "Federal Elections 2012 Results." Accessed May 7, 2020. https://transition.fec.gov/pubrec/fe2012/2012pres.pdf.

Federal Election Commission (FEC). n.d. "Fred Dalton Thompson." Accessed May 7, 2020. https://www.fec.gov/data/candidate/S4TN00138/?cycle=1994&election_full =true.

Federal Election Commission (FEC). n.d. "Jim Cooper." Accessed May 7, 2020. https: //www.fec.gov/data/candidate/S4TN00096/.

Federal Election Commission (FEC). n.d. "Linda McMahon." Accessed May 8, 2020. https://www.fec.gov/data/candidate/S0CT00151/?cycle=2010&election_full =false.

Federal Election Commission (FEC). n.d. "Richard Blumenthal." Accessed May 8, 2020. https://www.fec.gov/data/candidate/S0CT00177/?cycle=2010&election_full =true.

Federal Election Commission (FEC). n.d. "Official 2020 Presidential General Election Results." Accessed May 25, 2021. https://www.fec.gov/resources/cms -content/documents/2020presgeresults.pdf.

"Feinstein, Boxer Win California Senate Nominations; Seymore, Herschensohn Get GOP Bids." 1992. Facts on File Worlds News Digest, June 4.

Flinn, John. 1986. "Now Clint's Got Himself a Whole Town." *San Francisco Examiner*, April 9.

Franken, Al. 2017. *Al Franken: Giant of the Senate*. New York: Twelve.

Franklin, Bob. 2004. *Packaging Politics: Political Communication in Britain's Media Democracy*. 2nd ed. London: Arnold.

Gajanan, Mahita. 2017. "Kellyanne Conway Defends White House's Falsehoods as 'Alternative Facts.'" *Time Magazine*, January 22. Accessed May 27, 2020. https:// time.com/4642689/kellyanne-conway-sean-spicer-donald-trump-alternative-facts/.

Gallup Poll. June 2012. Retrieved January 17, 2013 from the iPOLL Databank, The Roper Center for Public Opinion Research, University of Connecticut. http://www .ropercenter.uconn.edu/data_access/ipoll/ipoll.html.

Garrett, Robert T., and Gromer Jeffers Jr. 2021. "Matthew McConaughey May Be a Viable Candidate for Texas Governor; Poll Shows Actor Ahead of Abbott." *Dallas Morning News*, April 18. Accessed April 19, 2021. https://www.dallasnews.com /news/politics/2021/04/18/matthew-mcconaughey-may-be-a-viable-candidate-for -texas-governor-poll-shows-actor-ahead-of-abbott/.

Garthwaite, Craig, and Timothy J. Moore. 2008. "The Role of Celebrity Endorsements in Politics: Oprah, Obama, and the 2008 Democratic Primary." University of Maryland Department of Economics. Accessed May 20, 2020. http://www.stat .columbia.edu/~gelman/stuff_for_blog/celebrityendorsements_garthwaitemoore .pdf.

Gerson, Michael. 2020. "This Is What Happens When Bigotry Dominates the Main Conservative Media Platform." *Washington Post*, June 8. Accessed June 11, 2020. https://www.washingtonpost.com/opinions/this-is-what-happens-when -bigotry-dominates-the-main-conservative-media-platform/2020/06/08/c1deaf50 -a9ba-11ea-a9d9-a81c1a491c52_story.html.

Gervais, Bryan T., and Irwin L. Morris. 2018. *Reactionary Republicanism: How the Tea Party in the House Paved the Way for Trump's Victory*. New York: Oxford University Press.

Gilbert, Scott F. 2021. "Systemic Racism, Systemic Sexism, and the Embryological Enterprise." *Developmental Biology* 473: 97–104. https://doi.org/10.1016/j.ydbio .2021.02.001.

Gill, Steve. 2007. *The Fred Factor: How Fred Thompson May Change the Face of the '08 Campaign*. Brentwood, TN: Music City News Publishing.

Global Broadcast Database. August 4, 2011.

Glynn, Kevin. 2000. *Tabloid Culture: Trash Taste, Popular Power, and the Transformation of American Television*. Durham, NC: Duke University Press.

Goffman, Erving. 1959. *The Presentation of Self in Everyday Life*. New York: Anchor Books.

Goffman, Erving. 2005. *Interaction Ritual: Essays on Face-to-Face Behavior*. New York: Routledge.

Golden Globes. n.d. "Clint Eastwood." Accessed June 10, 2019. https://www .goldenglobes.com/person/clint-eastwood.

Goldmacher, Shane. 2018. "Nixon Has the Buzz, but Cuomo Hits Convention with the Advantage." *New York Times*, May 22.

Goldmacher, Shane. 2018. "For Cynthia Nixon, What Went Wrong in New York Primary? (Clue: Governor Cuomo)." *New York Times*, September 14.

Gordon, Greg. 1998. "GOP Got Less for Its Money Than Expected." *Star Tribune* (Minneapolis, MN), November 5.

Gordon, Greg. 2006. "Minnesota Races Drawing Big Names to Lure Big Bucks; Fundraising for House Races has Drawn Such Personalities as Comedian Al Franken and Presidential Adviser Karl Rove." *Star Tribune* (Minneapolis, MN), July 19.

Greenburg, Zach O. 2017. "The Top-Earning Dead Celebrities of 2017."
    Forbes, October 30. Accessed May 20, 2020. https://www.forbes.com/sites
    /zackomalleygreenburg/2017/10/30/the-top-earning-dead-celebrities-of-2017/
    #56b5d9fd41f5.
Guardian. 2018. "Clueless Star Stacey Dash Drops Run for Office with 'Plantation
    Politics' Lament." March 31.
Haberman, Maggie, and Shira Toeplitz. 2010. "McMahon Rides Millions to Victory."
    Politico.com, August 10.
Haigh, Susan. 2010. "WWE Mogul Charges Into Conn. Political
    Smackdown." Associated Press, May 20.
Haigh, Susan. 2010. "Ex-WWE Exec Wins GOP Primary for Conn. Senate Seat."
    Associated Press, August 11.
Haigh, Susan. 2010. "McMahon Has No Regrets Over $50M Conn. Senate Race."
    Associated Press, November 12.
Haigh, Susan, and Pat Eaton-Robb. 2010. "Conn. Republicans Endorse McMahon for
    US Senate." Associated Press, May 22.
Hall, Michelle. 1988. "The New Democrats in the House." *Washington Post*,
    December 27.
Hamedy, Saba. 2018. "'Clueless' Star Stacey Dash Withdraws from Congressional
    Race." CNN.com, March 30.
Hannity, Sean. 2011. "The Great American Panel Discusses Why the Left Hates
    Success and Why Wall Street Bankers Are Never Punished, and Discusses the Rick
    Perry N-word Controversy." Fox News Network, October 3.
Hare, Breeanna. 2012. "Stacey Dash Takes Heat for Being Pro-Romney." CNN Wire,
    October 9.
Harvey, Mark. 2017. *Celebrity Influence: Politics, Persuasion, and Issue-Based
    Advocacy*. Lawrence: University of Kansas Press.
Hauser, Tom. 20002. *Inside the Ropes with Jesse Ventura*. Minneapolis: University
    of Minnesota Press.
Hearn, Alison. 2008. "'Meat, Mask, Burden': Probing the Contours of the Branded
    'Self.'" *Journal of Consumer Culture* 8 (2): 197–217.
Heil, Emily. 2018. "Former 'Clueless' Actress Stacey Dash Files Paperwork to Run
    for Congress." *Washington Post*, February 26. Accessed May 5, 2022. https://
    www.washingtonpost.com/news/reliable-source/wp/2018/02/26/stacey-dash-files
    -paperwork-to-run-for-congress/.
Held, Amy. 2018. "Snapchat's Stock Sinks After Rihanna Denounces Domestic
    Violence Ad." *National Public Radio*, March 17. Accessed May 20, 2020. https://
    www.npr.org/sections/thetwo-way/2018/03/17/594593132/snapchat-s-stock-sinks
    -after-rihanna-denounces-domestic-violence-ad.
Herrnson, Paul S. 2008. *Congressional Elections: Campaigning at Home and in
    Washington*. 5th ed. Washington, DC: CQ Press.
Hersh, Eitan. 2020. *Politics Is for Power: How to Move Beyond Political Hobbyism,
    Take Action, and Make Real Change*. New York: Simon and Schuster.
Hesse, Monica. 2022. "Arnold Schwarzenegger Tries to Show Russians a Different
    Kind of Strongman." *Washington Post*, March 17. Accessed March 19, 2022. https:

//www.washingtonpost.com/lifestyle/2022/03/17/arnold-schwarzenegger-russia -ukraine-video/.

Hibbard, James. 2010. "'Sarah Palin's Alaska' Breaks TLC Ratings Record." *Hollywood Reporter*, November 15. Accessed May 28, 2020. https://web.archive .org/web/20110805114926/http://www.hollywoodreporter.com/blogs/live-feed/ sarah-palins-alaska-breaks-tlc-45421.

Hitsch, Günter J., Ali Hortaçsu, and Dan Ariely. 2010. "What Makes You Click?— Mate Preferences in Online Dating." *Quantitative Marketing and Economics* 8 (4): 393–427. https://doi.org/10.1007/s11129-010-9088-6.

Hoeschen, Kathy. 1986. "Jobst No Longer Wants Equal Time." *Des Moines Register*, April 9.

Hoeschen, Kathy. 1986. "Grandy, Hodgson Clash on 'Star Wars,' Deficit." *Sioux City Journal*, October 18.

Holmes, Su, and Sean Redmond, eds. 2006. *Framing Celebrity: New Directions in Celebrity Culture*. New York: Routledge.

Holston, Noel. 1990. "Night and Day: Election as Much Fun as Holiday for 'CCCO's Eskola." *Star Tribune* (Minneapolis, MN), November 9.

Horowitz, Jason. 2010. "Senate Smackdown!; WWE's Linda McMahon Wants to Put a Grip on Open Conn. Seat." *Washington Post*, February 22.

Hotakainen, Rob. 2006. "Coleman-Franken Talk Isn't Only Thing Getting Serious; As Speculation Continues About the GOP Senator and Radio Host Facing Off in 2008, Both Are Working Hard to Raise Money." *Star Tribune* (Minneapolis, MN), February 27.

Hotakainen, Rob. 2006. "Al Franken: Formidable Fundraiser; The Potential 2008 U.S. Senate Hopeful is Helping DFLers and Candidates Around the Country." *Star Tribune* (Minneapolis, MN), September 17.

Hotakainen, Rob. 2007. "Franken Saying He'll Run for Senate; The Liberal Radio Show Host and Comedian Began Telephoning Democrats with His Decision in Recent Days." *Star Tribune* (Minneapolis, MN), February 1.

Hotakainen, Rob, and Patricia Lopez. 2007. "Campaign2008; Senate; Coleman's Seat: Pols Already Chattering; Some Democrats Worry Ciresi and Franken Don't Have the Clout to Win What's Viewed as a Vulnerable GOP Seat." *Star Tribune* (Minneapolis, MN), February 13.

Huddart, Stephen. 2005. *Do We Need Another Hero? Understanding Celebrities' Roles in Advancing Social Causes*. Montreal: McGill University.

Hughey, Matthew W. 2014. "White Backlash in the 'Post-Racial' United States." *Ethnic and Racial Studies* 37 (5): 721–30. https://doi.org/10.1080/01419870.2014 .886710.

Hughey, Matthew W., and Gregory S. Parks. 2014. *The Wrongs of the Right: Language, Race, and the Republican Party in the Age of Obama*. New York: New York University Press.

Hyde, John. 1986. "'Issue' of Grandy Dominates Contests." *Des Moines Register*, November 1.

Hyde, John. 1986. "National GOP Backs Grandy in 3-Way Race." *Des Moines Register*, April 26.

Hyde, Marina. 2009. *Celebrity: How Entertainers Took Over the World and Why We Need an Exit Strategy*. New York: Random House.

Indiana, Gary. 2005. *Schwarzenegger Syndrome: Politics and Celebrity in the Age of Contempt*. New York: New Press.

"Industry Impact; Losses by Key Communications Policymakers Help Tip Senate Balance of Power." 1986. *Communications Daily*, November 6.

Inglis, Fred. 2010. *A Short History of Celebrity*. Princeton, NJ: Princeton University Press.

International Business Times. 2012. "Election Day 2012: Roseanne Barr Makes Final Push for Votes as Third-Party Candidate." *International Business Times News*, November 6.

Internet Movie Database (IMDb). n.d. "Ben Jones." Accessed May 6, 2020. https://www.imdb.com/name/nm0427549/?ref_=nv_sr_srsg_0.

Internet Movie Database (IMDb). n.d. "Caitlyn Jenner." Accessed October 2, 2021. https://www.imdb.com/name/nm0421063/?ref_=nv_sr_srsg_0.

Internet Movie Database (IMDb). n.d. "Clint Eastwood Awards." Accessed June 10, 2019. https://www.imdb.com/name/nm0000142/awards.

Internet Movie Data Base. n.d. "Fred Dalton Thompson." Accessed February 4, 2020.https://www.imdb.com/name/nm0000669/?ref_=nv_sr_srsg_0.

Internet Movie Database (IMDb). n.d. "Fred Grandy." Accessed March 11, 2021.https://www.imdb.com/name/nm0334948/?ref_=nv_sr_srsg_0.

Internet Movie Database (IMDb). n.d. "Ronald Reagan." Accessed June 13, 2018. http://www.imdb.com/name/nm0001654/bio.

Jackson, Sarah J. 2014. *Black Celebrity, Racial Politics, and the Press: Framing Dissent*. New York: Routledge.

Jenkins, Henry, III. 2005a. "Never Trust a Snake: WWF Wrestling as Masculine Melodrama." In *Steel Chair to the Head: The Pleasure and Pain of Professional Wrestling*, edited by Nicholas Sammond, 33–66. Durham, NC: Duke University Press.

Jenkins, Henry, III. 2005b. "Afterward, Part I: Wrestling with Theory, Grappling with Politics." In *Steel Chair to the Head: The Pleasure and Pain of Professional Wrestling*, edited by Nicholas Sammond, 295–316. Durham, NC: Duke University Press.

Johnson, Carolyn Y., Laurie McGinley, Josh Dawsey, and Christopher Rowland. 2020. "Trump Sets Goal of Hundreds of Millions of Coronavirus Vaccine Doses by January, but Scientists Doubt It." *Washington Post*, May 15. Accessed May 24, 2020. https://www.washingtonpost.com/health/2020/05/15/trump-coronavirus -vaccine-january/.

Jones, Jeffrey P. 2013. "Politics and the Brand: *Saturday Night Live's* Campaign Season Humor." In *Saturday Night Live and American TV*, edited by Nick Marx, Matt Sienkiewicz, and Ron Becker, 77–92. Bloomington: Indiana University Press.

Justin, Neal. 2007. "Critic's Choice." *Star Tribune* (Minneapolis, MN), March 28.

Kam, Cindy D., and Elizabeth J. Zechmeister. 2013. "Name Recognition and Candidate Support." *American Journal of Political Science* 57 (4): 971–86. http://www.jstor.org/stable/23496668.

Kamin, Blair. 1986. "Grandy Goes for it Despite Hollywood Image." *Des Moines Register*, March 3.

Kaplan, Robert M. 1978. "Is Beauty Talent? Sex Interaction in the Attractiveness Halo Effect." *Sex Roles* 4 (2): 195–204. https://doi.org/10.1007/BF00287500.

Kendi, Ibram X. 2019. "The Day 'Shithole' Entered the Presidential Lexicon: In Insulting Certain Countries, Trump Revealed the Hierarchy He Imposes on the World." *Atlantic*, January 13. Accessed May 27, 2020. https://www.theatlantic.com/politics/archive/2019/01/shithole-countries/580054/.

Kennedy, Mark. 2019. "'When They See Us' Actors Revisit the Central Park Five Case." *Canadian Press*, May 23.

Kim, Seung Min, Josh Dawsey, and Brady Dennis. 2020. "Trump's Inaccurate Assertion of 'Total' Authority Sparks Challenge from Governors." *Washington Post*, April 14. Accessed May 24, 2020. https://www.washingtonpost.com/politics/trumps-inaccurate-assertion-of-total-authority-sparks-challenge-from-governors/2020/04/14/46f3a03c-7e51-11ea-8013-1b6da0e4a2b7_story.html.

Kimmel, Michael. 2013. *Angry White Men: American Masculinity at the End of an Era*. New York: Nation Books.

Kittle, Robert A., and Timothy Murphy. 1980. "Photo Report; On the Stump with Ronald Reagan." *U.S. News & World Report*, October 13.

Kranish, Michael, and Marc Fisher. 2016. *Trump Revealed: The Definitive Biography of the 45th President*. New York: Scribner.

Krasniewicz, Louise, and Michael Blitz. 2006. *Arnold Schwarzenegger: A Biography*. Westport, CT: Greenwood Press.

Kreidler, Mark. 1986. "Eastwood Gunning for Votes." *San Diego Union-Tribune*, January 31.

Kunen, James S. 1985. "Iowa-Born Actor Fred Grandy, Alias Love Boat's Gopher Smith, Plots a Course for Washington." *People Magazine*, December 16. Accessed March 9, 2021. https://people.com/archive/iowa-born-actor-fred-grandy-alias-love-boats-gopher-smith-plots-a-course-for-washington-vol-24-no-25/.

Lasswell, Harold D. 1976. *Power and Personality*. New York: W.W. Norton.

Letterman, David. 1987. *The David Letterman Show.* November 13. Accessed July 1, 2019. https://www.youtube.com/watch?v=7msTqzjZ7PU.

Levine, Mike. 2019. "'No Blame?' ABC News Finds 36 Cases Invoking 'Trump' in Connection with Violence, Threats, Alleged Assaults. President Donald Trump Insists He Deserves No Blame for Divisions in America." ABC News, August 14. Accessed May 27, 2020. https://abcnews.go.com/Politics/blame-abc-news-finds-17-cases-invoking-trump/story?id=58912889.

Levy, Melissa. 1998. "Yes, It's Jesse (the Doll) Ventura; Proceeds from Official Merchandise May Help Fund Campaigns." *Star Tribune* (Minneapolis, MN), December 24.

Lipper, Hal. 1988. "'Hairspray' Holds with Some Teasing from John Waters." *St. Petersburg Times* (Florida), March 15.

Littler, Jo. 2008. "I Feel Your Pain: Cosmopolitan Charity and the Public Fashioning of the Celebrity Soul." *Social Semiotics* 18 (2): 237–51. https://doi.org/10.1080/10350330802002416.

Longoria, Richard T. 2018. *Janus Democracy: Transconsistency and the General Will*. Albany, NY: SUNY Press.

Longoria, Richard T. Summer 2022. "George Murphy: A Celebrity Politician." *Southern California Quarterly* 104 (2): 201–27.

Lopez, Patricia. 2007. "At The Fair: Politics on a Stick; Fairgoers Get a Taste of the Candidates Up Close and Personal; During the 12-day Run, Politicians Strut Their Stuff and Try to Convert Fleeting Contacts into Lasting Impressions." *Star Tribune* (Minneapolis, MN), August 29.

Los Angeles Times. 1986. "'Feeling Good,' Eastwood Cites Need to Avoid Dewey Image." April 8.

Los Angeles Times. 1966. "White Backlash Aided His Rivals, Brown Declares." June 17.

Los Angeles Times. 1966. "Reagan Will Speak in Santa Monica." October 20.

Lucker, G. William, William E. Beane, and Robert L. Helmreich. 1981."The Strength of the Halo Effect in Physical Attractiveness Research." *Journal of Psychology Interdisciplinary and Applied* 107 (1): 69–75. https://doi.org/10.1080/00223980 .1981.9915206.

Mabery, D.L. 1989. "Jesse 'The Body' Ventura Hopes Role Will Punch Up Acting Career." *St. Cloud Times*, November 5.

Machiavelli, Niccolò. 1995. *The Prince*. New York: Penguin.

Magnuson, Karen M. 1982. "Reagan Plays Peoria." United Press International, October 21.

Majic, Samantha, Daniel O'Neill, and Michael Bernhard. 2020. "Celebrity and Politics." *Perspectives on Politics* 18 (1): 1–8. https://doi.org/10.1017/ S1537592719004602.

Mansfield, Stephanie. 1981."Watergate; The Reagan Renaissance." *Washington Post*, May 28.

Marcus, Ruth. 1986. "American Journal; For Eastwood, It's Ballots, Not Bullets." *Washington Post*, April 1.

Marcuse, Herbert. 2013. *One-Dimensional Man: Studies in the Ideology of Advanced Industrial Society*. New York: Routledge.

Marinucci, Carla, and Steven Shepard. 2021. "Caitlyn Jenner Running for California Governor." Politico.com, April 24. Accessed October 2, 2021. https://www.politico .com/news/2021/04/24/caitlyn-jenner-running-for-california-governor-484537.

Mark, Julian. 2022. "Stacey Abrams Said She'd Become U.S. President by 2040. She Became President of United Earth Much Sooner." *Washington Post*, March 18. Accessed March 19, 2022. https://www.washingtonpost.com/nation/2022/03/18/ stacey-abrams-star-trek-discovery-cameo/.

Markham-Smith, Ian, and Liz Hodgson. 1999. *The Outrageous Jerry Springer*. London, UK: Blake Publishing.

Marlantes, L. 2011. "Rick Perry Slips on Immigration Banana." *Christian Science Monitor*, September 30.

Marshall, P. David. 1997. *Celebrity and Power: Fame in Contemporary Culture*. Minneapolis: University of Minnesota Press.

Marx, Nick, Matt Sienkiewicz, and Ron Becker. 2013. *Saturday Night Live and American TV*. Bloomington: Indiana University Press.

Masterson, Karen M. 2020. "Trump Says He's on a Miracle Covid-19 Drug. People Who Take His Advice May Die." *Washington Post*, May 19, 2020. Accessed May 24, 2020. https://www.washingtonpost.com/outlook/2020/05/19/trump-hydroxychloroquine-science/.

Mazer, Sharon. 2005. "'Real Wrestling' / 'Real' Life." In *Steel Chair to the Head: The Pleasure and Pain of Professional Wrestling*, edited by Nicholas Sammond, 67–87. Durham, NC: Duke University Press.

McAuliffe, Bill. 1998. "FYI; Ventura and His Predecessors." *Star Tribune* (Minneapolis, MN), November 5.

McCarthy, Rebecca. 1992. "Primary '92 Jones Loses Bid for Re-Election in Heated 10th District Race He Blames Johnson's Negative Ads." *Atlanta Journal and Constitution*, July 22.

McCord, Mary. 2020. "Trump's 'LIBERATE MICHIGAN!' Tweets Incite Insurrection. That's Illegal." *Washington Post*, April 17. Accessed May 24, 2020. https://www.washingtonpost.com/outlook/2020/04/17/liberate-michigan-trump-constitution/.

McDonald, Paul. 2006. "The Star System: The Production of Hollywood Stardom in the Post-Studio Era." In *Framing Celebrity: New Directions in Celebrity Culture*, edited by Su Holmes and Sean Redmond, 167–81. New York: Routledge.

McDougal, Dennis. 1998. *The Last Mogul: Lew Wasserman, MCA, and the Hidden History of Hollywood*. New York: Crown Publishers.

McGinniss, Joe. 2011. *The Rogue: Searching for the Real Sarah Palin*. New York: Crown Publishers.

McEnroe, Paul. 1990. "'The Body' Politicked and Ventura is Mayor-Elect." *Star Tribune* (Minneapolis, MN), November 8..

McKinley, Jesse. 2018. "Cynthia Nixon, Battling Cuomo, Wins Endorsement of Progressive Die-Hards." *New York Times*, April 14.

McKinley, Jesse and Shane Goldmacher. 2018. "Progressives Grudgingly Offer Ballot Line to Gov. Cuomo After Backing Cynthia Nixon." *New York Times*, October 3.

Mecum, Lauralee. 1988. "Bono Has More Than $53,000 in Campaign." *Desert Sun*, April 1..

Miga, Andrew. 2009. "WWE CEO Linda McMahon Wades into Conn. Senate Race." Associated Press, September 16.

Milbank, Dana. 2019. "Trump Finds a Cure for His Small-Hands Problem." *Washington Post*, January 22. Accessed May 27, 2020. https://www.washingtonpost.com/opinions/with-enough-facetune-skill-and-creativity-trumps-team-can-make-anything-possible/2019/01/22/05d6015e-1e84-11e9-8e21-59a09ff1e2a1_story.html.

Mills, C. Wright. 2000. *The Power Elite*. New York: Oxford University Press.

Minzesheimer, Bob. 1994. "Sonny Bono Hopes Next Stage is Congress / The Former Entertainer Now a GOP Front-Runner." *USA Today*, October 10.

Modesti, Kevin. 2018. "Actress of 'Clueless' Fame Running for House." *Long Beach Press-Telegram* (Long Beach, CA), February 27.

Morain, Dan. 2003. "Isolation, Caution Cost Davis Dearly." *Los Angeles Times*, October 8.

Morain, Dan, and Joel Rubin. 2003. "Financially, the Recall Was Business as Usual." *Los Angeles Times*, October 10.

Morgan, Piers. 2012. "Romney Surging in Ohio; Actress Bashed for Supporting Romney; 28 Days Before Election; Interview with Hulk Hogan." CNN, October 9.

Muir, Kate. 1994. "California's Got Him, Babe." *Times* (London), November 18.

Murray, Steve. 2007. "79th Annual Academy Awards: Oscar Goes Global—and Long; Drawn-Out Ceremony Takes Its Time Getting to Big Awards." *Atlanta Journal-Constitution*, February 26.

National Journal. 2009. "McMahon Confirms Interest in Senate Race." *National Journal's Congress Daily*, August 17.

Needham, Catherine. 2005. "Brand Leaders: Clinton, Blair and the Limitations of the Permanent Campaign." *Political Studies* 53 (2): 343–61. https://doi.org/10.1111/j .1467-9248.2005.00532.x.

Neumann, Sean. 2021. "Kanye West Spent $13.2 Million—Including $12 Million of His Own—for 2020 Campaign." *People Magazine*, February 25. Accessed May 25, 2021. https://people.com/politics/kanye-west-spent-more-than-13-2-million-on -his-2020-run/.

New York Times Editorial Board. 2017. "President Trump's Big-Money Establishment; Editorial." January 24.

Newmyer, Tory, and Brent D. Griffiths. 2020. "The Finance 202: Trump Team's Contradictory Messages Risk Undermining Push to Reopen the Economy." *Washington Post*, May 11. Accessed May 24, 2020. https://www.washingtonpost .com/news/powerpost/paloma/the-finance-202/2020/05/11/the-finance-202-trump -team-s-contradictory-messages-risk-undermining-push-to-reopen-the-economy /5eb88b9488e0fa17cddf7188/.

Ng, Roxana. 1993. "'A Woman out of Control': Deconstructing Sexism and Racism in the University." *Canadian Journal of Education/Revue canadienne de l'éducation* 18 (3): 189–205. https://doi.org/10.2307/1495382.

Nisbett, Richard E., and Timothy D. Wilson. 1977. "The Halo Effect: Evidence for Unconscious Alteration of Judgments." *Journal of Personality and Social Psychology* 35 (4): 250–56. https://doi.org/10.1037/0022-3514.35.4.250.

Norman, Jane. 1986. "Candidates Meet in Lively Debate." *Des Moines Register*, October 18..

Norman, Jane. 1986. "Fred Grandy Is a Wealthy Man." *Des Moines Register*, May 9..

Norman, Jane. 1986. "Biden Reports Congress Wary of Farm Claims." *Des Moines Register*, October 24..

Norman, Jane. 1986. "Grandy Still Trying to Shed 'Actor' Image." *Des Moines Register*, October 27..

Norman, Jane. "Iowans Accept Grandy's Return from Hollywood." *Des Moines Register*, November 5..

Norman, Jane, and John Hyde. 1986. "Grassley Rolls to 2nd Senate Term." *Des Moines Register*, November 5..

North Woods Advertising. 2009a. "'Action Figure'—Jesse Ventura for Governor (MN)." July 13. Accessed December 23, 2018. https://www.youtube.com/watch?v =TjU948M0ARw.

North Woods Advertising. 2009b. "'Jesse The Mind'—Jesse Ventura for Governor (MN)." July 13. Accessed December 23, 2018. https://www.youtube.com/watch?v =zSACk65D3pk.

Ochoa, Melissa Kumari. 2019. "Systemic Sexism in Our Everyday Lives." PhD diss., Texas A&M University.

O'Donnell, John R., and James Rutherford. 2016. *Trumped!: The Inside Story of the Real Donald Trump—His Cunning Rise and Spectacular Fall*. Hertford, NC: Crossroad Press.

O'Donnell, Kelly. 2007. "Fred Thompson Appears on 'The Tonight Show' to Announce His Plans to Seek Republican Party Nomination." NBC News Transcripts, September 6.

Ogden, Ruth S. 2013. "The Effect of Facial Attractiveness on Temporal Perception." *Cognition and Emotion* 27 (7): 1292–304. https://doi.org/10.1080/02699931.2013 .769426.

Olorunnipa, Toluse, and Josh Dawsey. 2020. "Trump's Abrupt Reversal on Georgia's Reopening Plan Highlights Growing Tensions with Kemp." *Washington Post*, April 24. Accessed May 24, 2020. https://www.washingtonpost.com/politics /trump-kemp-georgia-coronavirus-reopen/2020/04/24/116f6ebe-863f-11ea-a3eb -e9fc93160703_story.html.

O'Shaughnessy, Nicholas. 1999. "Political Marketing and Political Propaganda." In *The Handbook of Political Marketing*, edited by Bruce I. Newman, 725–40. London: Sage.

Palermo, Joseph A. 2008. "Ann Coulter Starts Early with Racist Slurs Against Obama." *Huffington Post*, February 15. Accessed May 27, 2020. https://www .huffpost.com/entry/ann-coulter-starts-early-_1_b_86849.

Palin, Sarah. 2009. *Going Rogue: An American Life*. New York: HarperCollins.

Pallotta, Frank. 2016. "Fox Commentator: Oscar Flap 'Ludicrous' and Get Rid of Black History Month." CNN Wire, January 20.

Parker, Kathleen. 2022. "Volodymyr Zelensky, the Modern Warrior-Artist." *Washington Post*, March 15. Accessed March 16, 2022. https://www.washingtonpost.com/ opinions/2022/03/15/volodymyr-zelensky-modern-warrior-artist/.

Pasek, Josh, Tobias H. Stark, Jon A. Krosnick, Trevor Tompson, and B. Keith Payne. 2014. "Attitudes Toward Blacks in the Obama Era: Changing Distributions and Impacts on Job Approval and Electoral Choice, 2008–2012." *Public Opinion Quarterly* 78 (SI): 276–302. http://www.jstor.org/stable/24545951.

Pasek, Josh, Tobias H. Stark, Jon A. Krosnick, and Trevor Tompson. 2015. "What Motivates a Conspiracy Theory? Birther Beliefs, Partisanship, Liberal-Conservative Ideology, and Anti-Black Attitudes." *Electoral Studies* 40 (December 2015): 482– 89. https://doi.org/10.1016/j.electstud.2014.09.009.

Patterson, Thomas E. 2019. *How America Lost Its Mind: The Assault on Reason That's Crippling Our Democracy*. Norman: University of Oklahoma Press.

Payne, James L. 1980. "Show Horses & Work Horses in the United States House of Representatives." *Polity* 12 (3): 428–56. https://doi.org/10.2307/3234215.

Payne, Sebastian. 2014. "The Nine Lives of Sarah Palin." *Washington Post*, July 28. Accessed May 28, 2020. https://www.washingtonpost.com/news/the-fix/wp/2014/07/28/the-nine-lives-of-sarah-palin/?arc404=true.

Pels, Dick. 2003. "Aesthetic Representation and Political Style." In *Media and the Restyling of Politics: Consumerism, Celebrity, and Cynicism*, edited by John Corner and Dick Pels, 41–66. London: Sage.

"People." 1985. *Facts on File World News Digest*, 13 December 1985.

Peterson, David. 2007. "Candidate Franken Shows Flashes of the Comedy Career He Left Behind; Seeking to Morph from Cutup to U.S. Senator, the DFL Hopeful Returned to His Old School, Where the Cutup Kept Poking Through." *Star Tribune* (Minneapolis, MN), March 4.

Pew Hispanic Center National Survey of Latinos. November 2011. Retrieved January 10, 2013 from the iPOLL Databank, The Roper Center for Public Opinion Research, University of Connecticut. http://www.ropercenter.uconn.edu/data_access/ipoll/ipoll.html.

Picardie, Justine. 1988. "Look: On the Campaign Trail with Sonny—The Re-emergence of a Sixties Singing Star." *Sunday Times* (London), January 24.

Pilkington, Ed. 2020. "Electoral College: How Trump Could Lose the Popular Vote and Win Again." *Guardian*, January 12. Accessed May 27, 2020. https://www.theguardian.com/us-news/2020/jan/12/trump-electoral-college-2020-election-popular-vote.

Pins, Kenneth. 1986. "6th District Race Is Seen as a Toss-Up: Poll Finds Hodgson, Grandy Neck-and-neck." *Des Moines Register*, October 22..

Pittsburgh Post-Gazette. 1994. "Just an Act?; Thespian-Politicians Deserve the Benefit of the Doubt." *Pittsburgh Post-Gazette* (Pennsylvania), November 15.

Pomerantz, Dorothy. 2011. "The Top-Earning Dead Celebrities." *Forbes*, October 25. Accessed May 20, 2020. https://www.forbes.com/sites/dorothypomerantz/2011/10/25/the-top-earning-dead-celebrities/#2cf4112b64e3.

Powers, William F. 1994. "The Politician's Pickup Lines; Fred Thompson, Driving Home a Campaign of Illusion and Disillusion." *Washington Post*, October 21.

Putnam, Jackson K. 2006. "Governor Reagan: A Reappraisal." *California History* 83 (4): 24–45. https://doi.org/10.2307/25161839.

Rabidoux, Greg. R. 2009. *Hollywood Politicos, Then and Now: Who They Are, What They Want, Why It Matters.* New York: University Press of America.

Rahman, Abid. 2017. "Stacey Dash Out at Fox News." *Hollywood Reporter*, January 22.

Rao, Sonia. 2020. "Michelle Obama Will Be the Focus of the Upcoming Netflix Documentary 'Becoming.'" *The Washington Post*, April 27. Accessed May 6, 2022. https://www.washingtonpost.com/arts-entertainment/2020/04/27/michelle-obama-netflix-documentary-becoming/.

Raphael, Jackie. 2017. "Paul Newman: Posthumous Philanthropy and Persona." In *Becoming Brands: Celebrity, Activism and Politics*, edited by Jackie Raphael and Celia Lam, 137–48. Toronto: WaterHill Publishing.

Raphael, Tim. 2009. "The Body Electric: GE, TV, and the Reagan Brand." *TDR: The Drama Review* 53 (2): 113–38. https://www.jstor.org/stable/25599477.

Recording Academy Grammy Awards. 2003. "Winners: 46th Annual Grammy Awards (2003)." Accessed May 6, 2019. https://www.grammy.com/grammys/awards/46th-annual-grammy-awards.

Recording Academy Grammy Awards. n.d. "Kanye West." Accessed June 18, 2021. https://www.grammy.com/grammys/artists/kanye-west/6900.

Reilly, Kaitlin. 2021. "Dwayne Johnson Reacts to Poll About Him Running for President." *E! News*, April 10. Accessed April 14, 2021. https://www.msn.com /en-us/movies/celebrity/dwayne-johnson-reacts-to-poll-about-him-running-for -president/ar-BB1fvZr1?li=BBnb2gh.

Reinhold, Robert. 1992. "THE 1992 CAMPAIGN: Politics' Cutting Edge; Californians Making Political Waves That May Wash Over Nation by Fall." *New York Times*, June 4.

Relman, Eliza. 2019. "The 25 Women Who Have Accused Trump of Sexual Misconduct." *Business Insider*, October 9. Accessed May 27, 2020. https://www .businessinsider.com/women-accused-trump-sexual-misconduct-list-2017-12.

Richey, Lisa Ann, and Stefano Ponte. 2011. *Brand Aid: Shopping Well to Save the World*. Minneapolis: University of Minnesota Press.

Ringham, Eric. 1998. "Ventura Victory Shows the Limits of Speech." *Star Tribune* (Minneapolis, MN), November 5.

Robehmed, Natalie. 2017. "Celebrity 100: The World's Highest-Paid Celebrities of 2017." *Forbes*, June 12. Accessed May 20, 2020. https://www.forbes.com/sites/ natalierobehmed/2017/06/12/celebrity-100-the-worlds-highest-paid-celebrities-of -2017/#ee1953f4d92a.

Roberson, Peter. 1994. "Bono Campaign Among Debt Leaders at $399K." *States News Service*, December 21.

Rojek, Chris. 2004. *Celebrity*. London: Reaktion Books.

Ronald Reagan Presidential Library. n.d. "Ronald Reagan Filmography." Accessed June 14, 2018. https://www.reaganlibrary.gov/sreference/ronald-reagan-s -filmography.

Roos, Meghan. 2021. "Caitlyn Jenner Says Failed California Recall 'Opened My Eyes to Political Life.'" *Newsweek*, September 28. Accessed October 2, 2021. https:// www.newsweek.com/caitlyn-jenner-says-failed-california-recall-opened-my-eyes -political-life-1633619.

Ross, Steven J. 2011. *Hollywood Left and Right: How Movie Stars Shaped American Politics*. Oxford, UK: Oxford University Press.

Rossi, Jason. 2018. "Clint Eastwood: What's His Net Worth, and Does He Have Any Oscars?" *Cheat Sheet*, December 16.

Royce, Graydon, and Neal Justin. 2005. "Home of the Brave; An Oral History of Dudley Riggs' Brave New Workshop." *Star Tribune* (Minneapolis, MN), April 29.

Rucker, Philip, and Ashley Parker. 2019. "The Brand Label That Stokes Trump's Fury: 'Racist, Racist, Racist.'" *Washington Post*, August 11. Accessed May 27, 2020. https: //www.washingtonpost.com/politics/the-brand-label-that-stokes-trumps-fury-racist -racist-racist/2019/08/11/fd5573d2-bad9-11e9-b3b4-2bb69e8c4e39_story.html.

Rybak, Deborah Caulfield. 2005. "Country, Christian Radio Stations Gain in Latest Arbitron Ratings." *Star Tribune* (Minneapolis, MN), February 2.

Rybak, Deborah Caulfield. 2005. "Left of Dial Radio Is Doing All Right." *Star Tribune* (Minneapolis, MN), March 31.

Sammond, Nicholas. 2005a. "Introduction: A Brief and Unnecessary Defense of Professional Wrestling." In *Steel Chair to the Head: The Pleasure and Pain of Professional Wrestling*, edited by Nicholas Sammond, 1–22. Durham, NC: Duke University Press.

Sammond, Nicholas. 2005b. "Squaring the Family Circle: WWF *Smackdown* Assaults the Social Body." In *Steel Chair to the Head: The Pleasure and Pain of Professional Wrestling*, edited by Nicholas Sammond, 132–66. Durham, NC: Duke University Press.

Sanbonmatsu, Kira. 2002. "Gender Stereotypes and Vote Choice." *American Journal of Political Science* 46 (1): 20–34. https://doi.org/10.2307/3088412.

San Francisco Examiner. 1967. "Shirley Third in Spending." November 14.

San Francisco Examiner. 1986. "No frills: Eastwood Swearing-In." April 16.

San Jose Mercury News. 1994. "Bono's Riposte." November 19.

Sanoff, Alvin P. 1980. "It Takes More Than a Candidate to Win White House." *U.S. News & World Report*, April 28.

Schickel, Richard. 1996. *Clint Eastwood: A Biography*. New York: Vintage Books.

Schwartz, John. 1988. "Even Wild Dogs Couldn't Keep Them Away." *Newsweek*, 21 November 1988.

Schwarzenegger, Arnold, with Peter Petre. 2013. *Total Recall: My Unbelievably True Life Story.* Enhanced Edition. New York: Simon and Schuster.

Schweiger, Gunter, and Michaela Adami. 1999. "The Nonverbal Image of Politicians and Political Parties." In *The Handbook of Political Marketing*, edited by Bruce I. Newman, 347–64. London: Sage.

Scott, Ian. 2011. *American Politics in Hollywood Film*. Edinburgh: Edinburgh University Press.

Seager, Susan. 1988. "Sonny Bono Elected Mayor of Palm Springs." United Press International, April 13.

Seidman, Robert. "Conspiracy Theory with Jesse Ventura Delivers 1.6 Million Viewers, truTV's Biggest Audience Ever for a New Series Launch." TVbytheNumbers.com, December 3. Accessed August 23, 2018. https://web.archive.org/web/20110413053637/http://tvbythenumbers.zap2it.com/2009/12/03/conspiracy-theory-with-jesse-ventura-delivers-1-6-million-viewers-trutv%E2%80%99s-biggest-audience-ever-for-a-new-series-launch/35201.

Shafer, Jack. 2019. "The Fake Feud Between Trump and Fox: The Pro-Wrestling Origins of the President's Latest Twitter Spat." *Politico Magazine*, August 30. Accessed May 27, 2020. https://www.politico.com/magazine/story/2019/08/30/donald-trump-fox-news-227994.

Shales, Tom, and James A. Miller. 2002. *Live From New York: An Uncensored History of Saturday Night Live*. New York: Little, Brown and Company.

Sheffield, Matthew. 2019. "Voters Overwhelmingly Want GOP to Move on from Border Wall Fight." *The Hill*, April 1. Accessed May 27, 2020. https://thehill.com

/hilltv/what-americas-thinking/436723-voters-overwhelmingly-want-gop-to-move -on-from-border-wall.

Shepard, Steven. 2017. "Poll: Majority of Voters Back Trump Travel Ban." Politico.com, July 5. Accessed May 27, 2020. https://www.politico.com/story/2017 /07/05/trump-travel-ban-poll-voters-240215.

Sherman Jake. 2007. "Franken Raises Some Serious Money; DFL Senate Candidate has $1.9 million - Setting the Stage for an Expensive Race." *Star Tribune* (Minneapolis, MN), July 10.

Sherman, Jake. 2007. "Coleman, Ciresi Stockpile Money for Senate Runs." *Star Tribune* (Minneapolis, MN), July 3.

Shinada, Mizuho, and Toshio Yamagishi. 2014. "Physical Attractiveness and Cooperation in a Prisoner's Dilemma Game." *Evolution and Human Behavior* 35 (6): 451–55. https://doi.org/10.1016/j.evolhumbehav.2014.06.003.

Sidoti, Liz. 2010. "2010 Situation Grows More Difficult for Democrats." Associated Press, January 3.

Silver, Marc. 2014. "Is There Anything Real About 'Amazing America with Sarah Palin'?" *Washington Post*, April 3. Accessed May 28, 2020. https:// www.washingtonpost.com/express/wp/2014/04/03/amazing-america-sarah-palin -sportsman-channel/.

Singh, Devendra. 1995. "Female Judgment of Male Attractiveness and Desirability for Relationships: Role of Waist-to-hip Ratio and Financial Status." *Journal of Personality and Social Psychology* 69 (6): 1089–101. https://doi.org/10.1037/0022 -3514.69.6.1089.

Sioux City Journal. 1986. "Grassley, Grandy are Top Fundraisers." July 17.

Sioux City Journal. 1986. "We Endorse." October 30.

Sioux City Journal. 1986. "Grassley Spends $3 Per Vote." December 11.

Smith, Ben, III. 1994. "Election '94 Redrawn Districts Sparked GOP Gains." *Atlanta Journal and Constitution*, November 12.

Smith, Dane, and Dean Barkley. 1998. "Diary of an Upset; Jesse Ventura's Amazing Run for Governor Has Drawn Lots of Attention from the Outside. Here's a Look at It from the Inside." *Star Tribune* (Minneapolis, MN), November 8.

Smith, Will. 2018. "One Thing Arnold Schwarzenegger Told Me That I'll Never Forget." Will Smith Vlog, January 3. Accessed May 25, 2020. https://www.youtube .com/watch?v=eIAtHvzjk98.

Sonny Bono Debate. n.d. Accessed July 15, 2019. https://www.youtube.com/watch ?v=0IlMBdaEUNo.

Springer, Jerry, and Laura Morton. 1998. *Ringmaster!* New York: St. Martin's Press.

Stanley, Timothy. 2014. *Citizen Hollywood: How the Collaboration between LA and DC Revolutionized American Politics*. New York: Thomas Dunne Books.

Stanyer, James. 2007 *Modern Political Communication*. Cambridge: Polity Press.

Star Tribune (Minneapolis, MN). 1990. "Ventura Leads in Brooklyn Park Mayor Race." November 7.

Star Tribune Editorial Board. 2005 "Al Franken: 'We Have to Win on Values.'" *Star Tribune* (Minneapolis, MN), December 11.

Stein, Mark A. 1986. "Eastwood Wins Easy Victory in Carmel Vote." *Los Angeles Times*, April 9.

Stein, Mark A. 1986. "Clint Gets a Call from Central Casting." *Los Angeles Times*, April 10.

Stelter, Brian. 2015. "Fox News Suspends Two Commentators for Profanity While Criticizing Obama." CNN Wire, December 7.

Sternberg, Ernest. 1998. "Phantasmagoric Labor: The New Economics of Self-Presentation." *Futures* 30 (1): 3–21. https://doi.org/10.1016/S0016-3287(98)00003-2.

Stevens, Stuart. 2020. *It Was All a Lie: How the Republican Party Became Donald Trump*. New York: Knopf.

Stevenson, Adlai E. 1958. "The Swift, Wise, and Ready." *Centennial Review of Arts & Science* 2: 385–95. https://www.jstor.org/stable/23737542.

Stokes, Donald E., and Warren E. Miller. 1962. "Party Government and the Saliency of Congress." *Public Opinion Quarterly* 26 (4): 531–46. https://www.jstor.org/stable/2747304.

Stoll, Laurie Cooper. 2013. *Race and Gender in the Classroom: Teachers, Privilege, and Enduring Social Inequalities*. Lanham, MD: Lexington Books.

Stoller, Gary. 2012. "Murphy Holds Off McMahon in Connecticut Brawl; Bitterly Fought Contest Marked by Months of Mudslinging." *USA Today*, November 7.

Strauss, Valerie. 2020. "Here's the Limited Guidance Trump Allowed the CDC to Give to Schools and Child-Care Centers About Safely Reopening." *Washington Post*, May 15. Accessed May 24, 2020. https://www.washingtonpost.com/education/2020/05/15/heres-limited-guidance-trump-allowed-cdc-give-schools-child-care-centers-about-safely-reopening/.

Street, John. 2001. *Mass Media, Politics and Democracy*. Basingstoke: Palgrave Macmillan.

Street, John. 2002. "Bob, Bono and Tony B: The Popular Artist as Politician." *Media, Culture & Society* 24 (3): 433–41. https://doi.org/10.1177/016344370202400309.

Street, John. 2003. "The Celebrity Politician: Political Style and Popular Culture." In *The Media and the Restyling of Politics*, edited by John Corner and Dick Pels, 85–98. London: Sage.

Street, John. 2004. "Celebrity Politicians: Popular Culture and Political Representation." *British Journal of Politics and International Relations* 6 (4): 435–52. https://doi.org/10.1111/j.1467-856X.2004.00149.x.

Street, John. 2012. "Do Celebrity Politics and Celebrity Politicians Matter?" *British Journal of Politics and International Relations* 14 (3): 346–56. https://doi.org/10.1111/j.1467-856X.2011.00480.x.

Street, John. 2019. "What Is Donald Trump? Forms of 'Celebrity' in Celebrity Politics." *Political Studies Review* 17 (1): 3–13. https://doi.org/10.1177/1478929918772995.

Strickland, Ronald. 2017. "Clint Eastwood's Identity Politics." In *Becoming Brands: Celebrity, Activism and Politics*, edited by Jackie Raphael and Celia Lam, 70–82. Toronto: WaterHill Publishing.

Stuever, Hank. 2003. "Candidate with A Diff'rence; Gary Coleman Is Campaigning for Governor, and for Respect." *Washington Post*, August 24.

Sturdevant, Lori. 2007. "The Place to Take the Pulse of Minnesota; The Dual Disasters of August May Be Giving Sen. Coleman a Respite from Political Damage Over Iraq." *Star Tribune* (Minneapolis, MN), September 2.

Sturdevant, Lori. 2008. "He's Got Their Interest. He's Seeking Their Loyalty. Even a Celebrity Needs a Personal Touch to Succeed at Minnesota's Caucuses." *Star Tribune* (Minneapolis, MN), February 3.

Sturdevant, Lori. 2008. "Franken's 'I'm Sorry' Was a Key First Step; Endorsee Still Has Work to Do Among Skeptical DFL Legislators—and a Recent Rival Might Help." *Star Tribune* (Minneapolis, MN), June 9.

Struyk, Ryan, and Lauren Pearle. 2017. "Fact-Checking Trump's Repeated Unsubstantiated Claim of Widespread Voter Fraud: The White House Says Trump Believes Millions Voted Illegally." ABC News, May 11. Accessed May 27, 2020. https://abcnews.go.com/Politics/fact-checking-trumps-repeated-unsubstantiated-claim-widespread-voter/story?id=45021067.

Sultan, Niv M. 2017. "Election 2016: Trump's Free Media Helped Keep Cost Down, but Fewer Donors Provided More of the Cash." Center for Responsive Politics, April 13. Accessed May 27, 2020. https://www.opensecrets.org/news/2017/04/election-2016-trump-fewer-donors-provided-more-of-the-cash/.

The Sunday Mail. 1986. "'Dirty Harry' to Stand for Mayor." *Sunday Mail*, February 2.

Surawski, Melissa K., and Elizabeth P. Ossoff. 2006. "The Effects of Physical and Vocal Attractiveness on Impression Formation of Politicians." *Current Psychology* 25 (1): 15–27. https://doi.org/10.1007/s12144-006-1013-5.

Tacheron, Donald G., and Morris K. Udall. 1966. *The Job of the Congressman*. Indianapolis: Bobbs-Merrill.

Talamas, Sean N., Kenneth I. Mavor, and David I. Perrett. "Blinded by Beauty: Attractiveness Bias and Accurate Perceptions of Academic Performance." PLoS ONE 11 (2). https://doi.org/10.1371/journal.pone.0148284.

Television Academy. n.d. "Al Franken." Accessed May 6, 2019. https://www.emmys.com/bios/al-franken.

Television Academy. n.d. "Cynthia Nixon." Accessed May 14, 2020. https://www.emmys.com/bios/cynthia-nixon.

Television Academy. n.d. "Fact and Figures for 2018 Nominations." Accessed May 6, 2019. https://www.emmys.com/sites/default/files/Downloads/70th-nominations-facts-figures-v2.pdf.

Television Academy. n.d. "Roseanne." Accessed May 7, 2020. https://www.emmys.com/shows/roseanne.

Television Academy. n.d. "The Sonny and Cher Comedy Hour." Accessed June 19, 2019. https://www.emmys.com/shows/sonny-cher-comedy-hour.

Temple Black, Shirly. 1988. *Child Star: An Autobiography*. New York: McGraw-Hill.

Thompson, Fred. 2010. *Teaching the Pig to Dance: A Memoir of Growing Up and Second Chances*. New York: Crown Forum.

Thorndike, Edward L. 1920. "A Constant Error in Psychological Ratings." *Journal of Applied Psychology* 4 (1): 25–29. https://doi.org/10.1037/h0071663.

Totman, Sally. 2017. "The Emergence of the 'Super-Celebrity Activist': George Clooney and Angelina Jolie." In *Becoming Brands: Celebrity, Activism and Politics*, edited by Jackie Raphael and Celia Lam, 21–31. Toronto: WaterHill Publishing.

Tourse, Robbie W.C., Johnnie Hamilton-Mason, and Nancy J. Wewiorski. 2018. *Systemic Racism in the United States*. Cham, Switzerland: Springer International.

Townsend, John Marshall, and Timothy Wasserman. 1998. "Sexual Attractiveness: Sex Differences in Assessment and Criteria." *Evolution and Human Behavior* 19 (3): 171–91. https://doi.org/10.1016/S1090-5138(98)00008-7.

Trott, William C. 1987. "People." *United Press International*. February 20.

Trott, William C. 1987. "Glimpses." *United Press International*, April 6.

Trump, Donald. 2005. *Trump: The Art of the Deal*. New York: Ballantine Books.

Tsaliki, Liza, Christos A. Frangonikolopoulos, and Asteris Huliaras. 2011. "Making Sense of Transnational Celebrity Activism: Causes, Methods and Consequences." In *Transnational Celebrity Activism in Global Politics: Changing the World?*, edited by Liza Tsaliki, Christos A. Frangonikolopoulos, and Asteris Huliaras, 295–311. Bristol: Intellect.

Tsaliki, Liza, Christos A. Frangonikolopoulos, and Asteris Huliaras, eds. 2011. *Transnational Celebrity Activism in Global Politics: Changing the World?* Bristol: Intellect.

Turner, Graeme. 2014. *Understanding Celebrity*. 2nd ed. London: Sage.

TV Ratings Guide. n.d. Historical Ratings Database—Saturday Night Live. Accessed May 22, 2019. www.thetvratingsguide.com.

Tyson, Alec, and Shiva Maniam. 2016. "Behind Trump's Victory: Divisions by Race, Gender, Education." Pew Research Center, November 9. Accessed May 27, 2020. https://www.pewresearch.org/fact-tank/2016/11/09/behind-trumps-victory -divisions-by-race-gender-education/.

United Press International. 1986. "Actor Announces for Mayor of Carmel." January 30.

United Press International. 1988. "Sonny Bono Files Papers to Run for Mayor." February 1.

USA Today. 1994. "Capitol Christmas from 'Murphy.'" December 12.

Vakil, Caroline. 2021. "Romney Compares Trump's False Election Claims to 'a Bit Like WWF.'" *The Hill*, June 27. Accessed June 27, 2021. https://thehill.com /homenews/sunday-talk-shows/560431-romney-says-trumps-republicans-claims -that-election-was-rigged-a.

van Deerlin, Lionel. 1988. "Sonny Might Win If He Can't Be Seen." *San Diego Union-Tribune*, April 7.

Vandermaas-Peeler, Alex, Daniel Cox, Maxine Najle, Molly Fisch-Friedman, Rob Griffin, and Robert P. Jones. 2018. "Partisan Polarization Dominates Trump Era: Findings from the 2018 American Values Survey." Public Religion Research Institute, October 29. Accessed May 27, 2020. https://www.prri.org/research /partisan-polarization-dominates-trump-era-findings-from-the-2018-american -values-survey/.

van Krieken, Robert. 2012. *Celebrity Society*. New York: Routledge.

Van Susteren, Greta, and Adam Housley. 2003. "Interview with Actor Gary Coleman." Fox News Network, August 8.

van Zoonen, Liesbet. 2003. "After Dallas and Dynasty We Have . . . Democracy: Articulating Soap, Politics, and Gender." In *Media and the Restyling of Politics: Consumerism, Celebrity, and Cynicism*, edited by John Corner and Dick Pels, 99–116. London: Sage.

van Zoonen, Liesbet. 2005. *Entertaining the Citizen: When Politics and Popular Culture Converge*. Lanham, MD: Rowman & Littlefield.

Vaughn, Stephen. 1994. *Ronald Reagan in Hollywood: Movies and Politics*. Cambridge: Cambridge University Press.

von Sternberg, Bob. 1998a. "Exit Polling Shows Ventura Fueled Surprising Turnout." *Star Tribune* (Minneapolis, MN), November 4.

von Sternberg, Bob. 1998b. "Ventura Is a Master of Reinvention." *Star Tribune* (Minneapolis, MN), November 4.

von Sternberg, Bob. 2005. "You Can Go Home Again—If You've Got Senate Ambitions." *Star Tribune* (Minneapolis, MN), May 20.

Wallace, Amy and Cynthia Ducanin. 1988. "Jones Defeats Swindall in Bitter 4th District Race." *Atlanta Constitution*, November 9.

Walsh, Kenneth T. 1987. "When It's Citizen Reagan Again; California Dreamin.'" *US News & World Report*, March 16.

Walsh, Kenneth T. 2008. "The Most Consequential Elections in History: Ronald Reagan and the Election of 1980." *US News & World Report*, September 25. Accessed June 25, 2018. https://www.usnews.com/news/articles/2008/09/25/the-most-consequential-elections-in-history-ronald-reagan-and-the-election-of-1980.

Wang, Vivian. 2018. "Cynthia Nixon Puts Legalizing Marijuana Front and Center of Campaign." *New York Times*, April 11.

Warnke, Melissa B. 2020. "Democratic and Republican National Conventions: From Clint Eastwood Palling Around with a Chair to Al and Tipper Gore's Headline-Grabbing Smooch, These Are the Most Memorable Moments from RNCs and DNCs Past." *Vanity Fair*, August 18. Accessed April 23, 2021. https://www.vanityfair.com/hollywood/2020/08/dnc-rnc-most-memorable-moments.

Washington Post. 1994. "State by State; U.S. Senate." November 10.

Weber, Max. 1947. *The Theory of Economic and Social Organization*, edited by Talcott Parsons. New York: Free Press.

Weekly Standard. 2003. "Leakers, Gary Coleman, and More." October 20.

Wheeler, Mark. 2013. *Celebrity Politics: Image and Identity in Contemporary Political Communications*. Cambridge, UK: Polity Press.

Weiner, Rachel. 2012. "Chris Murphy Beats Linda McMahon in Ct. Senate." *Washington Post*, November 7. Accessed May 7, 2022. https://www.washingtonpost.com/news/post-politics/wp/2012/11/06/ap-chris-murphy-beats-linda-mcmahon-in-connecticut/.

Wemple, Erik. 2014. "Sarah Palin's Sportsman Channel Show Renewed for 2015." *Washington Post*, July 7. Accessed May 28, 2020. https://www.washingtonpost.com/blogs/erik-wemple/wp/2014/07/07/sarah-palins-sportsman-channel-show-renewed-for-2015/.

Weprin, Alex. 2022. "Former President Obama to Narrate Netflix National Parks Docuseries." *Hollywood Reporter*, March 15. Accessed March 27, 2022. https://www.hollywoodreporter.com/tv/tv-news/barack-obama-host-narrate-netflix-series-1235111584/.

West, Darrell M., and John Orman, J. 2003. *Celebrity Politics*. Upper Saddle River, NJ: Prentice Hall.

Westphal, David. 1986. "Iowa Candidates Received $1 Million from PACs." *Des Moines Register*, October 29.

Whereatt, Robert. 1998. "Ventura's Office Asks for Public Donations." *Star Tribune* (Minneapolis, MN), November 19.

Wheway, Daniel. 2017. *The Sonny and Cher Guide*. Rakuten Kobo.

Willis, Doug. 1990. "Actor Ralph Waite Pushes 'Waltons' Values on Campaign Trail." Associated Press, October 18.

Wills, Garry. 2017. *Reagan's America: Innocents at Home*. New York: Open Road Media.

Wilstein, Steve. 1986. "Eastwood Holds First Meeting as Mayor." Associated Press, May 6.

Winegar, Karin. 1989. "'The Body' Speaks His Mind." *Star Tribune* (Minneapolis, MN), August 7.

Witosky, Tom. 1986. "Celebrity an Issue in 6th District." *Des Moines Register*, May 28.

Witte, Brian. 2012. "Mass. Doctor Wins Green Party's Presidential Nod." Associated Press State & Local Wire, July 14.

Wolf, Z. Byron. 2018. "Trump's Attacks on Judge Curiel Are Still Jarring to Read." CNN Politics, February 27. Accessed May 27, 2020. https://www.cnn.com/2018/02/27/politics/judge-curiel-trump-border-wall/index.html.

Woodard, Colin. 2011. *American Nations: A History of the Eleven Regional Cultures of North America*. New York: Viking.

Working Families Party. n.d. "About." Accessed May 15, 2020. https://workingfamilies.org/.

Wray, J. Harry. 1999. "Though a Glass Darkly: Television and American Electoral Politics." In *The Handbook of Political Marketing*, edited by Bruce I. Newman, 439–54. London: Sage.

Wright, Esmond. 1989. *Benjamin Franklin: His Life as He Wrote It*. Cambridge, MA: Harvard University Press.

Wright, Lauren A. 2019. *Star Power: American Democracy in the Age of the Celebrity Candidate*. New York: Routledge.

Yandel, Gerry. 1992. "Today's Radio Tips Hometown Sound." *Atlanta Journal and Constitution*, September 17.

Yang, Maya. 2022. "White House Tells Dr Oz and Herschel Walker to Resign from Fitness Council." *Guardian*, March 24. Accessed March 27, 2022. https://www.theguardian.com/us-news/2022/mar/24/dr-oz-herschel-walker-president-sports-council.

Yoon, Robert. 2012. "America One Step Closer to President Roseanne." CNN Wire, August 5.

Young, Robert. 1988. "The Stars' Desert Paradise." *Sun Herald* (Sydney, Australia), February 14.

Zipporah, Mwendwa Mildred, and Hellen K. Mberia. 2014. "The Effects of Celebrity Endorsement in Advertisements." *International Journal of Academic Research in Economics and Management Sciences* 3 (5): 178–88. http://dx.doi.org/10.6007/IJAREMS/v3-i5/1250.

Index

About the Author

Richard T. Longoria is Associate Professor of Political Science at The University of Texas Rio Grande Valley. He earned his PhD in Government and Politics from the University of Maryland, College Park.

www.ingramcontent.com/pod-product-compliance
Lightning Source LLC
Chambersburg PA
CBHW022306280326
41932CB00010B/1007